LITERAR

PUBLISHING

IN THE

TWENTY-FIRST

CENTURY

LITERARY

PUBLISHING

IN THE

TWENTY-FIRST

CENTURY

Edited by Travis Kurowski,
Wayne Miller & Kevin Prufer

MILKWEED EDITIONS

Published 2016 by Milkweed Editions
Printed in Canada
Cover design by Mary Austin Speaker
16 17 18 19 20   5 4 3 2 1
First Edition

Milkweed Editions, an independent nonprofit publisher, gratefully acknowledges sustaining support from the Jerome Foundation; the Lindquist & Vennum Foundation; the McKnight Foundation; the National Endowment for the Arts; the Target Foundation; and other generous contributions from foundations, corporations, and individuals. Also, this activity is made possible by the voters of Minnesota through a Minnesota State Arts Board Operating Support grant, thanks to a legislative appropriation from the arts and cultural heritage fund, and a grant from the Wells Fargo Foundation Minnesota. For a full listing of Milkweed Editions supporters, please visit www.milkweed.org.

Library of Congress Cataloging-in-Publication Data

    Names: Miller, Wayne, 1976- editor. | Prufer, Kevin, editor. | Kurowski, Travis, editor.
    Title: Literary publishing in the twenty-first century / edited by Wayne Miller, Kevin Prufer & Travis Kurowski.
    Description: First edition. | Minneapolis, Minnesota : Milkweed Editions, 2016.
    Identifiers: LCCN 2015033778 Y ISBN 9781571313546 (paperback) | ISBN 9781571319227 (ebook)
    Subjects: LCSH: Literature publishing--United States--History--21st century. | Authorship--History--21st century. | Authors and publishers--United States--History--21st century. | BISAC: LITERARY COLLECTIONS / Essays.
    Classification: LCC Z480.L58 L58 2016 Y DDC 070.50973/0905--dc23
    LC record available at http://lccn.loc.gov/2015033778

Milkweed Editions is committed to ecological stewardship. We strive to align our book production practices with this principle, and to reduce the impact of our operations in the environment. We are a member of the Green Press Initiative, a nonprofit coalition of publishers, manufacturers, and authors working to protect the world's endangered forests and conserve natural resources. *Literary Publishing in the Twenty-First Century* was printed on acid-free 100% postconsumer-waste paper by Friesens Corporation.

CONTENTS

INTRODUCTION

At the turn of the millennium, back when only one in three American adults reported using email at home, the editors of this volume were just beginning careers in literary publishing. Kevin Prufer and his colleague R. M. Kinder were publishing some of the earliest issues of *Pleiades: A Journal of New Writing*. Wayne Miller was a graduate student starting to edit poetry for the literary journal *Gulf Coast*, while Travis Kurowski was still an undergraduate, about to join the staff of *West Wind Review* as a fiction reader. By that point, all three of us had heard a range of voices deriding the big-box bookstores that had popped up more or less everywhere throughout the previous decade. *Fence* and *McSweeney's* had just launched in 1998, changing the look and feel of American literary magazines about as much as *The Paris Review* did when it first appeared in 1953. Lightning Source, an early print-on-demand publisher, had been established in 1997 but had yet to alter in any significant way how presses would cut costs and keep books in print, as well as how individual authors might self-publish. A few pioneering online literary magazines were gaining readership— *Cortland Review, Jacket,* and *La Petite Zine* among them—and desktop publishing was in something of a second generation: Quark had unseated PageMaker as the dominant software, but InDesign—released in 1999—had yet to make a splash.

In 2000, Nielsen's BookScan was instituted, turning each author, no matter how big or small, into a data set of his/her book sales. That same year, Stephen King published online his novella *Riding the Bullet*—the first high-profile e-book— and books as diverse as Mark Z. Danielewski's *House of Leaves*, Susan Sontag's *In America*, David Sedaris's *Me Talk Pretty One Day*, Kazuo Ishiguro's *When We Were Orphans*, Joseph Brodsky's *Collected Poems*, and J. K. Rowling's *Harry Potter and the Goblet of Fire* garnered large-scale interest. According to a 2000 article by MH Munroe, in 1998–99 there had been sixty publishing mergers and acquisitions with more than $20 billion spent in the process. Meanwhile, by 2000 a marked increase in the number of literary agents and agencies had cemented the agent's role as both gatekeeper and medium between a growing number of aspiring authors and an increasingly hierarchical publishing structure. The 2000 Association of Writers & Writing Programs (AWP) Conference in Kansas City was attended by just fifteen hundred people—about 10 percent of the number of attendees in 2015—and the Council of Literary Magazines and Presses (CLMP) established for the first time an online presence. In four years, Foetry.com would begin to investigate perceived corruption in poetry book contests—which by 2000 had already become the primary way that first collections were acquired—and in just three years lending libraries would start to offer to the general public e-books of popular fiction and nonfiction.

It's clear, now, that many of the seeds of our current publishing moment had already been sowed by the turn of the millennium. Print-on-demand, e-books, online publications and marketing strategies, long-term digital tracking of sales, corporate mergers, box stores, blockbuster young-adult fiction, graphic novels, powerful agents, and organizations such as AWP were already well in the mix and growing. It would nonetheless take more than a decade for these new technologies, methods, and means to change irrevocably—and to continue to change—the publishing environment today.

In 2011, just before we started work on this volume, Amazon—currently America's largest bookseller and the elephant in the room for so many discussions about literary publishing—made two enormous announcements. In May,

the online retailer reported that its sales of e-books had sur-
passed those of regular books. Just a few weeks later, the
company revealed it had hired Laurence Kirshbaum—former CEO of the Time Warner Book Group—to head its
own book-publishing venture, effectively joining under one
corporate roof roles previously reserved for publishers, editors, distributors, and retail stores.

At that particular moment, Amazon seemed steadily
ascendant. In September of that year the big-box bookstore
Borders—one of Amazon's two largest competitors—closed
the last of its more than five hundred retail outlets after
declaring bankruptcy. For the previous decade, the number of independent bookstores had been declining precipi-
tously, having been put out of business at least in part by the
expansion of box stores and online vendors such as Amazon.
Between 2000 and 2007, approximately one thousand
independent bookstores closed in the United States.

Jump forward to 2015—just as we're getting ready to
send to Milkweed Editions the completed manuscript of
Literary Publishing in the Twenty-First Century—and these details
have shifted significantly. In 2014, Kirshbaum departed
Amazon, whose publishing arm has, thus far, failed to
achieve the sort of commercial success competing publishers no doubt feared. At the moment, e-book sales appear to
have plateaued, and independent bookstores are resurgent, a
situation provoking much discussion in the literary marketplace. According to a September 2014 article in *Slate*, sales at
independent bookstores have grown at a rate of 8 percent for
three years in a row, and the number of independent bookstores signing on as members of the American Booksellers
Association is up 20 percent.

This is the unpredictable world of twenty-first-century publishing—a paradoxical place in which more and
more Americans each year possess a Master of Fine Arts

(MFA) in creative writing, yet the percentage of American non–book readers has tripled since 1978. According to the CLMP website there are approximately six hundred regularly publishing literary magazines in the United States (not counting online journals!), and a general estimate is that the number of U.S. literary magazines has *tripled* just in the last thirty years—yet since the turn of the millennium most newspapers across the country have gutted or shuttered entirely their "books" sections. For decades, the largest, most influential publishing houses have consolidated under massive corporate umbrellas, yet thanks to the advent of desktop publishing programs new independent journals and book presses pop up at such a rate it's nearly impossible to keep up with them.

Meanwhile, the Internet has revolutionized how literature is discovered, marketed, and read; print-on-demand technology has substantially reduced the costs of short-run printing; online publishing has made significant gains in readership; VIDA: Women in the Literary Arts has in a short time drawn national attention to questions of gender parity in literary publications; and each year the AWP conference attracts more than twelve thousand writers and seven hundred presses, magazines, and literary organizations from across the country. All this while every year another article comes out declaring the death of American poetry, fiction, literature, and publishing. How do editors and publishers keep up with—and adapt to—this shifting and contradictory world? What, if anything, remains constant?

In 1980, Bill Henderson, founding editor of the Pushcart Press, gathered a group of prominent writers and editors to discuss American publishing toward the end of the twentieth century. The resulting volume, *The Art of Literary Publishing*, helped define the roles and problems publishers would face for the next twenty years. It could not, however, predict today's situation, which includes new technologies remaking the geographies of publishing as much as Johannes Gutenberg did five centuries ago and at a quicker pace.

With that in mind—and with Henderson's book as both something of a model and an earlier publishing discussion to build on—we started recruiting contributors who could address twenty-first-century literary publishing from a range of perspectives. In an effort to round out our picture, we also tracked down a few previously published essays that seemed salient to our purpose.

The resulting volume includes essays on contemporary publishing from the perspective of literary journals (Sven Birkerts of *AGNI*, and Jessica Faust and Emily Nemens of the *Southern Review*), small and university presses (Donna Shear of the University of Nebraska Press, John O'Brien of Dalkey Archive, Daniel Slager of Milkweed Editions, and Emily Louise Smith of Lookout Books), major New York presses (Gerald Howard of Doubleday), international journals (Gabriel Bernal Granados, Kristin Dykstra, and Robert Tejada of *Mandorla* and Megan M. Garr of *Versal*), book critics (Jessa Crispin of *Bookslut*), digital publishers (Richard Nash of Cursor, Byliner, and Small Demons), and literary agents (Chris Parris-Lamb, interviewed by Jonathan Lee). Other included essays address the increasingly prominent publishing of comics and graphic novels (Douglas Wolk), the effect Amazon has had on the current publishing and bookselling climate (Steve Wasserman), questions of diversity and inclusion in today's publishing world (Erin Belieu, Daniel José Older), the increased prevalence of writing contests in the publishing of poetry and short fiction (Kevin Larimer), and various business and operational strategies employed by literary publishers (Matthew Stadler and Jane Friedman).

Of course, we could have included more. Every invitation we sent to a contributor brought to mind two or three others who might offer counterpoints. But the idea behind *Literary Publishing in the Twenty-First Century* isn't to be exhaustive. Things are changing too quickly for that, and by the time this book comes out whole new sets of issues and questions may have arisen that our contributors couldn't have predicted. The point, instead, is to suggest to readers something of the enormous and expansive range of forces at work in the literary marketplace at a time when our sense of what it means to publish a literary magazine, to be an author, to direct a press, or to buy a book is changing more quickly than it ever has before. (Though it's also important to note that the technology of the printed book—the codex—has remained remarkably consistent for nearly two thousand years.) The twenty-three prominent editors, agents, authors, and publishers gathered here offer readers a snapshot of the multifaceted, ever-shifting conversation surrounding literary publishing today—a conversation that, years from now, we hope will have built a substantial piece of the framework for some thriving literary moment that lies ahead.

TRAVIS KUROWSKI (York, Pennsylvania)
WAYNE MILLER (Denver, Colorado)
KEVIN PRUFER (Houston, Texas)

LITERARY

PUBLISHING

IN THE

TWENTY-FIRST

CENTURY

Sven Birkerts

Sven Birkerts is the editor of the journal AGNI *(based at Boston University) and the director of the Bennington Writing Seminars. His most recent book is* Changing the Subject: Art and Attention in the Internet Age *(Graywolf Press, 2015). The author of eight books, he has received grants from the Guggenheim and Lila Wallace-Reader's Digest foundations and awards for his essays and criticism from PEN and the National Book Critics Circle.*

Speaking at the Lahore Literary Festival early in 2014, Pakistani novelist Mohsin Hamid, author of *The Reluctant Fundamentalist* and *How to Get Filthy Rich in Rising Asia*, made the observation that modern technology and social media were having an effect on the styles of young writers, at one point asserting: "The way they write today is very different from how people used to write ten or fifteen years ago."

When I read this I did a double take. Not at Hamid's basic point about change—I think we all understand that a major transformation is underway—but at his time frame. Ten or fifteen years. I reflexively think of that period as part of the cultural present, a version of "just yesterday," right here in ready reach. But now I suspect that my thinking might be a holdover from an earlier way of measuring, that my impulse marks me out as old school right from the start. Those few years represent a newly significant increment on the timeline, and the fact that they do is one of the main background things we need to think about in considering literary publishing in the twenty-first century. Change itself is changing.

In truth, the whole of Hamid's simple sentence is worth study, proposing as it does both the extraordinary rate of technological change *and* the idea that new media might be exerting very real pressure on how young people write— which is also to say, on what writing will look like in years to come. Certainly these technological changes are altering the platforms on which that work will be written, published, and read.

. . .

TECHNOLOGICAL CHANGE, THE RATE OF. Before we conjecture anything about this future, we need a way to conceive of the momentum that is affecting everything, most especially our interactions with others: our communications. A bit of historical context is useful and eye-opening.

Let's agree that the time of a generation equals twenty-five years and do some quick computations. One accepted approximation holds that language developed some two hundred thousand years ago, while the harnessing of electricity happened in the middle of the eighteenth century, and the telephone was only invented in the middle of the nineteenth century. This means that over 8,070 generations came and went in succession between the earliest uses of language and the first transmission of the spoken word through a wire.

Eight thousand and seventy generations. Take a minute to ponder the weight of that interval. Ponder, too, the incalculable impact exerted by those eons of repetition on the collective human substrate (I hesitate to say "collective unconscious"), if there can be said to be such a thing.

It was only around 3000 BCE that the written sign was discovered. With this we can start to picture a more specific succession, a history: from the marks made in clay and then papyrus and vellum, to scrolls, the codex, the early laboriously printed books, and then those that began to pour forth as the press was mechanized; on to the paperback proliferation, and to the variety of screen devices.

The one basic constant of our processing of signs has been that the eyes move left to right and back (for most scripts, anyway), but we ought to ask how meaningful or determining *is* that constant? For it seems that, eye movements notwithstanding, a great deal—almost everything—has changed about reading. That is, about the mind that performs the deciphering action. And that much of that change has been caused by the mind's interaction with the various media.

We can narrow the context further in this matter of the rate of change. Nine words: "Mr. Watson, come here! I want to see you!" Thomas Edison patented the telephone in 1876. In other words, it was only five generations ago that we first mastered the art of flinging our voices across space. But telephones themselves did not become common in American homes until the early 1950s. Two and a half generations ago.

Changes, improvements: rotary dials gave way to touch-tone buttons, long-distance calling—at first a costly and involved procedure—became increasingly common. Wireless mobile phones, first pioneered in the early 1970s, were not commonly adopted until the 1990s. *One generation ago.* And consider how basic those instruments were when compared with the most up-to-date smartphones. What has happened in this latest generational increment, just in the last few years, has been the incorporation of digital computing power—the microprocessor, itself an epoch-making invention—into an instrument whose marvels we have barely begun to assess. Suddenly, in a historical flash, we have developed an affordable, pocket-sized instrument that we can use to make calls, text, take and send pictures, record sound and video, watch movies, find directions, look up information on the Internet, locate our friends, engage in social networking, listen to customized music streams, and read whatever we want . . .

.   .   .

I WAS ON THE SUBWAY the other morning, on my way to the airport, immersed in doing the crossword in Boston's little giveaway paper. At one point I looked up, and right then—before I could formulate any logical account or narrative—I got it. I realized that even in my persistent brooding about the onrush of all things digital, I had been naively conservative. I had pitched my thinking in terms of some pending "future." What I saw in that unprepared moment was that it was already in place. Every person in that car was either staring at a phone or reading pad, or standing with a faraway look in her eyes and a wire in her ear. The transformation is no longer just pending. Any person who puts words to the page—or any surface—must reckon with *this*. I mean the technology itself, before even looking to see what the various devices are delivering to their various consumers.

So far I've been talking about smartphones and iPads and other devices and not about the transformations of books and reading. But the nature of those technologies and our acclimatization to them has everything to do with this discussion of the outlook for literary books and literary reading. For like it or not, it is in the field of these devices and adaptations that all reading increasingly happens.

We are shaped by our reading, of course, but our reading is in every way shaped by who we are, and this is, at least in part, the product of how we live. We inhabit a great tangle of causes and effects, all crosshatched with the feedback loops of influence. The point is, too, that we don't yet know how these myriad causes and effects will transform books and reading. Certainly, though, one effect will be to disabuse us of the notion that the old model—to which some of us so fixedly cling—was a kind of given, rather than what now seems clearly to have been a remarkably long and stable phase.

We don't know how things will change, only that they will. We can try to anticipate, of course, based on the trends and tendencies of the present. But we have no way of being sure that the vector of these tendencies will not start twisting this way and that at the least technological provocation. Nor do we know—how can we?—how to factor in what is happening to us in our own systems. Neurobiology: the field is inventing itself with great velocity. How are we to guess possible new variables in a world that has been bringing forth surprises with each rotation?

What has emerged and is becoming increasingly clear is that the brain exhibits extraordinary plasticity, that it does *not* take the time of a generation to effect substantial changes in our mental processing. "Neurons that fire together, wire together"—we sing it like a nursery rhyme, and will until our attention spans shrink to the point where we can just recollect the keywords: *fire, wire*. But the odds are that we won't need to use our memories in that way. There will surely be digital prostheses that will make sure the words are there when we need them.

. . .

THOUGH HIS OBSERVATION WAS GENERAL, I think this is what Hamid is referring to when he talks about change. He means not just the technology, but changes in the writers' sensibilities *because* of their interactions with the technology; not just in their sensibilities, but—and maybe I'm adding this layer myself—in the whole conception and subject matter of literature. The literary.

.   .   .

ALREADY WE KNOW THAT PEOPLE don't read in the same way. Writer Nicholas Carr, we may remember, made a big splash, first with a cover article in the *Atlantic* and then in his book *The Shallows: What the Internet Is Doing to Our Brains*. In the article, which had the catchy title "Is Google Making Us Stupid?," he began on a note of personal worry. He had noticed in recent years an increasing difficulty in sitting down and reading a book in the old way. He found himself having a hard time focusing on any single text; he felt impatient, skittish, frustrated. He theorized that the difficulty might have to do with the fact that he spent the better part of every day working on a computer, doing all of the usual multitasking behaviors so familiar to all of us. Looking further, he began to test his hypothesis using all kinds of studies coming out in the burgeoning field of neuroscience. What he found and documented in his book was the striking corroboration of his intuitions. Our astonishingly "plastic" neural system adapts with great rapidity to its behavioral environment. Fire: wire. Which is to say: we are changing in tandem with the media that are bringing about the changes.

.   .   .

ONE READS THE TEA LEAVES. Or the newspaper—a similar process. Two articles reflecting on certain contemporary trends will at least suggest the kinds of developments I'm talking about—developments that, singly, exert impact, but that may also affect the psyche in unforeseeable combinations and further underscore Hamid's assertion about transformations of the practice of writing.

In a 2014 article in the *Washington Post,* "Books Are Losing the War for Our Attention," writer Matt McFarland opens by saying: "Technology has reshaped everything from how we communicate to how we find a mate or a job. Yet the experience of reading books remains largely untransformed, and the popularity of books has suffered in the face of flashier media formats that are perfected for our busy world."

McFarland follows with statistics on the declining number of book readers, and voices the common fear that though books can still bring us essential kinds of knowledge and understanding, they cannot do so if they sit unopened on shelves. He underscores his concern by quoting Russell Grandinetti, vice president of Amazon Kindle content: "Most people walk around with some kind of device or have access to some kind of device that allows them to choose how to use their time. . . . In a world with that much choice, books need to continue to evolve to compete for someone's time and interest."

What to do? "One possibility," writes the author, "would be to integrate more multimedia into e-books, which don't offer the same dynamic story-telling as HTML and Web sites." That has always seemed to me to be the obvious and inevitable next thing, a development from which going back will be very difficult, especially given what we are learning about our highly supple neural networks. The integration of videos, graphics, and sound—not to mention other kinds of interactive links—into standard text content would obviously affect the neural dynamics of the reading act in untold ways, most of them challenging further our already challenged faculty of attention. But McFarland does not linger here—though one easily could—to spell out a range of possible scenarios that might not finally feel all that futuristic. The real question, not addressed in the article, is the extent to which such amped-up e-presentations would undermine the ostensibly separate process of reading traditional—literary—books in the traditional way.

Considering possible industry responses to the loss of readers, McFarland goes on to discuss Spritz, a new Boston-based start-up devoted to the speeding up of reading through a process that combines rapid-fire flashing of words in what have been shown to be "optimal recognition points"—the gist being that the eye stays steady while the words flash past at strategically calculated rates. Research claims that comprehension is not "negatively affected at speeds up to 400 words per minute." A novel like *The Catcher in the Rye,* he writes, "could be read in three hours and four minutes." The contested word here, obviously, is "read," for the impact on literary reading would certainly be considerable. Salinger's colloquially based *Catcher in the Rye* is one thing, and a story by, say, Lydia Davis is quite another. And even if the work in question is not forbidding in its structure or syntactical expression, we should remember that all literary writing asks us to savor the nuances of diction.

Just a few days after McFarland's piece appeared, David Streitfeld published an article in the business section of the *New York Times* on the new growth industry of fiction serialized for readers who read on their phones. Wattpad is a new storytelling app that seems to be having huge success. Streitfeld writes: "Wattpad is a leader in this new storytelling environment, with more than 2 million writers producing 100,000 pieces of material a day for 20 million readers on a intricate international social network." The material he documents is entertainment, mainly, goods served up for quick consumption that have little to do with the literary, but . . .

Though I am not necessarily thinking in terms of any direct influences on the future of literary reading and writing, these kinds of developments cannot but have an effect, insofar as they condition the reflexes and expectations of readers and the thinking of the strategists at publishing houses, etc. On this front, Wattpad represents several things, and they can be itemized. One is the further imposition of assembly-line rhythms and dynamics on at least one sector of the book culture. A second is the intensification of the new ethos of ephemerality, bringing the former conception of book reading—wherein a book was a means of preservation as well as dissemination of text—up against the assumption of steady evanescence that is a feature of most Internet writing.

A third—and possibly most nervous-making—element of Wattpad is its demolition of the hitherto fairly sacrosanct division between author and reader, a division that is in at least one way analogous to the therapist/client divide. A key feature of the latter—and, to a degree, the former, too—is that the separation enables, or encourages, a certain active projection on the part of client and reader, one that vitally informs both the therapy and the act of reading. But the author/reader division of labor appears to be under threat as well, at least in this one sphere.

Writing about a woman named Anna Todd, who uses Wattpad to post episodes of a saga called "After," Streitfeld notes how after posting Chapter 278, "the first comment appeared 13 seconds after the chapter was uploaded." And: "By the next day there were 10,000 comments: always brief, overwhelmingly positive, sometimes coherent."

We need to consider the eventual likelihood of the merging of realms—and how the culture of social media is already pressing up against at least one fringe of the reading world. How long, and on what grounds, can literary publishing keep itself apart from changes moving through adjacent parts of its shrinking domain? Or maybe the real question is: what can we expect from literary publishing as market pressures and changed reading habits bring their inevitable transformations? Will the author be reduced to being a privileged component in what will start to resemble a communal narrative-making enterprise? And, given the basic level of discourse of screen media and the movement toward easy access and disposability, what will be the fate of those undertakings that present more complex material or venture artistically ambitious approaches?

There are so many imponderables. We can't be sure about the platforms, the staying power of the printed book, or the interests and aptitudes of the generations of future consumers of the word. We also don't know what those who persist in writing will be writing *about*, or what forms their expressions might take. Fragmented weaves, interactive hypertexts, narratives that make digital process itself the core of their presentation . . . will writers continue to treat character in familiar ways, or will the saturations of connectivity spawn new modes? The old constants of time and space—how will they signify in a virtual screen culture? What now-unimaginable hybridizations will flourish? What linguistic variations? How will the canonic works of the past be reprocessed? I won't make any guesses here.

· · ·

BUT I DO BELIEVE THAT insofar as there are truths and expressions that cannot be compromised, and that at least some people deem essential (in the spirit of William Carlos Williams on poetry: "Men die miserably every day for lack of what is found there"), the literary/artistic will survive in some interesting form(s). And if it were to die out, I'm confident that certain independent spirits would invent it again, and when they did it would feel like a revolution was at hand. At the same time, I don't see the literary as we have known it prevailing or even flourishing. With luck, it will survive for some time yet at the present scale, which is, in terms of societal influence and prestige, already much diminished from former times. But we should keep in mind that those were times when the seemingly sedate verbal art was not yet beset on every side by the seductions of easily accessible entertainment. In the future, literature will likely not command enough marketplace attention to make it commercially viable at any corporate level, but might rather become (and this is not a bad thing) an artisanal product that functions either as a vital inner resource or else as a status marker for its reduced population of consumers. What we might think of as old-school "serious" literature may come to function as a kind of code among initiates. At that point charges of elitism will not have to be defended against—they will have been fully earned.

Matthew Stadler

Matthew Stadler is the author of five books, editor of four more, and the recipient of a Guggenheim Fellowship and a Whiting Writer's Award. In 2001 he cofounded Clear Cut Press; in 2009 he cofounded Publication Studio, a print-on-demand press that has now spawned eight "sibling studios" in a number of different cities. "The Ends of the Book" was given as a lecture at Yale University's Beinecke Library in 2012.

The crisis in publishing is the collapse of the book as a commodity, as a nexus for shopping. That's it. That's the bottom line that has destroyed livelihoods and can wreck corporations. Ironically, this catastrophe also blinds publishers to a vibrant resurgence in the culture of reading. Reading and shopping have never been a good match—I would say they are opposites. As the publishing industry struggles to configure new sites of shopping and rescue an economy that used to support writers by selling books, vibrant new communities of reading emerge, both online and in small-run printed books. For those of us who love reading, for those of us who are sick and tired of shopping, this is a remarkable time rife with opportunity. The question we're faced with is not, as so many publishers believe, how to rescue shopping; the question is how to make a viable economy in a culture of reading.

In 2009 I learned of cheap, hand-operated machines that can make sturdy perfect-bound books one at a time, fast and at low cost. I bought them and, with a friend, set up shop in a storefront in Portland, Oregon. Like a lot of people, we knew some great writers whose work we loved and thought should be published. We became publishers by printing, binding, and selling their books directly to the readers who wanted them. We also offered the books for sale as e-books, and we let anyone read and annotate them for free online in a digital "free reading commons." We made a website to sell and circulate the books globally, while also hosting the social life of the books back home at our storefront. Friends visited and liked what they saw. In eight other cities, mostly in North America, friends bought similar machines and opened up their own shops. The nine shops together comprise what we call Publication Studio. In five years, we've published three hundred new titles, all of them profitable. Publication Studio has made a viable, unsubsidized, for-profit economy based on reading. This is the story of how.

READING AND SHOPPING

Reading is a specific practice. We know it best as reading books, but it's a practice that we can apply generally. Reading is open-ended, provisional, conversational. It's not solitary, but deeply collective. We might be alone with a book, but the book fills our heads with other voices and puts our thoughts into conversation, not only with the writer but with countless other readers, real and imagined. Immersed in reading, the self dissolves and mixes with others. We take comfort in the flickering, light-dappled margin, where we stand both inside and outside of the text. It is a liminal space. The relationships of reading are multivalent, empathetic—they entail recognition across difference. Texts have many readers, divergent participants positioned at the edges of a shared central space; we recognize each other in common across that space, not erasing difference but living in it.

Such relationships are not limited to books, but can also play out in the world.

Reading can shape an economy. I call that practice "publication." I'm going to draw things in sharp contrast to clarify the practice. Publication is the creation of new publics in a culture of reading. It includes the production and circulation of books, the management of a digital commons, and a rich social life of gathering and conversation with books and readers. All of these activities together construct a space of conversation, a public space, which beckons a public into being. Shopping—which is the prevailing culture of our time, and which drives most of the choices now being made in the publishing industry—corrodes and evacuates publics. So, real publication begins by quieting the noise of shopping.

The culture of shopping is pervasive. What exactly does it do to you? Shopping stages the repeated performance of the self along rigorously organized lines. The purchase is its pivotal moment. Every minute of every day shopping positions us on the verge of a purchase, a consumer choice. We stand ready, groomed for this moment by constantly cycling messages about our taste and its meanings. You know these messages—announcements addressing you by name; mail slots stuffed with personal offers; objects that beckon you, eliciting your enactment of taste within very narrow, in fact dictated, confines. The act of choosing becomes a repeated affirmation of your selfhood and liberty.

Shopping positions you alone in the spotlight, center stage, performing the correct, repeated display of your taste. It atomizes us. Shopping is the opposite of reading.

Readers naturally quiet the noise of shopping. We're distracted, which deafens us, and we fail to act. We go on reading. Not just books, but all those open, inconclusive relationships that reading entails. Beckoned to move into the spotlight and decisively exercise our taste, to consume, we instead dawdle in ambivalance, in the lingering incompleteness of the text. We keep circling, reading, rereading, cycling into the next book even before we've finished the last, so that the two books remain open, and then more; ten, fifteen books opened or bookmarked, cluttering the room. We stay engaged. The clerk asks us what we'd like to buy, and we look up, half-focused in the space of reading, and we answer with a question. We invite the clerk into a conversation that might never be completed. These are the pleasures of reading, and if given serious attention, they shape an economy called "publication."

Publication with Friends

About four years ago a woman named Jacqueline Suskin told me she'd been collecting old photographs from tag sales, thrift stores, even from the piles of garbage people leave in the street after cleaning out a basement or an attic. Mostly snapshots of travel and families. She had scores of them. The photos were haunting, not only because Jacqueline was drawn to haunting images, but because of the way they reached her. Many were bent and torn, deeply marked by the neglect and time that separated them from the lives they came from. Jacqueline had been writing poems from these photos.

She gave me a manuscript. The poems were lovely. Deft slight things that graced the images by remaining quiet and understated. The language was bold, sometimes funny, and drew attention to itself, though the speaker did not—she framed and tended the slight margin the world had left around these photos, conducting her business of writing there and leaving the spotlight to the pictures. Jacqueline's poems were modest, but I got lost in them. It was an odd book. Jacqueline wanted to print each photograph in full color, opposite each poem. I kept going back to three or four poems that stuck with me, and I grew to love the book.

In traditional publishing there's a moment when the pleasure of reading must stop. Usually that moment is marked by the sad sentence, "I love your book, but I can't publish it." The disappointed writer concludes that the editor is either a coldhearted liar or a fool. In fact the editor is neither. The editor is someone who sincerely loves books, but lives in a special kind of hell where hundreds, if not thousands, of talented writers are motivated to send her their very best work, which she is obliged to read, often to love, and to reject over and over and over. The sentence she writes a dozen times a day, in all sincerity, is "I love your book, but I can't publish it." This is publishing's hellish negative to shopping's moment of affirmation—the repeated performance of the discerning self saying "no" to what she loves. It is anathema to readers.

"Publication"—an economy based in reading—extends the pleasures of reading deeper. Having read a book, the editor's reply is either "I love your book, I want to publish it" or "I don't love your book, good luck." Because we make our books one at a time as they are purchased, and we organize our work around the relationship of one reader to one book, any book we love can be published profitably. We make books for readers who want them, so we have costs only when we also have income from selling the book.

I emailed Jacqueline and said, "I love your book, we want to publish it." She was thrilled. I explained that this meant we would make books for anyone who wanted them, but one at a time; and we would only send books to stores if the stores bought them, agreed to keep them and sell them, and never return them. We offered the stores a 40 percent discount so they could make their customary profits. Jacqueline would get half the profit on every book we sold. The way things got priced, that meant she made about four dollars on each sale. The book is eighty pages, lovely and modest, like the poems, and it's called *The Collected*.

It turned out Jacqueline had friends in Portland. She wanted to come up from Arcata, California, the pot-growing capital of the United States, where she lived and did her work as "poem store." (Poem Store is a project she shares with poet Zachary Houston. They set up a typewriter on the street and write poems for strangers, on themes of the customer's choosing; you pay what you want.) Why not bring Poem Store north and have a Portland launch party for *The Collected*? Jacqueline would read and her friend's band would play. We'd invite all our friends. Jacqueline likes to travel, and we agreed it was a great idea and started planning the party, spreading the word, and making books to sell at the event.

Agreements in traditional publishing are a little different. Let's say it's a good day in publishing, and that rare pleasure has appeared, the letter or phone call saying, "I love your book, we want to publish it." The editor offers a contract and an advance—which is a wager, money bet against future sales—in exchange for the writer's promise to not allow anyone else to publish the same work. The standard publishing contract pivots on this prohibition—the writer is paid for agreeing to not offer her work to others. (Advances can be big or small, and are becoming less common, but the promise of exclusivity remains at the core of the publishing contract.) Without an exclusive right to publish, the old wisdom goes, the market will be flooded and profits will be lost.

Given the bet that the publisher has made—in the form of any advance payments, printing and distribution of a print run, and pushing that run into stores or book media quickly enough to sell copies before the book is old or irrelevant—the need for exclusive rights makes sense. But it is an ugly way to begin a crucial relationship.

By contrast, publication—driven by a reader's hopes for the book he loves—begins with a nonexclusive contract. We ask the writer for permission to make our edition of her work. We welcome, encourage, and even help the writer find other publishers to make other editions and join in support of the writer's work. An economy shaped by one-at-a-time production, focused on the relationship of one reader to one book, makes money one sale at a time. For us, the "lost sale" is a meaningless fiction.

Further, for publication there are no hidden bets, no history of speculation weighing the fates of our books unequally. We don't have a thousand copies of Jacqueline's book in a warehouse or out in the stores waiting to be sold. We don't even have two copies. We have Jacqueline's permission to publish our edition, to make and sell copies as needed to readers who want the book, and we intend to keep doing so forever.

I wish the next turn in my story was the appearance of a second excited publisher who also loved Jacqueline's work and called to say, "Yes, we'd like to publish an edition too." Sadly it's not. And when that second publisher does call, it is more likely that they'll say, "We love your book and would you please stop working with Publication Studio, so that we can take over and do a proper job of publishing you?" But that day has not yet come; so, instead, let me tell you about the party.

It was a great party. Jacqueline's dad came from Cincinnati, and brought a lot of booze. A local café made snacks that could have been meals, and everyone crowded into this weird skater/crafty gallery that's down the street from us, where they like books and thought it would be cool to have a poetry reading. Jacqueline is an excellent reader.

She showed some of the photos on slides as she read. The friend's band was called "and and and" and they were awesome. By the time they played we'd drunk all the liquor and people were dancing on tables. The place is tiny, so it was packed. The gamble we took—making forty copies ahead of time for the party—paid off. We sold all forty.

This was a good start. Given the way that we work it could also be the end. Maybe Jacqueline really prefers staying home. You know writers. She's working on a new book. The party was fun and, hey, she made $160. But why do more? As it turns out, Jacqueline is a restless and social person. Over the next year she made similar events in dozens of other cities and sold hundreds of books. Some of the parties were in bookstores that now carry her work. And other stores heard about it and ordered the book from us. I'll tell you more about *The Collected* in a second, but first let's look at that new book that Jacqueline is working on. Let's say it's a novel, or just a good long story, and it's brilliant—smart, empathetic, fierce, like Jacqueline's poems. And this time the good news comes: Knopf wants to publish their edition alongside the Publication Studio edition Jacqueline insists on. (I'm imagining here.)

At this point a second difference between publishing and publication appears. Having leapt bravely into the future of nonexclusive rights, Knopf must still make a guess, a wager, that will oblige them to pursue certain time-pressured strategies on behalf of the book. How many to print? Thousands? Tens of thousands? What if Terry Gross interviews Jacqueline? What if Michelle Obama gets ahold of the book and loves it? What season is best to bring it out? Who is the market for this book, and how to reach them in the three- or four-month window that a new book has to spark interest and sell enough copies to stay in print?

At Publication Studio, our challenge is a little

more manageable. No bets weigh on our books. The day Jacqueline approves the final design and we're all happy with it, we print one and marvel at it. It's a wonderful day. That copy goes to Jacqueline, of course. Then we print a second one and we send it to Joy Williams. (Again, just imagining, "for instance . . .") She knows Jacqueline's work, met her on the street at a Poem Store in Florida. Joy likes the work and they've kept in touch; so Jacqueline scribbles a note to include with the book when we pop it in the mail. We take our time. Publication, the creation of a public shaped by reading, is not time pressured.

This economy is starting to look a lot like an older model of publishing. Book lovers writing to friends whom they think might love a new book, or a not-so-new one. It's an economy where the ease, surprises, and readerly indirection of old publishing (as recent, say, as Bennett Cerf's Random House or James Laughlin's New Directions) were the product of lower profit pressures, steadier backlist sales, or simply wealth. The opportunity to return to that model—to publish what we love at a pace that befits our enduring care for it—now extends to those of us with very little money, no subsidies, and no backlist.

Through the efficiencies of one-at-a-time production and the broad reach of digital circulation and the Internet, Publication Studio has been able to make profitable strategies for three hundred new titles, channeling all of our earnings directly back into the social life of the book. We've made and sold more than twenty-five thousand books, with zero returns, directly to readers and through fifty or so bookstores around the world, stores that work with us because they saw our books and wanted them. Echoing our excitement and loyalty *as readers* those stores also agree to never return the books we send to them. They buy our books because they believe the books are worth buying.

The Collected is in stores in Paris, Berlin, London, and many cities across North America. We've sold around three hundred copies. Most of the copies sold at events where Jacqueline reads. It helps that she loves to travel and she's a good reader. But as the books sell and circulate, online orders and interest from bookstores both rise. Instead of the apocalyptic model of traditional publishing, where the book is visible everywhere for three or four months before disappearing completely, its last bubbles rippling the surface of the remainder tables before going under completely, Jacqueline's book remains visible in the hands of those who love it, and who will speak for it. Its presence is a low, rich hum that has grown, not a loud shout followed by a startling silence.

PUBLICATION WITH STRANGERS

If publication is the creation of new publics, how does this constitute a "public?" How can three hundred books make a difference? And how can a writer live on so little money?

First the money. Jacqueline lives the way that most published poets do. She works various jobs and hopes for prizes while depending on the peripatetic life of her book to spread the word. Sometimes we think that famous poets make money from their work, but they mostly make money by being famous, not by selling books. Heather McHugh, a MacArthur fellow and a leading figure in American letters, tells me no book of hers has ever made more than $5,000 dollars. And that's the high end of the poetry economy.

Writers, not just poets but all literary writers—up to and including the famous ones—do not make a living selling books. They could make a living on the winning end of a publisher's foolish advance, but more often than not, the big advance is a dangerous endgame, one that is becoming increasingly rare. Writers make their money elsewhere, with prizes and teaching and gigs that stem from their achievements as writers. So, books are crucial, but book sales do not comprise a living wage, even for most well-known writers. It's important to dispel the myth of "making it" so that younger writers can turn away from that false promise.

In publication, our writers will make money from the books we sell. They'll make their fair share, but they won't make a living. So it is for writers in these times. Publishers should aim not to be wasteful, and to be sure everyone profits equally. And they should concentrate their energy on the more important question of publication: How do they make new and lasting publics?

How do publics grow from such small numbers? The publics that matter, that can shape or change our lives and the fate of books, do not depend on numbers. The misconception that they do—that publics become significant only as they get bigger, mass movements catalyzing when the sheer size of a crowd or a vote or a poll overwhelms the size of opposition to it—begins in an age-old confusion of publics and markets. The first naming of "the public" as an identifiable political force came simultaneously with the emergence of mass markets as a force shaping European economies in the late eighteenth century. What we have come to regard as democratic forces, "the people"—this abstraction that is measured in numbers, of bodies in a crowd, votes at an election, or units sold—is actually the buying power of effectively interchangeable consumers positioned at the end of a new economic form, global capitalism, that requires vastly expanding markets to sustain its core engines of growth.

I won't expect anyone to be swayed by my thumbnail history. But look at the discussion of "the public" that's encapsulated by Jürgen Habermas in his mid-twentieth-century analysis of these concepts, and you'll see the confusion between markets and publics that I am speaking of. The point that's relevant here is to separate the two. We want to know how to make new publics, not markets. And to do so, we must focus on the quality of relationships, not on their number. Mistaking publics for markets, we have wrongly assumed that their power or importance can be measured by a head count.

A plaza of holiday shoppers, no matter how crowded or busy, does not constitute a public. The atomized shoppers lack the crucial recognition of one another, the capacity to see each other and act in common. When we engage strangers as people, when we find ourselves partly by finding their selves, we catalyze a public. When we withdraw that recognition and categorically exclude or erase them, we retreat into something that is not public. Usually it is a market. The catalyzing or erasure of publicness is palpable. You can feel it as you enter a plaza or a crowd, and either recoil from strangers, withdrawing in revulsion, or engage and act toward these strangers as you would toward those you know. In this spark of recognition, of common humanity across difference, you feel a public kindled; you feel its flame grow.

There is no preexisting public. Publics begin in willful actions, an invitation, an event. A public can arise in any defined space that is open to strangers—a street, a meeting hall, a plaza or park, or a book—and is best supported by small, formally clear settings where there is an obvious threshold to be crossed. An invitation to join, literal or implied, is crucial. A good example is the cover of a book, which can be opened or closed.

We catalyze publics when we make and circulate books. The book held in a stranger's hands welcomes him into a space shared by others. A used book might even bear a former reader's marks, notes scribbled in the margins. I sometimes find used copies of my own books annotated by readers whose fanciful conclusions I can only marvel at. "Bird imagery here," throughout the margins of my first novel, *Landscape: Memory*, seemed to me to be evidence of some misguided undergraduate instructor who had assigned my book in the hopes of "teaching it." In another copy I found the exclamation "omg" beside the book's first detailed description of oral sex. The notation thrilled me. I pictured a wide-eyed reader, rapt with fascination, a complete stranger for whom this event had meant as much as it had meant to me.

My grandmother read these same sex scenes, decades ago, and she sent me a heartwarming note, thanking me for portraying a romance between two boys "without any graphic sexual content." She'd read the whole book, closely; but what she did not want to see did not impose itself on her. In this way, books are especially welcoming public spaces; they offer everything, but don't force it on you. You can flip ahead, glaze over, or close the book and sigh.

My book's public includes my grandmother and misguided undergraduates, clutching their marked-up copies, and the book groups who adopted it, and the nervous teens whose counselors put it on lists of "gay and lesbian youth novels," and the travelers who find it in one hostel and leave it, later, in another. Books travel through the world collecting strangers. They are public spaces. Readers meet in the margins, at the edge of a text they share in common. You know this moment of recognition—in a crowded subway car or on the benches of a public park, when you see a stranger reading the same obscure book that has meant the world to you. It's a powerful and unfailing link. Books make publics. And these publics grow, especially if we organize our work to help them grow, rather than killing books young if they fail to achieve certain market metrics, the metrics of shopping.

Some books will circulate widely and their publics grow large. Our Walter Benjamin books, with Carl Skoggard's superb new translations, have an international readership that grows each month, without the kind of social life or support that Jacqueline Suskin brings to her books. In this case, the books themselves speak clearly. Joe Holtzman, Carl Skoggard's partner, and the founder and designer of *Nest* magazine, where I worked, designed the covers. We told Carl no printed covers, only recycled file folders and rubber stamps. He told Joe and the results were brilliant. The books sell anywhere we place them.

Other books aren't meant to travel. My neighbors in Portland, the painters Chris Johanson and Johanna Jackson, painted a mural on the side of our local grocery store. It's beautiful. They made ten watercolor studies for the mural. They letterpressed the pages with a local printer, and hand-painted thirty-six sets of them. We bound the sets as books, thirty-six copies. Almost all are in the hands of neighbors and friends now, but a few are in Amsterdam and Berlin, and there's one in the Beinecke Library collection of American literature.

Other books travel and grow significant publics, but they do so unpredictably over time. They live out the social life of the book, within lives shaped by reading, not shopping. There's no telling where they will go, only that each book will have its own unique life and its own public, however big or small. Publication, the economy we've shaped around the relationships of reading, can treat each book on its own terms, giving them attention and producing books for sale when needed, and letting them lie idle when not.

Publication as an Economy

In 2011 I published my fifth novel, *Chloe Jarren's La Cucaracha*, using Publication Studio, this apparatus I'd been touting to my colleagues. I got in touch with friends in a dozen cities, people who had read my books and knew my work. Six of those friends were running Publication Studios, making books, hosting events, hosting the economy of publication. In each city we set up a dinner—one big table of forty to fifty people, with a local chef who was game for an unusual gig, great food and drink, and sometimes a special guest, usually another writer, with whom I'd have a conversation as part of our gathering. Seats at the tables cost forty-five to seventy-five dollars, depending on what the chef had in mind. They were lavish. The price covered everything: all the booze and wages for the servers and chef, and, importantly, a copy of my book. We set the ticket price by figuring out the total costs of the event, including the cost of the book, and dividing that by the number of seats. Anywhere Publication Studio had a space, they made the books fresh in editions unique to the event, date-stamped, as we do with all our books.

In two weeks, having these big dinners almost every night in San Francisco, Dallas, Mexico City, Guanajuato, Los Angeles, Vancouver (British Columbia), Toronto, North Adams (Massachusetts), New York, Seattle, and Portland, I met five hundred people and sold five hundred books (and made five dollars on each book sold). It was exhausting, thrilling, and buoying. The connections I made over the long hours at these dinner tables meant more than most I've made reading to bookstore audiences, where shoppers sit and try to decide if my book is worth buying. And pragmatically, they mean much much more. We don't just make sales. We meet readers, a more enduring thing.

It helped that I'd published four books before and had had some earlier success. I doubt that many first-time authors could do what I did. But if we make an economy based in reading, shift our attentions away from shopping and the allure of a big publisher's gamble, and back onto the relationships that mean so much to us, writers will begin to see and engage the potentials I was lucky enough to find that summer. They're there. The audience is as ready for change as we are; they're ready to be addressed as readers sharing the common space of a book, strangers ready to recognize each other across difference.

This is publication, the creation of new publics. We're fortunate to live in a time when it has become robustly possible, even for those of us without means or investors, equipped only with our love of books. The printed book—made and sold one at a time to readers who want them—turns out to be the best, indeed irreplaceable, instrument of publication (better, even, than its temperamental, disappearing cousin, the e-book), even if it might be a poor driver of sales.

From Publishing to Publication

We still shop in a culture of reading, just as we still read in a culture of shopping. The skilled reader might be bad at shopping, too slow and indecisive, just as skilled shoppers are often lousy readers (too impatient to finish, not to read but to "have read" and to get on to the next book). But the two coexist. A culture of reading makes an economy that is, like reading itself, slower than shopping. It's conversational, open-ended, interested in detail, difference; it goes on and on, back and forth; it accepts what is available, rather than unilaterally demanding satisfaction. Shops like Henry, in Hudson, New York; Ooga Booga, in Los

Angeles; or hundreds more in scores of other cities, show us the viable economy of a culture of reading. It's relaxing and always interesting. Yes, it's slow, but big things happen, and it's steady.

The simultaneous viability—even thriving—of this reading economy amidst the prevalent economy of shopping is probably most obvious today in the food industry. The food industry is dominated by what's called agribusiness, the massive companies like Monsanto that reward industrial-scale farming by linking those suppliers to vast distribution networks and global markets where consumers become accustomed to the convenience of brand-name, prepackaged foods—foods whose origins and economy the consumer remains unaware of.

Amid this dominant culture of industrial-scale food production, there is a multiheaded, multirooted, swiftly spreading sort of blackberry vine called "slow food," which has many different versions in different nations and cultures. The essence of slow food is that the person who eats knows something about the place their food comes from, who produces it, and how it gets to the table. This knowledge—more so than any strict rules about scale or distance—defines slow food. It's not really that slow. Since the easiest version is to grow food in your backyard and eat it (or, similarly, to visit the nearest farmer or yard with good food and buy theirs and eat it), slow food can actually be a lot faster than agribusiness. The difference is in the knowledge one has and in the relationships that lead to it. These are relationships of reading—open-ended, conversational, back and forth, enduring, curious, never unilaterally demanding.

Publication, the economy I've been describing, is the book's equivalent of "slow food." It's local. It's made by hand by people who care. It carries the best-quality work in the world, and (because literature travels well) publication gives us access to the entire world of books, not just what is geographically near at hand. I like this economy because I love reading. It is just as viable as slow food. It exists and can thrive, regardless of the fate of traditional big publishing. My hope is that anyone who values a culture of reading above that of shopping will actively join in the economy of publication. First we do so by insisting on nonexclusive contracts. Second, we discourage gambling on big print runs. Third, we extend the pleasures of reading as deeply into this economy as they can possibly go.

Reading is not just that thing we do with books, on those luxurious evenings when we've cancelled plans at the last minute, set a fire in the fireplace, and sit down to read without obligation until bedtime: it is also the thing we do throughout the day in all of our relationships and interactions—with our economy. We can be readers rather than always shoppers.

Steve Wasserman

Steve Wasserman, former editor of the Los Angeles Times Book Review, *served as editorial director of Times Books and publisher of Hill & Wang. He is a past partner of the Kneerim & Williams Literary Agency and is currently editor-at-large for Yale University Press. "The Amazon Effect" was first published in the May 29, 2012, issue of the* Nation.

From the start, Jeff Bezos wanted to "get big fast." He was never a "small is beautiful" kind of guy. The Brobdingnagian numbers tell much of the story. In 1994, four years after the first Internet browser was created, Bezos stumbled upon a startling statistic: the Internet had been growing at the rate of 2,300 percent annually. In 1995, the year Bezos, then thirty-one, started Amazon, just 16 million people used the Internet. A year later, the number was 36 million, a figure that would multiply at a furious rate. Today, more than 1.7 billion people, or almost one out of every four humans on the planet, are online. Bezos understood two things. One was the way the Internet made it possible to banish geography, enabling anyone with an Internet connection and a computer to browse a seemingly limitless universe of goods with a precision never previously known and then buy them directly from the comfort of their homes. The second was how the Internet allowed merchants to gather vast amounts of personal information on individual customers.

The Internet permitted a kind of bespoke selling. James Marcus, who was hired by Bezos in 1996 and would work at Amazon for five years, later published a revealing memoir of his time as Employee #55. He recalls Bezos insisting that

the Internet, with "its bottomless capacity for data collection," would "allow you to sort through entire populations
with a fine-tooth comb. Affinity would call out to affinity:
your likes and dislikes—from Beethoven to barbecue sauce,
shampoo to shoe polish to *Laverne & Shirley*—were as distinctive as your DNA, and would make it a snap to match you
up with your 9,999 cousins." This prospect, Marcus felt,
"was either a utopian daydream or a targeted-marketing
nightmare."

Whichever one it was, Bezos didn't much care. "You
know, things just don't grow that fast," he observed. "It's
highly unusual, and that started me thinking, 'What kind
of business plan might make sense in the context of that
growth?'" Bezos decided selling books would be the best
way to get big fast on the Internet. This was not immediately obvious: bookselling in the United States had always
been less of a business than a calling. Profit margins were
notoriously thin, and most independent stores depended on
low rents. Walk-in traffic was often sporadic, the public's
taste fickle; reliance on a steady stream of best sellers to keep
the landlord at bay was not exactly a surefire strategy for
remaining solvent.

Still, overall, selling books was a big business. In 1994
Americans bought $19 billion worth of books. Barnes &
Noble and the Borders Group had by then captured a
quarter of the market, with independent stores struggling to make up just over another fifth and a skein of
book clubs, supermarkets, and other outlets accounting
for the rest. That same year, 513 million individual books
were sold, and seventeen best sellers each sold more than 1
million copies. Bezos knew that two national distributors,
Ingram Book Group and Baker & Taylor, had warehouses
holding about 400,000 titles and in the late 1980s had
begun converting their inventory list from microfiche to

a digital format accessible by computer. Bezos also knew that in 1992 the Supreme Court had ruled in *Quill Corp. v. North Dakota* that retailers were exempt from charging sales tax in states where they didn't have a physical presence. (For years, he would use this advantage to avoid collecting hundreds of millions of dollars in state sales taxes, giving Amazon an enormous edge over retailers of every kind, from bookstores to Best Buy and Home Depot. In recent months, however, Amazon, under mounting pressure, has eased its opposition and reached agreements with twelve states, including California and Texas, to collect sales tax.) "Books are incredibly unusual in one respect," Bezos said, "and that is that there are more items in the book category than there are items in any other category by far." A devotee of the Culture of Metrics, Bezos was undaunted. He was sure that the algorithms of computerized search and access would provide the keys to a consumer kingdom whose riches were as yet undiscovered and barely dreamed of, and so he set out to construct a twenty-first-century ordering mechanism that, at least for the short term, would deliver goods the old-fashioned way: by hand, from warehouses via the Postal Service and commercial shippers.

. . .

ONE OF AMAZON'S CONSULTANTS WAS publishing visionary Jason Epstein. In 1952 Epstein founded Anchor Books, the highbrow trade-paperback publisher; eleven years later he was one of the founders of the *New York Review of Books*, and for many decades was an eminence at Random House. His admiration for Bezos was mixed with a certain bemusement; he knew that for Amazon to really revolutionize bookselling, physical books would have to be transformed into bits and bytes capable of being delivered seamlessly. Otherwise, Bezos would have built only a virtual contraption hostage to the Age of Gutenberg, with all its cumbersome inefficiencies. But Epstein could not fathom that the appeal of holding a physical book in one's hand would ever diminish. Instead, he dreamed of machines that would print on demand, drawing upon a virtual library of digitized books and delivering physical copies in, say, Kinkos all across the country. The bookstores that might survive in this scenario would be essentially stocking examination copies of a representative selection of titles, which could be individually printed while customers lingered at coffee bars awaiting the arrival of their order. Ultimately, Epstein would devote himself to this vision.

Bezos looked elsewhere, convinced that one day he could fashion an unbroken chain of ordering and delivering books, despite the deep losses Epstein warned he'd have to sustain to do so. But first he had to insert the name of his new company into the frontal lobe of America's (and not only America's) consumers. Like all great and obsessed entrepreneurs, his ambitions were imperial, his optimism rooted in an overweening confidence in his own rectitude. He aimed to build a brand that was, in Marcus's phrase, "both ubiquitous and irresistible." A decade before, while a student at Princeton in the mid-1980s, he had adopted as his credo a line from Ray Bradbury, the author of *Fahrenheit 451*: "The Universe says No to us. We in answer fire a broadside of flesh at it and cry Yes!" (Many years later, the octogenarian Bradbury would decry the closing of his beloved Acres of Books in Long Beach, California, which had been unable to compete with the ever-expanding empire of online bookselling.) A slightly built, balding gnome of a man, Bezos often struck others as enigmatic, remote and odd. If not exactly cuddly, he was charismatic in an otherworldly sort of way. A Columbia University economics professor who was an early boss of

Bezos's said of him: "He was not warm. . . . It was like he could be a Martian for all I knew. A well-meaning, nice Martian." Bill Gates, another Martian, would welcome Bezos's arrival to Seattle, saying, "I buy books from Amazon.com because time is short and they have a big inventory and they're very reliable." Millions of book buyers would soon agree.

As the editor of the *Los Angeles Times Book Review,* I had watched Bezos's early rise with admiration, believing that whatever complications he was bringing to the world of bookselling were more than compensated for by the many ways he was extending reader access to a greater diversity of books. After all, even the larger sixty-thousand-square-foot emporiums of Barnes & Noble and Borders could carry no more than 175,000 titles. Amazon, by contrast, was virtually limitless in its offerings. Bezos was then, as he has been ever since, at pains to assure independent bookstores that his new business was no threat to them. He claimed that Amazon simply provided a different service and wasn't trying to snuff bricks-and-mortar stores. Independent booksellers weren't so sure.

. . .

IN THE MID- TO LATE 1990S, when online bookselling was in its infancy, Barnes & Noble and Borders were busy expanding their empires, often opening stores adjacent to long-established community bookstores. The independents were alarmed by these and other aggressive strategies. The chain stores could give customers deeply discounted offerings on a depth of stock made possible by favorable publishers' terms not extended to independents. Clerks at the chains might not intimately know the tastes and predilections of the surrounding neighborhood, but the price was right: lower was better, lowest was best.

The death toll tells the tale. Two decades ago, there were about 4,000 independent bookstores in the United States; only about 1,900 remain. And now, even the victors are imperiled. The fate of the two largest U.S. chain bookstores—themselves partly responsible for putting smaller stores to the sword—is instructive: Borders declared bankruptcy in 2011 and closed its several hundred stores across the country, its demise benefiting over the short term its rival Barnes & Noble, which is nonetheless desperately trying to figure out ways to pay the mortgage on the considerable real estate occupied by its 1,332 stores across the nation. It is removing thousands of physical books from stores in order to create nifty digital zones to persuade customers to embrace the Nook e-book readers, the company's alternative to Amazon's Kindle. Persistent rumors that Barnes & Noble's owners wish to sell regularly sweep the corridors of publishing. But the very idea of owning a bookstore strikes most savvy investors as forlorn. In recent weeks, Microsoft Corp. decided to challenge Amazon by investing $605 million in Barnes & Noble's digital-book business, an arrangement that calls for sharing revenue from e-book sales and other content.

For many of us, the notion that bricks-and-mortar bookstores might one day disappear was unthinkable. Jason Epstein put it best in *Book Business*, his incisive 2001 book on publishing's past, present, and future, when he offered what now looks to be, given his characteristic unsentimental sobriety, an atypical dollop of unwarranted optimism: "A civilization without retail bookstores is unimaginable. Like shrines and other sacred meeting places, bookstores are essential artifacts of human nature. The feel of a book taken from the shelf and held in the hand is a magical experience, linking writer to reader."

That sentiment is likely to strike today's younger readers as nostalgia bordering on fetish. Reality is elsewhere.

Consider the millions who are buying those modern Aladdin's lamps called e-readers. These magical devices, ever more beautiful and nimble in design, have only to be lightly rubbed for the genie of literature to be summoned. Appetite for these idols, especially among the young, is insatiable. For these readers, what counts is whether and how books will be made available to the greatest number of people at the cheapest possible price. Whether readers find books in bookstores or a digital device matters not at all; what matters is cost and ease of access. Walk into any Apple store (temples of the latest fad) and you'll be engulfed by the near frenzy of folks from all walks of life who seemingly can't wait to surrender their hard-earned dollars for the latest iPad, Apple's tablet reader, no matter the constraints of a faltering economy. Then try to find a bookstore. Good luck. If you do, you'll notice that fewer books are on offer, the aisles wider, customers scarce. Bookstores have lost their mojo.

. . .

THE BOOKSTORE WARS ARE OVER. Independents are battered, Borders is dead, Barnes & Noble weakened but still standing, and Amazon triumphant. Yet still there is no peace; a new war rages for the future of publishing. The recent Justice Department lawsuit accusing five of the country's biggest publishers of illegally colluding with Apple to fix the price of e-books is, arguably, publishing's Alamo. What angered the government wasn't the price, but the way the publishers seemed to have secretly arranged to raise it. Many publishers and authors were flabbergasted, accusing the Obama administration of having gone after the wrong culprit. Scott Turow, president of the Authors Guild, denounced the suit, as did David Carr, the media critic of

the *New York Times*, who said it was "the modern equivalent
of taking on Standard Oil but breaking up Ed's Gas 'N'
Groceries on Route 19 instead." On its face, the suit seemed
an antitrust travesty, a failure to go after the "monopolistic
monolith" that is, as the *Times* put it, "publishing's real nem-
esis." In this view, the biggest threat is Amazon's willingness
to sell e-books at a loss in order to seduce millions of unwit-
ting consumers into the leviathan's cornucopia of online
goods and services. What is clear is that "legacy publishing,"
like old-fashioned bookselling, is gone. Just as bookselling
is increasingly virtual, so is publishing. Technology democ-
ratizes the means of both production and distribution. The
implications for traditional publishers are acute.

Amazon, not surprisingly, is keen to sharpen its competitive edge, to use every means at its disposal to confound, sty-
mie, and overpower its rivals. It is well positioned to do so:
the introduction of the Amazon Kindle in 2007 led to a startling surge in e-book sales, which until then had been insig-
nificant. Soon it was not unusual to see e-book sales jump by
400 percent over the previous year. An estimated 3 million
e-readers were sold in 2009, the year Amazon began to sell
its Kindle 2, the first e-reader available globally. Bezos called
the Kindle a response to "the failings of a physical book. . . .
I'm grumpy when I'm forced to read a physical book because
it's not as convenient. Turning the pages . . . the book is always
flopping itself shut at the wrong moment." Millions of people
agreed and millions of Kindles were bought (though Amazon
refuses to reveal exact numbers). Competing devices—including the Nook and the iPad, to name but two of the most
prominent—began to proliferate and to give Amazon's Kindle
a run for its money, thanks to the e-book pricing arrangement
between some publishers and Apple that attracted the ire of
the Justice Department. Barely a year after Apple launched
the iPad, it had sold more than 15 million worldwide. Just

three years ago, only 2 percent of Americans had an e-reader or a tablet; by January of this year, the figure was 28 percent. And Amazon, despite watching its market share drop from 90 percent of the American e-book market in 2010 to about 55–60 percent today, reached a milestone just under three years after the Kindle was introduced. "Amazon.com customers now purchase more Kindle books than hardcover books," Bezos crowed, "astonishing when you consider that we've been selling hardcover books for 15 years, and Kindle books for 33 months."

How the digital age might alter attention spans and perhaps even how we tell one another stories is a subject of considerable angst. The history of writing, however, gives us every reason to be confident that new forms of literary excellence will emerge, every bit as rigorous, pleasurable, and enduring as the vaunted forms of yesteryear. Perhaps the discipline of tapping 140 characters on Twitter will one day give rise to a form as admirable and elegant as haiku was in its day. Perhaps the interactive features of graphic display and video interpolation, hyperlinks and the simultaneous display of multiple panels made possible by the World Wide Web will prompt new and compelling ways of telling one another the stories our species seems biologically programmed to tell. Perhaps all this will add to the rich storehouse of an evolving literature whose contours we have only begun to glimpse, much less to imagine.

. . .

ONE THING, HOWEVER, IS CERTAIN, and about it publishers agree: e-book sales as a percentage of overall revenue are skyrocketing. Initially such sales were a tiny proportion of overall revenue; in 2008, for instance, they were under 1 percent. No more. The head of one major publisher told me that in 2010 e-book sales accounted for 11 percent of his house's revenue. By the end of 2011 it had more than tripled to 36 percent for the year. As John Thompson reports in the revised 2012 edition of his authoritative *Merchants of Culture*, in 2011 e-book sales for most publishers were "between 18 and 22% (possibly even higher for some houses)." Hardcover sales, the foundation of the business, continue to decline, plunging 13 percent in 2008 and suffering similar declines in the years since. According to the Pew Research Center's most recent e-reading survey, 21 percent of American adults report reading an e-book in the past year. Soon one out of every three sales of adult trade titles will be in the form of an e-book. Readers of e-books are especially drawn to escapist and overtly commercial genres (romance, mysteries and thrillers, science fiction), and in these categories e-book sales have bulked up to as large as 60 percent. E-book sales are making inroads even with so-called literary fiction. Thompson cites Jonathan Franzen's *Freedom*, published in 2010 by Farrar, Straus & Giroux, one of America's most distinguished houses and one of several American imprints now owned by the German conglomerate Holtzbrinck. Franzen's novel sold three-quarters of a million hardcover copies and a quarter-million e-books in the first twelve months of publication. (Franzen, by the way, detests electronic books, and is also the guy who dissed Oprah when she had the gumption to pick his earlier novel, *The Corrections*, for her popular book club.) Did Franzen's e-book sales depress his hardcover sales, or did the e-book iteration introduce new readers to his work? It's hard to know, but it's likely a bit of both.

The inexorable shift in the United States from physical to digital books poses a palpable threat to the ways publishers have gone about their business. Jason Epstein got it right two years ago when he wrote, "The resistance today by publishers to the onrushing digital future does not arise from fear of disruptive literacy, but from the understandable fear of their own obsolescence and the complexity of the digital transformation that awaits them, one in which much of their traditional infrastructure and perhaps they too will be redundant." Traditional publishers, he argued, have only themselves to blame, many (perhaps even most) of their wounds having been self-inflicted. They have been too often complacent, allergic to new ideas, even incompetent. Their dogged and likely doomed defense of traditional pricing strategies has left them vulnerable to Amazon's predatory pricing practices. Peter Mayer, former CEO of Viking/Penguin and now owner and publisher of the independent Overlook Press, agrees: "Publishers clearly need to newly prove to readers and authors the value that publishers add." That value, he concedes, is no longer a given.

The inability of most traditional publishers to successfully adapt to technological change may be rooted in the retrograde editorial and marketing culture that has long characterized the publishing industry. As one prominent literary agent told me, "This is a business run by English majors, not business majors." A surpassing irony: for years many of us worried that the increasing conglomeration of publishers would reduce diversity. (We were wrong.) We also feared bloated overheads would hold editors hostage to an unsustainable commercial imperative. (We were right.) But little did we imagine that the blunderbuss for change would arrive in the form of an avaricious imperium called Amazon. It is something of a surprise to see so many now defending the practices of corporate publishers who, just yesterday, were excoriated as philistines out to coarsen the general culture.

Epstein, for one, doesn't fear Amazon, writing recently that the company's "strategy, if successful, might force publishers to shrink or even abandon their old infrastructure."

Thus will publishing collapse into the cottage industry it was "in the glory days before conglomeration." Epstein insists that the dialectic Amazon exemplifies is irreversible, "a vivid expression of how the logic of a radical new and more efficient technology impels institutional change."

Not very long ago it was thought no one would read a book on a computer screen. That assumption is now demonstrably wrong. Today, whether writers will continue to publish the old-fashioned way or go over to direct online publishing is an open question. How it will be answered is at the heart of the struggle taking place between Amazon and traditional publishers.

. . .

JEFF BEZOS GOT WHAT HE WANTED: Amazon got big fast and is getting bigger, dwarfing all rivals. To fully appreciate the fear that is sucking the oxygen out of publishers' suites, it is important to understand what a steamroller Amazon has become. Last year it had $48 billion in revenue, more than all six of the major American publishing conglomerates combined, with a cash reserve of $5 billion. The company is valued at nearly $100 billion and employs more than 65,000 workers (all nonunion); Bezos, according to *Forbes*, is the thirtieth wealthiest man in America. Amazon may be identified in the public mind with books, but the reality is that book sales account for a diminishing share of its overall business; the company is no longer principally a bookseller. Amazon is now an online Walmart, and while 50 percent of its revenues are derived from music, TV shows, movies and, yes, books, another 50 percent comes from a diverse array of products and services. In the late 1990s Bezos bought IMDb.com, the authoritative movie website. In 2009 he went gunning for bigger game, spending nearly $900 million to acquire Zappos.com, a shoe retailer. He also owns Diapers.com, a baby-products website. Now he seeks to colonize high-end fashion as well. "Bezos may well be the premier technologist in America," said *Wired*, "a figure who casts as big a shadow as legends like Bill Gates and the late Steve Jobs."

With the introduction last fall of the Kindle Fire, Bezos is pushing an advanced mobile portal to Amazon's cloud universe, which hosts Web operations for a wide variety of companies and institutions, including Netflix, the *New York Times*, NASA's Jet Propulsion Laboratory, Tina Brown's *Newsweek/Daily Beast*, PBS, Virgin Atlantic, and the Harvard Medical School, among others. As *Wired* put it, when you buy the Kindle Fire, "you're not buying a gadget—you're filing citizen papers for the digital duchy of Amazonia." For his part, Daniel Ellsberg of Pentagon Papers fame recently renounced his "citizenship," pulling the plug on his Amazon Prime membership and calling for a boycott of Amazon after he discovered that the company had buckled under pressure from Washington and scrubbed WikiLeaks from its Web servers. Not unlike small independent bookstores, bricks-and-mortar retailers such as Walmart, Home Depot, and Best Buy are feeling the ground give way beneath them. Target is fighting back, declaring that it will no longer sell Kindles, clearly dismayed by Amazon's brazen promotion of a price-checking app as a means of competing with many of the goods that Target sells.

Amazon has sixty-nine data and fulfillment centers, seventeen of which were built in the past year alone, with more to come. For the thousands of often older migratory baby boomers living out of RVs, who work furiously at the centers filling customer orders at almost literally a breakneck pace, it is, by all accounts, a high-stress job. These workers are the Morlocks who make possible Amazon's vaunted customer service. Last fall, the *Morning Call* investigated their plight in one of Amazon's main fulfillment warehouses in Allentown, Pennsylvania. It found that some employees risked stroke and heat exhaustion while running themselves ragged try-ing to fulfill quotas that resemble the onerous conditions so indelibly satirized by Charlie Chaplin in *Modern Times*. Ambulances were routinely stationed in the facility's giant parking lot to rush stricken workers to nearby hospitals. Amazon, for its part, says such problems are exceptional, and indeed by OSHA's standards incidents of this kind are not the norm. Pursuing greater efficiencies, Amazon in March bought Kiva Systems Inc., a robot manufacturer, for $775 million. Kiva, founded in 2003 and backed by, among others, Bain Capital Ventures, claims that three to four times as many orders per hour can be packed up by a worker using its robots. For Bezos the Martian, the human factor is pesky. Now a more automated solution looms.

. . .

IN SPRING 2011 AMAZON ANNOUNCED that it was hiring publishing veteran Laurence Kirshbaum, former CEO of the Time Warner Book Group, to head Amazon Publishing in New York. Kirshbaum was all but condemned by many of his publishing comrades as an apostate. Others were puzzled: Why, they wondered, would Amazon, having so spectacularly led the e-book revolution and done so much, in the words of one of its spokesmen, to "re-invent reading," seek to become a player in the rearview world of publishing books on paper? Doing so would require building an entire infrastructure of editors, publicists, and even sales repre-sentatives who would be charged with convincing America's booksellers—by now allergic to the very idea of aiding their most agile adversary—to carry its books. Indeed, Barnes &

Noble, among other booksellers, promptly said it would not sell any book published by Amazon. (It should be remembered that Barnes & Noble had once tried to become a publisher itself through its purchase of Sterling Publishing, raising howls of "conflict of interest" from publishers. The perennial question of whose ox is being gored fairly begs to be asked here.) For its part, Amazon swiftly struck an alliance with Houghton Mifflin Harcourt to handle placing its books in physical stores. In a transparent subterfuge aimed at protecting its tax-avoidance strategies, Amazon intends to publish many of its books under a subsidiary imprint of Houghton's called New Harvest, thus keeping alive the increasingly threadbare fiction that it has no physical presence in states where it does business online.

Nine months after Kirshbaum's hire, judging by the number of deals concluded, his nascent operation rivals two of publishing's largest companies, the French-owned Hachette and the Murdoch-owned HarperCollins. Like his boss, Kirshbaum wants to get big fast. It remains to be seen, however, whether spending a reported $800,000 to acquire Penny Marshall's Hollywood memoirs is ultimately profitable; a number of the publishers I spoke with thought not and professed little anxiety at Amazon's big-foot approach. They are not inclined to join the hysteria that largely greeted Kirshbaum's defection, feeling that a recent *Bloomberg Businessweek* cover story depicting a book enveloped by flames had exaggerated by several orders of magnitude the actual threat posed by Amazon's new venture. If Amazon wants to burn the book business, as the magazine's headline blared, publishing books the old-fashioned way struck them as a peculiar way of going about it. Was there really a "secret plot to destroy literature," as the magazine alleged? It seemed far-fetched, to say the least.

At the same time, Amazon's New York foray might be seen as an effort to lure "legacy writers," assuring them of a hardcover trophy and a state-of-the-art digital edition, and as such part of an overall strategy to overcome resistance among established best-selling authors to publish with the online retail giant. As one senior publishing executive said, 40–60 percent of the sales for the Stephen Kings, Lee Childs, and John Grishams are still derived from Barnes & Noble, Walmart, and Costco. Such authors, he said, "were they to walk away from their traditional publishers, would be leaving a considerable fortune on the table." But as Amazon's six other publishing imprints (Montlake Romance, AmazonCrossing, Thomas & Mercer, 47North, Amazon Encore, The Domino Project) have discovered, in certain genres (romance, science fiction, and fantasy) formerly relegated to the moribund mass-market paperback, readers care not a whit about cover design or even good writing, and have no attachment at all to the book as object. Like addicts, they just want their fix at the lowest possible price, and Amazon is happy to be their online dealer.

James Marcus, now an editor at *Harper's*, sees a particular irony in Amazon's entry into book publishing. "When I first worked at Amazon in the mid 1990s," he recalls, "we were advised to think of publishers as our partners. I believe this directive was in earnest. But even then, a creeping contempt for the publishing industry was sometimes discernible. Weren't they stodgy traditionalists, who relied on rotary phones and a Depression-era business model? Well, the company is now a bona-fide trade publisher. There's no predicting how these books will fare, especially with many retailers refusing to sell them (an embargo that won't, of course, affect e-book sales, where Amazon still rules the roost). But Bezos may now discover that cutting out the middleman isn't all it's cracked up to be—that it's surprisingly easy to fail in the neo-Victorian enterprise of publishing, especially when it comes to finding readers for worthy books. Perhaps it's time for him to acquire a rotary phone, available in five retro colors and eligible for two-day Prime shipping on his very own site."

. . .

AMAZON'S ENTRY INTO PUBLISHING'S TRADITIONAL casino is a sideshow. More worrisome, at least over the long term, is the success of Amazon's Kindle Single program, an effort to encourage writers to make an end run around publishers, not only of books but of magazines as well. That program offers writers a chance to publish original e-book essays of no more than 30,000 words (authors agree to a bargain-basement price of no more than $2.99 in exchange for a 70 percent royalty and no advance). It has attracted Nelson DeMille, Jon Krakauer, William Vollmann, Walter Mosley, Ann Patchett, Amy Tan, and the late Christopher Hitchens as well as a slew of lesser-known scribblers, some of whom have enjoyed paydays rivaling or exceeding what they might have gotten were magazines like *Vanity Fair* or the *New Yorker* to have commissioned their work. Royalties are direct-deposited monthly, and authors can check their sales anytime—a level of efficiency and transparency almost unknown at traditional publishers and magazines.

The boundaries are blurring all over publishing, as various actors have belatedly roused themselves to the necessities and blandishments of the online world. The literary agency William Morris Endeavor, for example, has launched 212 Books, an e-publishing program designed to showcase its clients, such as the estimable David Frum, a former speech-writer for President George W. Bush, whose first novel is wittingly called *Patriots* (first-serial rights have been placed with the *Huffington Post*). Endeavor is also bringing out as a direct e-book the hapless James Frey's *The Final Testament of the Holy Bible*. J. K. Rowling, an empire unto herself, is releasing the Harry Potter series on her own terms and making it available through her own website, Amazon, Apple, and every other conceivable digital "platform" in the known universe. Sourcebooks Inc., a medium-sized independent publisher based in Naperville, Illinois, is starting an online bookstore to sell its romance novels directly to readers for a monthly fee. Other creative online inducements for writers are being hatched at a number of publishers, including Little, Brown.

. . .

SUCH EFFORTS HAVE SCANT CHANCE of preventing Amazon from bulldozing any real or perceived obstacles to its single-minded pursuit of maximum clout. It is big enough to impose increasingly harsh terms on both its competitors and its clients. As reported by the *Seattle Times*, it has even begun to compel tiny indie publishers to abandon their traditional short discounts and embrace punitive larger trade discounts. When Karen Christensen of Berkshire Publishing Group refused, Amazon "stopped placing orders, affecting 10% of her business."

The Independent Publishers Group, a principal distributor of about five hundred small publishers, recently angered Amazon by refusing to accept the company's peremptory demand for deeper discounts. Amazon promptly yanked nearly five thousand digital titles. Small-press publishers were beside themselves. Bryce Milligan of Wings Press, based in Texas, spoke for most when, in a blistering broadside, he lambasted Amazon, complaining that its actions caused his sales to drop by 40 percent:

Amazon seemingly wants to kill off the distributors, then kill off the independent publishers and book-stores, and become the only link between the reader and the author. . . . E-book sales have been a highly addictive drug to many smaller publishers. For one thing, there are no "returns." . . . E-book sales allowed smaller presses to get a taste of the kind of money that online impulse buying can produce. Already e-book sales were underwriting the publication of paper books-and-ink at Wings Press. . . . For Amazon to rip e-book sales away is a classic bait-and-switch tac-tic guaranteed to kill small presses by the hundreds. . . . There was a time not so long ago when "compe-tition" was a healthy thing, not a synonym for corpo-rate "murder." Amazon could have been a bright and shining star, lighting the way to increased literacy and improved access to alternative literatures. Alas, it looks more likely to be a large and deadly asteroid. We, the literary dinosaurs, are watching to see if this is a near miss or the beginning of extinction.

But Amazon isn't the only player willing to play hard-ball. Random House, for example, quietly began in March to charge public libraries three times the retail price for e-books, causing Nova Scotia's South Shore Public Libraries to call for a boycott and accuse the German-owned con-glomerate of unfair e-book pricing. It gets worse: according to the *New York Times*, "five of the six major publishers either refuse to make new e-books available to libraries or have pulled back significantly over the last year on how easily or how often those books can be circulated."

Jacob Stevens, the managing director of Verso, the distinguished independent press spawned by the London-based *New Left Review*, says of Amazon:

Having our backlist instantly and immediately available has so far outweighed the problems. For me, the problems become worse as Amazon moves from "just" being a big player in selling books to vertical control of entire sections of the industry. It all gets a bit Big Brother. It's easy to imagine Amazon muscling existing publishers out of the picture altogether and inviting authors and agents to deal directly with them. What would that do for the richness and diversity of our culture?

And yet Amazon gives $1 million a year, in grants of about $25,000 apiece, to a wide range of independent literary journals and nonprofit organizations, including the *Kenyon Review*, the newly launched online *Los Angeles Review of Books,* and even *One Story*, the nonprofit literary magazine devoted to the short story, which recently celebrated its tenth anniversary by honoring Ann Patchett, an outspoken critic of Bezos's business practices and a co-owner of an independent bookstore in Nashville. Amazon's contributions outstrip by a large factor any advertising dollars sent my way by traditional publishers during the nearly nine years I ran the *Los Angeles Times Book Review*. Of course, such largesse—less than a pittance of its $5 billion cash reserve—may be meant to ensnare its most articulate critics in a web of dependency. If so, Amazon will likely be surprised, as the editors of such journals have well-deserved reputations for biting the hand that feeds, and they prize their contrarian sensibilities.

Another bookselling veteran made uneasy by Amazon's colossal success is Andy Ross, who—having succeeded the venerable Fred Cody as the owner of Cody's Books in Berkeley until online competition forced its flagship location to close in 2006, after fifty years in business—now works in Oakland as a literary agent. He told me:

Monopolies are always problematic in a free society, and they are more so when we are dealing with the dissemination of ideas, which is what book publishing is about. In the realm of electronic publishing, Amazon until recently controlled about 90% of the market, a monopoly by almost anyone's definition. Most people bought their e-books in the proprietary Kindle file format that could only be purchased from Amazon and only read on the Kindle reader that was manufactured by Amazon. Other makers of e-book readers designed them to accept the open-source e-pub format that allowed customers to have a wider choice of retailers to supply them with e-books. Since then, Amazon's market share has been declining, but 60% of all e-books in America continue to be sold by Amazon in the Kindle file format. Amazon simply has too much power in the marketplace. And when their business interest conflicts with the public interest, the public interest suffers.

It's a fair point—one that also plagues Peter Mayer of Overlook Press:

> All sides of this argument need to think deeply—not just about their businesses, but also about their world. I grew up in a world in which many parts together formed a community adversarial in a microcosmic way but communal in a larger sense: authors, editors, agents, publishers, wholesalers, retailers, and readers. I hope, worried as I am about the current trajectory [of publishing], that we do not look back one day, sitting on a stump as the boy does in Shel Silverstein's *The Giving Tree*, and only see what has become a largely denuded wasteland.

. . .

Postscriptum (2015)

Hardly a month goes by without news of Amazon's continuing assault on the publishing industry. In the three years since I undertook a close look at Amazon's ambitions and practices for the *Nation*, the company has continued to conquer. Today, in 2015, nearly two-thirds of all American e-books are bought through the online retailer. (In the United Kingdom Amazon is estimated to sell about 80 percent of e-books.) Its share of all new books sold in the United States is a whopping 40 percent—an increase from 12 percent in just five years. Peter Hildick-Smith, head of Codex, a leading book-audience research firm, declares that Amazon is "the most powerful book retailer today by far." Traditional publishers are in an uproar, fearing that the Seattle-based firm will render them obsolete by enabling writers to end-run old-school "gatekeepers" by going directly to readers digitally.

The rise of the Internet was initially seen as a revolutionary boon, transforming a backward carriage trade into a modern engine of knowledge distribution, with the promise of democratizing literacy. Thus was the rise of Jeff Bezos's Amazon celebrated in many precincts. No longer would readers be hostage to geography; books could be ordered from anywhere and swiftly delivered. Plus, the prices charged were the lowest to be had. Convenience, cost, and excellent customer service won millions of readers, happy to throng in Bezos's big tent.

While big is not always bad, I found there was much about Amazon that was troubling: its labor practices, for one; its cutthroat business dealings, for another. Bezos once joked that Amazon ought to approach small publishers "the way a cheetah would pursue a sickly gazelle"—a remark, we now learn, that led to an effort inside Amazon dubbed the

Gazelle Project, designed to extract concessions from the weakest publishers (it's since been helpfully renamed the Small Publisher Negotiation Program). Brad Stone's revelatory book *The Everything Store: Jeff Bezos and the Age of Amazon*, as well as recent reports in the *New Yorker* by George Packer and in the *New York Review of Books* by Steve Coll, echo my original analysis and deepen my worst fears. As did a startling front-page story, published on August 15, 2015, in the *New York Times* by Jodi Kantor and David Streitfeld, which quoted a former Amazon human resources director as characterizing the company's internal culture as one of "purposeful Darwinism." In its zeal to foster innovation, Amazon was said to be "more nimble and more productive, but harsher and less forgiving" of employees who are unable to keep up. Bezos, for his part, was baffled by the paper's portrait of "a soulless, dystopian workplace" and said he didn't "recognize" the company the reporters described.

Today, Amazon so dominates the marketplace that it feels free to bulldoze the competition, dictating terms to suppliers and customers alike. With respect to publishing and bookselling, Amazon is increasingly a vertically integrated company, at once a bookseller, a reviewer, even a publisher, and as such it poses a uniquely disturbing threat. Fears that Amazon might bolster its own publishing, however, by hiring book veteran Laurence Kirshbaum, subsided when he resigned two years after joining Amazon, in the wake of his failure to jump-start the operation with big authors and big advances, which, in the event, resulted in big losses. Still, Amazon has achieved a worrying hegemony, having successfully laid siege to traditional bricks-and-mortar bookstores not only in the United States but also in Europe. In Germany, Austria, and Switzerland, Amazon has forced the media conglomerate Bertelsmann to shutter its core book clubs and retail stores. Sarah Simon, a media analyst with

Berenberg Bank in London, says Bertelsmann's bookselling business "has been largely superseded by online sales, where Amazon is the market leader." Amazon is also going after other important publishers like Piper, Carlsen, and Ullstein, all owned by the Swedish Bonnier Group. According to a recent report in *Der Spiegel*, Amazon is demanding that its share of the profit from every e-book sale rise from 30 percent of the retail price to 50 percent. Christian Schumacher-Gebler, the CEO of Bonnier Media Deutschland, worries that "Amazon is undermining our ability to survive." The European Commission is concerned about the legality of Amazon's tactics and has begun to investigate whether the company has, as the *New York Times* reported, "used its dominant position in the region's e-books market" to favor its own products over rivals'. The company has also drawn heat for its dodgy tax practices in Luxembourg, home to its European headquarters. Amazon also engaged in a widely reported and bitter struggle with Hachette, the French company that owns Little, Brown, among other American imprints. As a negotiating tactic to extract higher fees from the firm, it refused to sell many Hachette titles. Ultimately, Amazon and Hachette came to terms, but the prolonged battle left the combatants on the publishing side feeling bruised. Amazon had used a similar tactic with Time Warner's Warner Bros. studio by refusing to take pre-orders for selected movie titles in an effort to get better terms for the sale of movie discs, which it sells for little or no profit in order to compete with stores like Walmart and Best Buy.

The entire ecology of publishing is at risk. Conglomeration proceeds at a dizzying pace: Random House and Penguin (which includes, among other imprints, the Viking Press) merge; Hachette buys the Perseus Group (which includes both Basic Books and Nation Books). Little fish are gobbled up by bigger fish, and they, in turn, face even larger predators. There is blood in the water. But the Justice Department, seemingly mesmerized by visions of a digital utopia, is oddly blind to the threat to publishing posed by Amazon's growing monopoly, apparently regarding Amazon as a benign giant whose machinations, so far, offer more benefits than disadvantages. Amazon, for its part, insists that it has only readers' interests at heart and is merely providing books at the lowest possible price, absorbing huge losses in order to do so. Increasingly, this claim is revealed as a self-serving stratagem; as Coll writes, "The more Amazon uses coercion and retaliation as a means of negotiation, the more it looks to be restraining competition." Antitrust issues are not only about price and market share, but also the antidemocratic implications for both competition and the larger culture. When will the Justice Department wake up? There is precedent, after all. In 1948, the Supreme Court, in *United States v. Paramount Pictures, Inc.,* ordered the breakup of the old Hollywood studio system.

Amazon is hardly an online bookstore anymore. Books are a small fraction of its overall business—just 7 percent. From the start, Amazon understood that books were a loss leader whose chief benefit was to induce millions to enroll in the online Walmart the company wanted to become. In 2015, Amazon's revenue exceeded $100 billion, making it one of America's largest retailers, and the company now employs 220,000 workers, up 49 percent over 2014. Its market capitalization stands at more than $260 billion. Today, even the CIA finds itself compelled to outsource some of its data collection by availing itself of Amazon's powerful cloud servers (whose operating income was $521 million in 2015, up more than fivefold in a year), in a deal estimated at $600 million.

I remain optimistic that our species will continue to tell itself stories, for that's the way we extract meaning from our otherwise unruly lives. But just as utilities are rightly regulated because they provide an essential service every-one needs—water, gas, electricity—so too has the time come for closer scrutiny and regulation of a company that, like Standard Oil a century ago, provides an indispens-able service for a modern economy and a healthy culture. As Amazon gains market share, we ought not to abide its self-proclaimed conceit that unfettered growth is invariably in the consumer's interest. We ought to resist a narrow defi-nition of those interests. Just as a responsible energy pol-icy must strike a balance between the benefit to individuals and the consequences to the environment, so must a simi-lar calculus be applied to Amazon. (The French are exem-plary here, having long recognized that books, like bread, are necessary for any civilization worthy of the name; they subject both to price controls, thus permitting independent bookstores and bakeries to survive and thrive.) Amazon's right to offer readers the widest array of books at the most reasonable price is not in question. But such a right is not to be exercised at the expense of the fragile and essential con-tributions of authors, editors, and publishers to the general culture. Amazon ought no longer to be permitted to behave like a parasite that hollows out its host. A serious Justice Department investigation is past due.

Jessa Crispin

Jessa Crispin is editor-in-chief of the litblog/webzine
Bookslut, *founded in 2002. Her writing has appeared
in the* Washington Post, Chicago Sun-Times,
Guardian, *and* Toronto Globe and Mail, *among
other publications. She lives in Chicago.*

Remember when everyone was super upset about newspapers cutting their book review sections? People picketed. People with better things to do and ideas in their heads stood outside of newspaper offices and held up signs and said words through bullhorns and performed other related physical activities. Until, I'm guessing, their feet got tired and they all shrugged and went to Starbucks.

Most of these people's employment was in some way tied up in the newspaper book review section. Either they were writers worried about their next books not being covered and thereby boosting sales, or they were critics themselves, worried about their paychecks. I point this out to illustrate that there was no big public outcry that book review sections were being cut. A few readers may have written a letter here or there, or strayed into the picket line until their feet also got tired. But as a whole, the cutting of book review sections was met by the general public with a shrug.

This all happened several years ago. More and more book sections collapsed, more and more longtime critics were laid off. And still, no one outside of those inside the business of reviewing books quite noticed.

. . .

IT FEELS STUPID TO TALK about the crisis of book criticism when the entire industry is in crisis. We have no bookstores now, now that Borders bullied so many independent shops out of business and then died itself, now that Barnes & Noble is in its death throes, now that Amazon rules publishing and acts like a British landowner in nineteenth-century Ireland.

"Oh, you're starving to death? That's too bad, it's your own fault really. It's a shame you can't have any of that nice food you've been growing, because you know that's ours now. Because we said so. If you could go outside to die, that would be helpful, it makes such a mess when you go, you know."

Then there's the no-one-reads-anymore hysteria, the lack of supportive careers for apprenticing writers, the MFA death trap, etc. It feels self-indulgent as a critic to say, "But the whole critical structure has broken down, let's talk about that." The critic only comes into play when the books are actually produced and put onto the market, meaning their jobs are tied into this whole decaying, rotting mess of an industry. Which is why it's amazing that the only thing book critics really got exercised about was the cutting of newspaper review sections, not any of the rest of it. Surely there was another point where they could have placed their picket lines to do some good.

. . .

AND LET'S LOOK, FOR A MOMENT, at what the death of the newspaper review actually meant, because that keeps getting lost in the nostalgic haze of men who remember a simpler time, when literary culture was tied intimately into popular culture and authors could still be rock stars without writing about magicians or vampires or whatever. The death of the newspaper review meant the end of the literary authority who would declare that books by straight, white men are always the best of books. That books by the conglomerate publishing houses are the best of books. That literary culture exists only in New York City. That literary critical culture is a lofty, apolitical space of objective assessment. That is essentially what the critical culture told us for the fifty years of postwar literature (the peak for literary rock stars like Norman Mailer, John Updike, Vladimir Nabokov, et al.) and its seemingly never-ending influence.

Actually, there are some newspaper book review sections still in existence for some reason, but now the rowdy online culture regularly keeps tabs on them. They count up the number of books written by women and people of color and LGBTQ writers that are reviewed by the newspapers. Or the number of women, people of color, and LGBTQ reviewers who are hired to write the reviews. It is always a small fraction of the whole. And that is what all those people on the picket line fought to save: a sexist, racist, elitist system.

Some people still confuse the newspaper literary culture—a small subgroup, almost a fetish really—with literary culture as a whole. Mostly those people are the people the newspaper literary culture is both serving and comprised of, those silly people in the picket lines. White, straight, male New York writers and critics.

I can't imagine why that might be.

. . .

BUT ALSO ALARMING IS THE number of women, people of color, LGBTQ, radicals, and weirdos, all the wonderful et ceteras of the world, banging on the doors of the New York Times to be let in. As if inclusion will give them legitimacy. As if there isn't a fucking cover fee. As if that fee weren't parts of your human body.

I want to tell them: this world is not for you, you are better without it. Outside the gates, not in. This world was in fact, in part, designed specifically to keep you out. It does not want you. It will not nourish you.

And just because you gain entry for one fleeting moment, do not think for a second that you haven't stomped all over the even less desirables on your way in, don't think the system has suddenly become tolerant.

But people outside the city's walls long for entry; it is the setup. That is how the city controls the frontier.

More interesting would be to exist outside the walls, and learn how to raid the city for whatever it is you need.

. . .

JUST TO BE CLEAR, THE Internet is not the frontier in this particular metaphor. Some of it might qualify, but most of it is just suburbs. The most respected, the most quoted and blurbed from, the most prominent and respectable of the literary critical apparatuses online are run by white men. They write about books published by conglomerate publishers. They pretend literary culture exists solely in New York, although MFA programs will also get attention. Other than a few eye-rolls about Amazon hijinks, they too are apolitical.

The city sends the suburbs their goods, the suburbs are grateful. The suburbs praise the city, the city in turn nurtures and feeds the suburbs with advertising dollars, book advances, and entry visas.

People like to think they live on the frontier, that they are pushing boundaries and living rebelliously. Nobody *really* wants to be James Joyce, though. When it comes down to it. Totally inaccessible and publishing poison, forced to self-publish with the help of two (inadequately celebrated) lesbians, thought to be a madman, and still cursed to this day. No one really wants to be James Joyce, living in borderline poverty with an insane daughter and a layabout son, quietly changing the world but very rarely, if at all, acknowledged for it. So completely out on the frontier his books were confiscated and destroyed by multiple governments.

But everyone wants to think they're James Joyce, in their cozy teaching jobs, in mortgaged homes, writing about the same things that everyone else is writing about. They want to think themselves renegades but they still want to be regularly petted by the authority. They look at their surroundings, and they think, *I can see grass, I can see sky, this must be the frontier.*

It's not. Check your paystubs, it's not.

.   .   .

FOR A CRITICAL CULTURE TO be vital, it has to be aware of its placement in the system. It has to see that system as broken. It has to respond to its brokenness.

It makes sense to me that when the system goes wobbly, the critical culture responds by saying, "From now on, we will only run positive reviews." It is a long list of publications and critics who have come out saying this, from the *Believer* to Buzzfeed to assorted Internet communities.

But that of course is not criticism, it is enthusiasm. And enthusiasm only happens in long form when all uncertainties and unknowns have been weeded out. When expectations are met.

It is a way to regain control. Uncertainty causes anxiety, and when things are already uncertain due to a literary system in flux, it is easier to close off, to shut the gates, to only admit those whose entrance is guaranteed. To, you know, review your friends.

Anxiety's primary function is to ready the body for action and for change. It is a complicated uprooting process, the gathering together of energy and focus so that when you decide what to do, you are able to do it. But only reviewing positively, closing off the doors of each individual subculture, creating communities of enthusiasm—that is not making a decision. That is the opposite of it. You are shutting all the windows and doors and trapping your anxiety in there. Smiles become forced and plasticky, and the anxiety becomes, *Do I really belong here? Do they want me here? How can I ensure my placement here?*

· · ·

GIVE A PERSON ABSOLUTE FREEDOM and probably what they will do is just copy the person closest to them. The anxiety of making a decision under absolute freedom is too much to bear. There is surely only one way to do things right, and all of these other ways to do things wrong. It's why the Internet culture is just a copy of newspaper culture, but with a few *fucks* and *shits* thrown in.

The removal of the newspaper book review and the rise of the Internet literary culture gave us all absolute freedom. So we all just basically recreated newspaper culture, because it was easy to replicate and had worked for others for so long. Surely it was the right thing to do.

· · ·

IT'S HARD TO SAY WHAT value the literary critic provides to the larger culture. And I say this as someone who has spent the last twelve years of her life engaged in this activity. Don't think there weren't nights where I woke up with the thought "My entire purpose in life is to help people make decisions about which books to buy; I am simply part of someone's marketing strategy" chilling me to the bone.

There's the value that the literary critic can provide, but it is so often buried under the needs of that critic to tend to one's career and to boost friends' books, and that burning desire to make one's opinion heard. That value is: thinking a thought out loud, following it through centuries of other people's thoughts, synthesizing it with your own thoughts and experiences. Books are vehicles for ideas, but ideas have no purpose until they are forced into contact with minds and bodies and experiences. Critics can put ideas into action, through the juxtaposition of idea and world.

And books are deeply personal things. Wept over, treasured, passed along. Not external objects, their function is to become internal. Sometimes the fit needs adjusting; that is another thing that the literary critic can provide.

Literary critics have value. And yet sitting here I cannot come up with a single name of a critic who has played some sort of role in my life. Elizabeth Hardwick? But really only for her fiction, her essays never did that much for me. Jenny Diski? But really only her personal essays. I am struggling here. And yet surely there have been some.

Maybe it doesn't matter that I can't remember a name. There were books that got into my hands thanks to critics, and there were books I was able to think my way through thanks to some assistance. It is probably right that they disappeared in that act, their identities dissolving so that the author could take their place. One should probably distrust someone who tries to make their name as a critic, someone whose goal is to be known for performing this act.

I am trying to remember what dragged me into this role to begin with. Books had served me, I wanted to serve them back. It must have been as simple as that.

. . .

IF ALL WE ARE DOING as book critics is propping up those in power, the conglomerate publishers and the unthinkingly celebrated, we are failing at our jobs.

If all we are doing as book critics is pretending there is such a thing as objective assessment of literature, we are failing at our jobs.

If all we are doing as book critics is assisting people in making a choice as a consumer, we are failing at our jobs.

If all we are doing as book critics is looking at the book and not the system that it came out of, we are failing at our jobs.

. . .

I AM A SELF-HATING BOOK CRITIC who is failing at her job, daily. But the act of failing, and trying to understand that failure, is an interesting one to me. So I will keep at it, never quite getting it right.

THE VIEW FROM A UNIVERSITY PRESS

Donna Shear

Donna Shear has directed the University of Nebraska Press since 2009. From 2003 to 2009, she directed Northwestern University Press and has been in scholarly publishing for more than twenty years. She is a graduate of Rutgers College and holds an MBA from the University of Toronto.

The crowds gathered at the annual conference of the Association of Writers & Writing Programs (AWP), held in Seattle, Washington, February 27 through March 1, 2014. At airport baggage claims and hotel lobbies, at local restaurants and trendy bars, writers and poets, students and teachers, and friends and acquaintances hugged and kissed one another, happy to see one another again, ready to catch up. More than fourteen thousand had come for the conference—another record-breaking year for attendance.

In the exhibit hall, more than six hundred exhibitors lined up row after row. Many exhibitors were from MFA and PhD programs in creative writing, others were small independent presses or even larger commercial publishers. There were literary magazines and writer's workshops. Among the exhibitors were more than thirty university presses. The feel in the exhibit hall was not unlike a crowded souk in a Middle Eastern city: people making their way to various booths to sample the wares, perhaps even purchase something, bags in hand, stuffing more and more goodies into them.

The number of people squeezed into the exhibit hall or rushing off to hear talks ranging from "What Was Is: The Use of Present Tense in Creative Nonfiction" to

"Teaching Brief, Sudden, Flash, and Very Short Prose" to "Shouting in a Crowded Room: Challenges in Expanding Small Press Readership" added to the excitement. There were sessions on how to get published, how to market yourself, how to market your book, how to expand the market for small presses, and how to get a job teaching, especially a tenure-track job.

One session, "Fiction, Memoir, and the University Press," spoke to the role of university presses in the world of literary publishing. The tweets and Facebook postings from those university press people who attended reflected the excitement and hustle and bustle. Editors from university presses tweeted about awards received or made comments about the important role of university presses in the world of literary publishing.

As we look at literary publishing in the twenty-first century, we need to ask ourselves what that role should be—or if there should even be a role at all.

Today, not many university presses are flourishing. Sales have not increased—in fact, for many, sales have seen a steady decline over the last decade. University administration support for presses has been precarious for more than two decades. Libraries, particularly research and academic ones, used to be the largest purchasers of university press books, but now see stagnant or shrinking budgets. If academic librarians need to carefully parcel out tight budgets, most would not consider creative works a part of the essential canon of academic books that research libraries must acquire.

All across the supply chain—publishers, printers, wholesalers, retailers—we've seen consolidation as smaller players get swallowed up. The big players are getting bigger, exerting more and more market power, insisting on deeper discounts from publishers. The Internet has had some unintended consequences, too. For instance, the used-book market has had a devastating effect on publishers—online used-books transactions means the reader can easily search, find, and purchase a used book anywhere in the world, instead of having to scour used-book stores; the burgeoning "open access" movement on campuses and the liberal use of e-course reserves—often led by campus libraries—have all had a profound negative effect on university press sales.

The publishing landscape has shifted and it cannot be "business as usual" for university presses.

THE ROLE OF UNIVERSITY PRESSES IN TENURE AND PROMOTION

Traditionally, the role and mission of university presses has been to publish the research of scholars worldwide in the various disciplines within that university press's publishing program. The University of Nebraska Press is known for publishing in Native American and the American West, among other fields. Other university presses have expertise in philosophy or economics or political science or other areas of history.

The 120 or so university presses in the United States (despite some closings, this number has remained fairly stable) have found themselves charged with publishing the humanistic and social science scholarship of faculty from thousands of institutions. Acquisition editors at these presses scour the academy looking for new, important, and cutting edge work. The editors attend academic conferences—some as large as AWP, others much smaller—to listen to papers being presented by junior and other faculty, searching for the next big (or biggish) idea. The competition to snare a good project is usually between or among university presses. In cases where the book is part of the scholar's tenure or promotion packet, having a peer-reviewed book published by a good university press is crucial and may trump an offer from a commercial press.

But if we look at the publishing process for creative works, we see a very different set of criteria and a different publishing landscape. It seems logical that, with the growth of MFA and PhD programs at universities, the pressure on that faculty to publish is intense. After all, how can you teach writing—how can you hold out hope for your students that they will get published—if you cannot get published yourself? The University of Oregon's creative-writing department's guidelines for tenure—for just one representative example—say it quite blatantly:

> The most important evidence to support the case for achievement in research is . . . a book or books published since hire with a nationally recognized press or presses, including fine small presses.

Notice that no mention is made of "peer-reviewed publication," or reference at all to being published by university presses, as there would be in other disciplines. This is because publication with a commercial or independent press is its own recognition of the value of the work. That work has beaten out thousands of others, risen from the slush pile, and has been rewarded with publication by a major or well-respected independent press. Essentially, this stands in for peer review. And after publication, reviews and sales act to further validate the success of the work.

CREATIVE WORKS AND UNIVERSITY PRESSES

Let's take a look at three "genres" or categories of creative works, if you will: poetry, fiction (short and long), and memoir. The financial picture for university presses publishing creative works varies with the genres; some seem to perform better than others, but none of them perform well enough to be the savior for university press publishing. Because the financial performance is spotty, the decisions seem to be driven by the perception of mission. It behooves us in university press publishing to subject those missions to closer scrutiny given the financial realities.

POETRY AND UNIVERSITY PRESSES

Poetry, more than any of the other creative genres, seems to have the most compelling case, both in terms of mission and finances. Over the years, university presses have become important destination presses for the finest poets. University presses at places such as Wesleyan, Northwestern, Louisiana State, Iowa, Pittsburgh, and others have established reputations as among the best publishers of poetry. Look at the recent finalists and winners of the National Book Award in poetry: university press poets are well represented and have taken home the award many times. Louisiana State University (LSU) Press has won two Pulitzers in poetry. Some fine "boutique" publishers, such as Milkweed, Graywolf, and Copper Canyon, are competition, but very few larger commercial publishers have significant poetry lists. At LSU Press, which publishes fifteen to seventeen poetry titles each year, the stellar reputation that the press has garnered in poetry, as well as the strategic way it has honed its marketing of poetry titles over the years, has meant that poetry is profitable for them.

Many of their poetry books backlist nicely. When asked about how publishing poetry fits into the overall mission to publish scholarship, the director made two points: many of the poets LSU Press are indeed affiliated with universities, but, more important, she sees the "encouragement of the life of the mind" as being as crucial as the dissemination of other kinds of research or scholarship. The merger of the press with the *Southern Review* (a university-based literary magazine) a few years ago and the synergy between the two has meant more opportunities to publish the best poets. Other university presses have strong relationships with literary magazines on campus (Nebraska and *Prairie Schooner*, for instance) that help to keep the publication of poetry in alignment with the host institution's priorities. In the case of the University of Iowa Press, alignment with its host institution—which endeavors to be *the* university for fine creative writing—works well.

So for all those factors, many university presses make a strong case for poetry being mission driven, albeit a different mission than that of tenure and promotion. Indeed, the national recognition for the press when poetry wins big national or international awards—and thus, for the university itself—is also an intriguing benefit. Even so, poetry isn't a field to venture into if you aren't already established and it isn't a field with wild profit attached to it. While it is not an expensive field to publish in, it takes years to build up the reputation, backlist, and marketing expertise to be successful, and one could question whether there is room for new entrants.

FICTION AND THE UNIVERSITY PRESS

Fiction is, sadly, a far different animal, though, and one where university presses must take a hard, sobering look at their role in publishing it.

The supply of fiction far outpaces the demand. Everyone has heard the stories of the slush pile; certainly it has existed for decades. In the more than two decades I have been in scholarly publishing, many have argued that university presses have real opportunities in fiction because commercial houses have dropped the so-called midlist writer (the writer who sells steadily but isn't a blockbuster). One wonders if this is truly an opportunity. Given a press's limited resources of time and money, is it a rational decision to publish fiction? Press directors who publish fiction tell me that it is in fact a mission-based decision: often, it's to publish writers of their region, sometimes it's to publish underrepresented voices. But to think that the midlist writer who can't get published by a major commercial house belongs at a university press is a tougher justification.

We have the financial realities of publishing fiction. First, if the book is good enough to be published, it is probably agented. Agents (and to be clear, I like agents and respect their role in the process) require advances and higher royalties for their authors. Second, these books carry what is known as a "trade discount"; that is, the discount that the publisher has to give the bookstore or wholesaler or online retailer is deeper than on an academic book. The list price for the book is constrained by the consumer marketplace. Unlike a scholarly monograph, which retails upwards of fifty dollars, the paperback fiction book is topping out around twenty dollars; the hardcover at under thirty dollars. After the discount given to retailers or wholesalers, the net selling price for a paperback might be eleven dollars. Once you account for the production costs, the author royalties, the marketing and advertising of the book, the warehouse and fulfillment fees, and staff time, the only way fiction can be profitable is if it sells a lot of copies, which, unfortunately, for university presses, is seldom the case.

Why? The major challenge is finding the audience for a particular fiction work. Unlike poetry, where we know that other poets are the largest market for poetry, or we know which poets can be grouped together and who likes to read those kinds of poets and how we can reach them, there is no easy way to identify or reach that market with an unknown fiction author. Consider this: if you want a cookbook on Thai cooking, you go on Amazon and put that in the search bar. Several dozen titles will show up on your computer. But how to find fiction? Most likely, you aren't going to search for a fiction title that way. You will use reviews or best-seller lists or someone's recommendation, all of which means the book has already made some splash. And seldom does a university press book of fiction win national awards (although it does happen occasionally, which only continues to allow presses to think they can play in that field) or get reviewed in major national publications. To get to the point where the novel or short story collection is even noticed at all requires a lot of time and money on the part of the university press. With the low retail price, coupled with the deep discounts, the margins are just not there. Given that the finances are grim and that university presses are not first choices for fiction writers, university presses probably have no business being in the fiction arena.

Others disagree. One press director feels that one of the roles of university presses is to be a first publisher of promising writers who can't get an agent or get noticed with their first book or short story collection.

Is this a legitimate role for the university press? Is it, as the LSU Press director says, about the life of the mind? In these challenging economic times, should university presses take the financial risk to further someone's nonacademic career?

LITERATURE IN TRANSLATION AND OTHER UNDERREPRESENTED VOICES AND UNIVERSITY PRESSES

Many university presses are known for publishing literature in translation, a field that seldom makes money. The justification for publishing these works is that English-language readers need to be exposed to the literature of other countries. At Northwestern University Press, the renowned European Classics series brought fiction, poetry, and drama classics to an English-speaking audience. Many of those books were by Nobel laureates. Many have gone on to become solid performers—used in classroom course adoptions. Dozens of university presses continue to publish literature in translation, although one could argue that most of the classics have now been translated and newer, more contemporary works need the test of time to see if they are important enough to translate. It's a curious role for university presses because obviously it's completely disconnected from the tenure or promotion process. After all, the book has already been written and published in the author's own language—the press is making it more accessible to a larger audience, but the press is not helping an author with his academic career.

The outlets for publication of literature in translation are small. Very little foreign literature gets translated by commercial houses. There are a precious few independent presses that publish literature in translation (bless them), but university presses still pick up the bulk of it. Here's where it's difficult to decide whether or not it is a legitimate role of university presses: most literature in translation is expensive—the press has to license the rights from the foreign publisher plus pay for the translation—yet these books don't help very much in the tenure and promotion process, except, perhaps, for those faculty teaching in the field of translation studies. Sales tend to be extremely modest unless the book finds its way to syllabi or the author wins major literary recognition, which happens only rarely. It's not uncommon for a novel in translation to sell fewer than four hundred copies. Once in a blue moon, an author will win the Nobel Prize in Literature and the press will be sitting on the English-language publication rights, but it's not a good investment strategy to acquire and publish in translation with that hope in mind. Several foreign governments make translation grants available, as does the National Endowment for the Arts, but if the end result is that the book has sold just a few hundred copies, the press needs to assess whether this is truly a good use of press time and resources, even in furthering culture.

A few press directors are continuing or expanding their lists in fiction and memoir because they see a need to publish underrepresented voices. In one case, the press is expanding the publication of works by African American women writers. In another case, it's Latinas. In another, it is voices of the South (both fiction and nonfiction). Again, these press directors see this as mission driven, in much the same way as those who publish literature in translation see their role. As long as the host institution sees this as part of their press's mission, it's wonderful that these works are being brought to life. But presses must keep their financial eyes wide open to the reality of the fiscal impact of these kinds of books.

CREATIVE NONFICTION AND THE UNIVERSITY PRESS

Some of the finest writing we have published at University of Nebraska Press has been in memoir. A few of these books have been so poignant, so gut wrenching, and so powerful (and some even hilarious) that it is tragic that more people don't know about them. Sadly, the best-selling of these has netted a few thousand copies. Most sell under one thousand copies. Memoir faces the same financial scenario as fiction—low list prices, hard-to-find audiences, and challenging competition. Celebrity or political memoirs are not the same as literary memoir, where craft is as important, or more important, than the story that is being told. And as a fellow director says, "It's hard to sell memoir to a bookstore buyer with the sole argument that it is well written." Some memoir may justify itself because of the press's mission to tell "untold stories," but, again, as finances get tighter and tighter, I fear that most university presses publishing in this field will abandon it out of necessity.

AWP AGAIN

Just back from Seattle, Nebraska's editors are gushing about AWP. "Not a second to rest; the booth was jammed with people." "We sold out of so many books we brought." "Everyone says we are the destination press for memoir." "People love our covers."

And the exciting sales total: less than $5,000.

Hmm. While such a sales total may be more than acceptable at academic conferences, where editors are more concerned about finding new books or authors, if presses are deluged with creative works without soliciting them, then this is a fairly paltry sum, particularly when you consider the costs of exhibiting and the travel expenses of sending staff to a conference.

Literary publishing takes a lot of work, often without the financial reward. As the pressure mounts on university presses to justify their existence within the academy, it may not be feasible for presses to remain in the creative-works arena.

A highly informal survey of university press directors I did a few months ago showed that most who published in creative works saw it as a slog—and that it had always been a slog—but they had no intention of cutting back on their programs. As the twenty-first century moves along, they may not be able to remain so resolute.

Gabriel Bernal Granados, Kristin Dykstra & Roberto Tejada

An editor of Mandorla *and the author of numerous books and translations in Mexico, Gabriel Bernal Granados has received grants from the National Fund for Culture and the Arts, the Mexican Center for Writers, and the Rockefeller Foundation. He lives in Mexico City, where he is cofounder and director of the publishing house Libros Magenta.*

Kristin Dykstra is an editor of Mandorla. *Among numerous awards, she has received a fellowship from the National Endowment for the Arts and the Gulf Coast Prize in Translation. She is Distinguished Scholar in Residence at Saint Michael's College.*

Roberto Tejada is the founding editor of Mandorla. *The author of poetry collections and books on the visual arts, he is the Hugh Roy and Lillie Cranz Cullen Distinguished Professor at the University of Houston.*

Mandorla: *Nueva Escritura de las Américas* / New Writing *from the Americas* was a multilingual journal of poetry, poetics, and translation that brought multiple sites of cultural activity into print form. It was a publishing effort that, over the course of two decades (1991–2013) and a handful of editorial fluctuations, navigated the literary geographies of the American continents. The first issue, published in May 1991, established the journal's particular multilingual format. Composed primarily of English and Spanish, translated work appeared only in the target language; previously unpublished material was featured only in its original; and in the case of poetry in French or Portuguese, oftentimes with translations into Spanish and English. Mexico City, where the first five issues were edited and printed, was an advantageous site for the cultural debates connecting north and south in the face of privatization, trade agreements, labor flows, and other emergent realities in the region—changes that went hand in hand with profound technological, financial, political, and artistic transformations in the national life of Mexico and of most other Latin American countries. The name of the magazine—the term *mandorla* denoting the space created by two intersecting circles—stood for the possibility of alternative, overlapping, more porous exchanges between political and imaginative boundaries. The effects of globalization on the horizon of poetry and translation were the political backdrop for *Mandorla* even as it served, too, in the words of Brazilian modernist Oswald de Andrade, as the basis for the journal's "exercise of possibility."

As the magazine shape-shifted over the years, it grew from a modest independent annual, produced by a single editor (Roberto Tejada) and one guest editor (Esther Allen) to a long period of coeditorship (2004–2013), with a substantial editorial board and issues as voluminous as 662 pages in length. Since 2004, with renewed and developing energies, *Mandorla* appeared each year as a dynamic gathering of translations and original work, primarily poetry and poetics in English and Spanish, and as a forum for other fields of cultural interest to the Americas. Departing from a cross-cultural and interdisciplinary framework, *Mandorla* sought to join creative production to the crucial questions posed by ethnic studies and the "re-worlding" of Latin American and U.S. Latino studies from a global perspective. Its content spanned the literary, the visual, and the documentary, so as to draw comparisons between projects in the language arts, translation, and cultural poetics. Even as *Mandorla* made formal concerns primary in the exploration of languages, many writers and artists published in its pages addressed the varieties of culture, by offering accounts that differed from the expected social imperatives.

The following conversation between the editors of this final period tells the story of a publishing venture whose reputation made the journal a kind of password for literary excellence despite its relatively tenuous visibility even "at the margin of the margins" for journals devoted to the experiment of poetry in the United States. *Mandorla* found distribution by circuitous means in Latin America where it achieved stature disproportionate to the actual number of copies of the journal that circulated. Its commitment to advocacy was central to the task of what we viewed as intellectual citizenship in the expanded field of poetic practice: editorship as a means to facilitate artistic exchange, translation, and multiple forms of critical writing. Our efforts suggested larger questions about the cultural economies of attention and the place of poetry as meaningful pursuit capable of prompting action in contemporary life.

As editors with an appetite for integrity, our intent was to dodge or confuse the expected scripts of social and aesthetic selfhood in terms of geographical location and aesthetic alignments. The result came not without consequences; and ours was often a prodigal relationship to rigid Latino or U.S. American canons. Even as we suspected the magazine and our energies would eventually run their course, we did not foresee it would come so abruptly. Many reasons, primarily to do with the sustainability today of the print platform for a project of *Mandorla's* scope and purview, gave way to what became the final print issue: *Mandorla* 16, which appeared in December 2013. Thanks to the communication technology of Skype, and from the comfort of our respective homes, the following conversation took place on December 23, 2014, between Roberto Tejada in Houston, Texas; Kristin Dykstra in the Burlington, Vermont, area; and Gabriel Bernal Granados in Mexico City. The exchange was bilingual in a mode that reflected the structure of the journal, with Kristin and Roberto mostly speaking in English and Gabriel primarily in Spanish, though all of us code-switched from time to time, in our first attempt to untangle some of the relationships and processes that went into the making of *Mandorla: Nueva Escritura de las Américas / New Writing from the Americas.*

ROBERTO TEJADA: How else to begin but by pointing out that our conversation today will have been a technological and editorial first for us? It's remarkable that, despite our reliance as editors on high-speed electronic communication over the last ten years, tools that enabled us to work from our faraway analog locations, the three of us have never actually heard the sound of our own voices together in real time. We'll barely have space to talk about the many aspects important to us about *Mandorla* over the years but a reasonable starting point could be *Mandorla* 7—the journal's second articulation, when the three of us began to edit the magazine together. One of the facets we've all expressed in one way or another is that we've seen this transition of *Mandorla* as being coincident with a shift in culture, from global culture in late modernity to a very aggressive globalization. And somehow *Mandorla* had a share and function in all those moving parts; it had a stake in that mapping. To look back at that edition of 2004 from the perspective of 2014, I wonder what especially stands out for you from that process? What elements stand out particularly from our many-sided roles as writers, translators, and cultural advocates?

GABRIEL BERNAL GRANADOS: In a previous conversation you asked me whether there were any writers I thought we might have overlooked these ten years, poets who in an ideal future, we'd have included in *Mandorla*. The journal evolved as a living organism during the last decade; it encompassed a variety of voices and coordinates from the United States, Latin America, and the Caribbean. For example, there were significant contributions from Cuban writers thanks to the many bridges Kristin extended across to Cuban culture and its literature. I don't know whether to speak of omissions, insofar as *Mandorla* met its objective of sounding out, or providing an x-ray of what was happening in the literatures of the Americas, not just during these ten years but prior to that as well. As a translator I had the opportunity to encounter the writing of many poets from the United States, work I hadn't known before or was just getting to know. And I wasn't alone: for most of the reading public in Mexico and the continent it featured writers who just weren't known south of the Rio Bravo, voices in an organic spiral movement launched by a magazine like *Mandorla*. So my relationship to the magazine as an editor was always one of surprise, marveled by the diversity of voices, the richness and vitality of both North American and Latin American.

KRISTIN DYKSTRA: I'd like to address these connections with some remarks as well on aggressive globalization. In terms of what Gabriel has mentioned, one starting point is the complex issue of globalization and its negative and positive effects. I'm glad that Gabriel commented candidly on the magazine's aim to provide greater visibility to certain U.S. writers. Thanks to Gabriel's leadership, we were able to engage meaningfully with writers from Latin America, not just from the United States, with the Argentine poet Reynaldo Jiménez, for example, who eventually formed part of our editorial board and, together with other Latin American contributors, allowed the journal spaciousness and width of view. That was really important to me.

When we talk about literature from the United States venturing out into the world in the age of globalization, that's often framed as a conversation about mass-market publications like the novels of Tom Clancy or Danielle Steel, books that used to be sold in airports until now—so many of those airport bookstores have closed. The task of *Mandorla* was to sustain a completely other kind of writing, work not promoted through any commercial venue, to go out there, connect to readers with affinities for a different mode of writing in Latin America—I believe that's a different version of globalization and an important one to conceive. As well as another component of the project, to have those voices from Latin America play active roles, and to have Latin American writers and editors making important decisions regarding the content. Certain countries featured more prominently than others, and I don't think we would claim to have represented all of Latin America, obviously.

A different aspect that occurred to me points back to the public dialogue Roberto facilitated with the Mexican American essayist and intellectual Richard Rodriguez. It's never dull with Rodriguez, inasmuch as I disagree with much of what he says, but the most compelling things that he was saying came at the beginning of that exchange when he talked about the way the book, as an object, retains an importance, even as everybody is trumpeting the death of the book in certain western countries—especially in the global North. He was talking about countries where the book is still meaningful. It's meaningful as an object you hold in your hands and as a subject of thought and as a kind of thought that's not subjected to the temporality or the speed of globalization.

But he was also talking about economic discrepancies and the uneven process of globalization—regular or consistent connection to the Internet, for example—and how that relates to literary work. That important point has been made again and again for *Mandorla* while working with writers from Cuba, because the island has the lowest Internet connectivity in the hemisphere. It implies things that editors take for granted all the time—you know, that everyone has the software to work with PDFs—when in fact there is so little access as of now, although this is likely to change even in the next few years. An important reality: that you deal with those material questions of technology when you're engaged with people in other places. It's a corrective to those who buy into one particular vision of literature in the twenty-first century, or publishing in the twenty-first century.

That said, and in seeming contradiction, when we created a Facebook page for *Mandorla*, suddenly a host of Peruvian writers—some of whom we had published in the journal—were looking up the magazine and me on Facebook. This fascinating new mode of connection can be, all at once, a kind of intimate, detached, but always flexible thing. I know of some writers who found each other through that *Mandorla* page, saw each other's names again, reconnecting in a way that was not possible in the past. Another technological component was getting writers and their work into databases. Again, it's a limited readership, in terms of technology and reach to date. But it's possible for some audiences to access the electronic versions of *Mandorla*, to have access to those databases and the writers who were not previously included.

TEJADA: Absolutely. We'll come back to the question of whether *Mandorla* reached or approximated its objectives in the ways you've both related, to the degree that the journal may have—at least as a print publication—performed the necessary cultural task so as to think about a different future endeavor for *Mandorla*. I thought I might describe briefly how much changed in just twenty years. I mean the first issue in 1991 appeared at a time in Mexico when desktop publishing software had only just become available, so the first two issues of the journal were produced still using conventional typography—photo typesetting, paste-up layout technique, camera-ready pages, offset printing. Issue 3 was produced using the now obsolete software PageMaker. Particularly resonant was the way in which, by the time we rebooted *Mandorla* in 2004 with issue 7, it was possible not only to solicit original work but also to engage across geographical distances in the intensive exchange—editorial queries, even the minutest clarifications—necessary to guarantee the highest-quality translations. This point may seem terribly obvious in terms of larger literary enterprises, but for a small-scale effort, it was momentous. In 2004, with issue 7, our editorial working mode consisted of each of us acting independently but in consultation to secure contribu-tors for the forthcoming issue, and in a free-floating online conversation with each other as the issue came into shape. Kris centralized the production efforts at the Publications Unit in the English department of Illinois State University (ISU), and established as well the LitLine interface that finally provided *Mandorla* with a digital imprint.

DYKSTRA: I have to thank Charles B. Harris as one of the people who got that started. With his departure shortly thereafter, contemporary-literature programming at ISU changed. But by that time, the Publications Unit—which then went on to produce our magazine—had heard about us and took an interest. Tara Reeser was crucial to this process because she gathered all those graphic design templates from the magazine's earlier format, digital files in dire need of technological upgrading, and she went back and essentially recreated the entire format from scratch. All those files generated in PageMaker had to be translated into InDesign, making it possible as well to move forward with the database. Joining Tara later was Steve Halle: another indispensable contributor to *Mandorla*'s production team. Both of them invested huge amounts of time and an abundance of goodwill to the project. Tara and Steve brought excitement to the process I think because the journal was so different from anything they had been working on in that unit. I'd feel remiss in not acknowledging them here, as well as contributing editors Gabriel Gudding and Ricardo Cortez Cruz, stalwart local supporters.

TEJADA: They form part of a wide-ranging network of advocates who contributed to the journal in a variety of crucial ways—early companions, contributors, and constant enthusiasts of the magazine, like Forrest Gander, for instance. As well, the original typographical conception and print format were the inspiration of Mexico City designer Azul Morris. She founded the graphic design studio El Taller, and in the early 1990s we worked together at *Artes de México* magazine, on which she served as graphic designer, and I as part of the original editorial team. Azul generously donated her design talents to *Mandorla* and the look of the journal played no small part in its critical reception at the time. Azul's typographical design for *Mandorla* inclined toward the classic: clean lines and ample white space, allowing for legibility, an elegance and clarity of the page. With content that often could be challenging, Azul opted for typographical restraint.

BERNAL GRANADOS: As for the content of the magazine, those first five issues reflected a distinctive editorial personality, Roberto, as though you were composing the chapters of a book, or piecing together the sections of a long poem, with the plurality and historical vision the journal sought to project in terms of Latin American and North American poetry; the presence in those first issues of Octavio Paz, or translators Eliot Weinberger and Clayton Eshleman, figures such as Guy Davenport, and poets like Jack Spicer or Nathaniel Tarn. Another key component was a younger generation of Mexican poets such as Alfonso D'Aquino, Coral Bracho, Carmen Boullosa, Ana Rosa González Matute, and David Huerta. Produced in Mexico throughout the 1990s, the magazine relocated when Roberto returned to the United States in 1997 after ten years of living and working in Mexico. Beginning with issue 6, the editorial means of production for *Mandorla* modified this personal vision, enhanced by the integration and active participation of Kristin and myself. Its handcrafted quality gave way to a more panoramic vision, at once global and omnivorous. This new viewpoint was more open ended and flexible, consistent with the migratory flows and cultural encounters taking place between the Spanish and English languages. There was an extraordinary permeability, more than we ever imagined.

DYKSTRA: That's a really nice way to say it.

TEJADA: I agree. Even as there were personal reasons, I think also there were historical reasons for this transition. The crafted and smaller-scale nature of those first issues remains indebted to journals like *El corno emplumado* and others in the tradition of the "little magazine." With the seismic shifts of global media on literary culture, the vertical axis for a literary project like *Mandorla* was no longer sustainable, and a more horizontal approach seemed the only viable way of accounting for those technological and cultural changes taking place between the United States and Latin America. In an important sense, I think the journal's electronic impact has been idiosyncratic compared to other literary journals, in that *Mandorla* arrived belatedly to the digital platform and, besides, our efforts were focused on coming to terms with the overwhelming amount of material that the journal could potentially contain within the limits of the print format. From a modest page count of just under two hundred pages, the amount of material we solicited, coedited, and published tripled from issues 7 to 16. With high-speed communication technologies, our constellation of writers and translators continued to expand, geographically and numerically, and so did the range back and forth between literary cultures. So, for example, today I was reviewing the U.S. American poets that Gabriel alone translated into Spanish, which makes for a very interesting list. It includes William Bronk, Peter Cole, Eleni Sikelianos, Dan Featherston, Lihn Dinh, Kent Johnson, Barbara Guest, Michael Burkhard, August Kleinzahler, Jayne Cortez, and Marjorie Welish. The entire list of contributors endures as an alternate mapping of U.S. American and Latin American poetries of the last thirty years—a cartography meant to trouble many of the certainties of what the ground looks like from a purely national perspective.

BERNAL GRANADOS: It's a changing constellation, lively and fluid. For example, it's important to underline what Kris was saying about Cuban literature today and the question of its availability, especially in light of President Barack Obama's announcement last week (December 17, 2014) to restore diplomatic relations with Havana; the links between energy, or the shortage thereof; and the way communication can wield influence in the contemporary world. Paradoxically, Cubans at this moment are some of the most cosmopolitan authors writing in Spanish. A significant number of Cuban intellectuals and writers don't reside on the island, but in Europe, or other countries in Latin America, and the level of permeability they have had is extraordinary compared with these other cultures. Even among the poets who decide to stay and live in Cuba, in Havana, there's a great openness to what's being produced in different parts of the world. As a project *Mandorla* provided a special lens, sometimes microscopic, onto literary formations, not only with regard to Cuban literature. From one's perspective here in Mexico, where access is often limited to literature from the Southern Cone (Argentina, Brazil, Chile, Paraguay, and Uruguay) in general, and from Brazil in particular, the journal featured, less frequently but whenever possible, the vitality and intelligence of Brazil's avant-gardism. That work, consistently surprising, was a reminder of the insufficient exchanges between Hispanophone and Lusophone literary cultures. Reynaldo Jiménez, one of *Mandorla*'s contributing editors, brought a wealth of knowledge regarding poetry from the Southern Cone and direct contact to some of its youngest writers. He opened doors to Brazilian poetry thanks to his efforts as the translator of Paulo Leminski's *Catatau*, which appeared just a few months ago in Argentina, and of the pivotal book by Haroldo de Campos, *Galáxias*, which we published here in Mexico (Libros Magenta).

TEJADA: The contrast between Cuba and Brazil is fascinating. Despite the differences in their histories, geographic location, and cultures of modernity, those two contemporary literary cultures have often experienced a form of isolation, be it political and technological in the case of Cuba, or linguistic in the case of Brazil.

DYKSTRA: Gabriel commented on the nations of the Southern Cone. One of the things that most interests me about the field of publishing is that it becomes a site of intersection between practice and theory. And I, frankly, cannot see myself involved with a project that is not located in that intersection. What do we mean by tossing around words like "global" or "transnational"? How many different approaches can we take to troubling long-established notions about culture, and what matters in terms of our locations for doing so?

I'm reminded of the poet and translator Daniel Borzutzky, who eventually joined us as a contributing editor. He first contacted us with translations of Jaime Luis Huenún. He had seen *Mandorla* and identified the journal among the few venues where he saw his work as a fit. At the time I had no idea who Daniel was but I came to learn that, although he was born here in the United States, he was of Chilean descent, and had already been at work translating the Chilean poet Raúl Zurita. For *Mandorla* he preferred to bring out a lesser-known writer, Huenún. Over the years Daniel's own work, as well as his Zurita translations, appeared in *Mandorla*. He also translated the work of Galo Ghigliotto, who writes a kind of abject cartography of Chile, focused on Valdivia, and which enters that nation's long traditions of landscape-oriented poetry, but in a uniquely contemporary way. These writers all form an affinity even as they reflect very distinct positions in Chile. As a contributing editor, Daniel reached out to writers in Chile, from different generations and from diverse aesthetics. This has profoundly impacted the directions of his own poetry and cultural commentary.

In terms of Cuba, there's a larger historic panorama at play. After 1989, as the island entered the Special Period, you see a change in modality: people leaving the island are no longer seen so strictly as exiles who are to be divided off, you know, and left out of traditions. You see more people opening up to this idea of a diaspora, and to the idea that Cuba may not be so singular, that Cuba actually has much in common with other countries—partly on account of its considerable diasporic population now. And you start to see people on the island, sometimes quietly, other times vigorously advocating for greater attention to those writers who are outside. I recall we had conscious editorial conversations around the fact that we wanted to project the notion of a greater Cuba; we sought to resist the geographically bounded concept of the nation in defining *who* writes Cuban literature. Cuba is presented in transnational forms through Pedro Márquez de Armas, Rolando Sánchez Mejías, Achy Obejas, and others.

The transition was openness to the view of the literary as being "on the move," linked, historically, to this aesthetic of fluidity we've addressed, and to the idea of clusters more than firmly bounded aesthetic territory. Recently, Roberto and I remarked how we definitely feel *Mandorla* submitted a point of view, irreducible to the singular editorial point of view or aesthetic, or to canons other magazines prefer to validate. I think one of the most exciting things for me was to find patterns—odd clusters of similar concerns—from very disparate authors. Absolutely unsolicited, but emerging in the last few issues of the journal, were these remarkably distinct imaginative modalities for treating animal-human relationships.

TEJADA: That's another coincidental but persuasive example of how *Mandorla* was inclined to capture an x-ray image of the present moment. As for submitting a point of view, one of great concern to *Mandorla*, from the beginning, was the question of how to think about *Latinidad*, about Latin America outside of Latin America; and in the United States, a long-standing tradition of writers of Latin American descent, whose work embodies exile, migration, and the resulting genealogies of dislocation and resettlement. The writing of *Latinidad* in the United States, whether in English, or in the interplay between Spanish and English, has a primary concern for language that is both formal and cultural. I recall the late Alfred Arteaga, the Chicano theorist and poet, whose work, which appeared in issue 3, pointed early on to this amalgamation of theory and practice—in the broadest terms, *Mandorla*'s point of view. Arteaga's challenging piece recast the postcolonial imagination by dismantling the image of Frida Kahlo as the quintessential ego ideal for Chicanismo. We could draw lines from that work to writers in later issues, including elena minor, Sesshu Foster, Valerie Martinez, Carmen Gimenez Smith, Rosa Alcalá, Urayoán Noel, Edwin Torres, Rodrigo Toscano, Mónica de la Torre (also a contributing editor), Robert Fernandez, Deborah Paredez, J. Michael Martinez, John Michael Rivera, Roberto Harrison, Farid Matuk, Emmy Perez, Francisco Aragon, Peter Ramos, and Daniel Borzutzky.

As for the interplay of theory and practice, at *Mandorla* we looked for less explanatory ways to incorporate commentary and scholarly criticism. James Pancrazio helped us to connect with various writers in this regard, and so did Juliet Lynd, whom we invited to join the board after featuring some of her criticism. I think it's telling that several of our contributing editors publish cultural commentary even if they have focused more on creative writing overall: Peter Ramos, for example, on James Wright's translations of César Vallejo; Joel Bettridge on the poetics of Harryette Mullen; and Susan Briante, with her writings elsewhere on cross-border optics. Important, too, were venue-specific collaborations between cover artists and writers: Sesshu Foster's "Interview with Juan Fish (Supposedly)" alongside photographs by Arturo Ernesto

Romo-Santillano; Andrea Giunta's writing on the artist Graciela Sacco; and Jeffrey Yang's poems in relation to images by Christine Nguyen. Also, those artists who contributed with statements or speculative fictions giving literary coloration to their practice: Paul Vanouse ("The Relative Velocity Inscription Device"), Thomas Glassford ("Homeland Insecurity), Yvonne Venegas ("Animal Artifice"), Liliana Porter ("Working Notes on Art and Politics"), Rubén Ortiz Torres ("The Past Is Not What It Used to Be"), the Brazilian photography collective CIA de Foto ("Carnival"), and Brian D. Collier ("Why Do Flying Carp Jump? An Inquiry by the Society for a Re-Natural Environment: SRNE").

BERNAL GRANADOS: Returning to Rodrigo Toscano's work—his poems in Spanish are often a violent staging of *Latinidad* as experienced in the United States—I'd mention another writer close to the magazine, Andrés Ajéns, whose writing reflects another form of *Latinidad*: the meaning of Latin America as being "foreign" to itself. Different variables are involved: immigration, the real and imaginative fact of the borderland, and the space of language as a conflicted field. These issues are very important to writers like Toscano and Ajéns whose cultural concerns modify into hybridized forms. Another example was the section "11 poetas del norte de México" ["11 Poets from the North of Mexico"] published in issue 13. The Mexican writer Julián Herbert assembled work, much of it written by poets under the age of thirty, into a mosaic of proposals and poetic voices, arguments and meditations about the geographical and cultural circumstance—cities, mass media, and other locations—of Mexican reality as experienced in proximity to the United States.

DYKSTRA: Critically, *Mandorla* sought to measure how the United States projects outwards; to link that issue into this conversation about visions of *Latinidad*, this projection of identity from the United States includes a stultifying history of segregation that has affected how Latinos are perceived in the United States, producing a repertoire of limited stereotypical ideas. U.S. Latina and Latino writing is capable of unsettling those attitudes and assumptions. The vision of a meeting place for a more challenging and multidirectional conversation was constitutive of the *Latinidad* our journal endorsed. Gabriel referred to *Latinidad* as it has been produced, and is recreated by, Latin Americans. Meanwhile, in the United States, *Latinidad* has been the construction of all these people who have come together in ways that were inconceivable from the perspective of one specific Latin American country. So there's a history, a comingling of demographics, that is very specific to the United States and has affected how we define who is an "American" writer in U.S. terms. We had grown tired of seeing that definition repeatedly constricted in the way that writing is projected outward from the United States.

I want to add, since I am not Latina, that we operated, I think, with a very flexible concept of the term "Latino," one that did not take lightly, for example, someone's relationship to different languages. Whether it was in English, Spanish, bilingual—or maybe even riddled with linguosensual phraseology, to play on terms from Edwin Torres—our aim was to provide a climate of self-determination for writers to defy the expectations projected onto them. If you write as a Latino in the United States—where the Latino or Latina is so often misconceived—you are often expected to perform certain scripts. So often I would hear writers express resistance to the pressures of producing a style of poetic personhood that may have been critical and energizing twenty years earlier but was not compelling for them now. From this starting point it's interesting to reflect that as a contributing editor, for example, Rosa Alcalá successfully solicited work for *Mandorla* by African American writers involved in very complex poetic projects. Like the poets Gabriel mentioned from Northern Mexico, many of these black writers also wrestle with social and cultural or political issues brought to the level of language so that these conflicts and dramas manifest compelling effects in the language itself. I'm thinking of John Keene, for example, and Evie Shockley, Tisa Bryant, and Khadijah Queen. Credit is due to Rosa for allowing us to prompt these connections. Duriel Harris arrived at ISU and gave us a great contribution with transnational impact, meditations on violence. And who could forget LaTasha Nevada Diggs? Contributing editor Urayoán Noel introduced us at an event at the Museo del Barrio in New York. It didn't take the editors long to agree that her writing should be, like John Keene's poem, the opening act of an issue (15).

TEJADA: I agree, and there's something to be said about the affinities between African American and Latin American modernity. *Mandorla* served as a hinge linking the work of Latino and African American writers in the hemisphere. There's a line that connects Langston Hughes, that great cosmopolitan, who spent significant time in Mexico, to poets like the late Jayne Cortez—translated into Spanish by Gabriel Bernal Granados in issue 14—not to mention Nathaniel Mackey, Will Alexander, and Jay Wright, all of whose work incorporates the histories, locality, politics, and imaginations of Latin America together with its peoples and cultures of African descent. And I think that, for example, it's very interesting that Latino writers have looked to organizations like Cave Canem, so that, out of Austin, Texas, you have Canto Mundo (founded by Norma Cantú, Pablo

Miguel Martínez, Celeste Guzmán Mendoza, Deborah Paredez, and Carmen Tafolla), pursuing similar collective concerns. These questions of *Latinidad* and the African diaspora point back to Cuba; to literary relations between Cuba, Mexico, and the United States.

DYKSTRA: Early in our conversation we began to reflect on situating editorial work in relation to specific historical coordinates. The recent announcements about U.S.-Cuba relations prompt me to say a bit more on how Cuba pragmatically did and didn't enter into our "literary" relations. To situate the magazine historically, the embargo of the United States against Cuba has absolutely conditioned our relationship to those writers in Cuba. To work around, through, against, and over that embargo has been a daily form of labor for many inside and out. Getting actual copies of *Mandorla* to Cuba was a part of that effort, related to that of having the lowest Internet connectivity in the hemisphere. I have been to writers' homes and looked at the local Internet access, which for most of them would be the equivalent of an extremely patchy dial-up service here. Frequently pirated, access was available only during certain times of day, when hopefully nobody would notice that there was a drain on the system, that somebody was pirating e-mail interface. If writers had access to enough dollars, they might be able to use a hotel's Internet café. But at ten dollars an hour for a salary of twenty dollars a month, it's not a viable form of access. Few had access to Adobe Acrobat products, making it unlikely that they could read PDFs from an issue of the magazine on a thumb drive; the media element was more or less null and void for Cuba in terms of dealing with the embargo. *Mandorla* circulated in Cuba thanks to traveling friends and colleagues who made room in their suitcases in order to accommodate issues of the journal. Publications are exempt from the embargo, so it was a burden, albeit a legal one. Hank Lazer, from the University of Alabama, traveled to Havana to meet with poets. He and some of his students carried one or two copies for me. In my own travels the most I have ever taken is eight. And every single copy was for somebody we published. I received requests from others for copies but never had enough. Reina María Rodríguez—whose home in downtown Havana has been a gathering point for writers— keeps copies around her place, and she's been known to give them away to a writer who she thinks could benefit from having a copy of the journal.

This commitment is one that I'm not sure is widely experienced by other literary magazines today—to try to really take on something like the embargo with all the practicalities and care involved to circulate the journal. Many Cuban writers cannot afford to buy books that have been translated into Spanish and sold elsewhere. Your average writer in Havana cannot afford to buy an edition of Gertrude Stein published in Spain, for example, or in Chile. Many Cuban poets have remarked on the high-quality Spanish translations featured in *Mandorla*— like those by Gabriel.

No small thanks are due to the faculty and Publications Unit at Illinois State University. Support came in the decision to help pay for the shipping in order to distribute the magazine internationally. And this was particularly important in the later voluminous issues: shipping costs for international mailing from the United States had suddenly skyrocketed. And so it became more and more expensive to send these boxes out—but we did it, sending boxes to Venezuela, Uruguay, Argentina, Peru, and Chile, among other countries. We also sent out copies when we invited many new contributors.

BERNAL GRANADOS: Getting the journal to Mexico was also a difficult task, even as the boxful of copies always found appreciative readers, and issues passed from hand to hand. We might have hoped for greater impact, but among the small community of writers and poets who make up the literary map of Mexico, the response was always enthusiastic.

TEJADA: I agree. The difficulties of print distribution limited the potential of the journal's short-term impact, not only in Mexico. But I wonder as well whether it had something to do with the aesthetic values.

BERNAL GRANADOS: The inclusive nature of the magazine did not persuade the narrower sectors of Mexico's poetry readership, but especially with the last several issues, the journal opened doors for younger poets dealing with provocative issues of a geopolitical, sexual, and literary nature. In the cultural climate of Mexico, often conservative, these younger poets found expressive affinities in a journal whose conception of poetry is based on mobility and change, where literature can unleash a series of transformations that affect a society's behavior. I think the magazine provided such a place. I recall how Luis Felipe Fabré, a leading figure of this newer generation of poets in Mexico, had one of his earliest publications feature in the opening pages of *Mandorla 6*, as did the work of Heriberto Yépez in a later issue. Prompting equal parts perplexity, surprise, and understanding, the magazine served as a vehicle for ideas of aesthetic and cultural concern.

DYKSTRA: At the most fundamental level the journal also stood for something, not unlike what Omar Pérez refers to as a poem's ideology. I don't want that to sound reductive in a political sense, though I don't think we need too fully to separate meanings either—there's the embodiment of a poem, and there's something that moves underneath the poem as well. If there's anything that, for me, translated across the different writers that I most enjoyed involving in the magazine, it's that coalescing of a text's specific object-hood to its underlying motion. So I think, for example, of John Keene, and his poem "How to Draw a Bunny" [featured in issue 14]. There's the reference of course to artist Ray Johnson and the palpable humor of the poem itself. But you can tell there are so many other levels on which that poem is moving, a multilayered sensation that provides completion, ironically, by producing a spark. In terms of reception, *Mandorla* offered a space for writers to identify each other, and to refer us to other writers. This process gave way to a meaningful sense of artistic community ever expanding from those initial constellations.

TEJADA: Yes, I think it's possible to survey all sixteen issues of the magazine—perhaps especially of the last ten years—and to so chart a complex network of mid-career writers across two continents, aligned by an "inward-looking" and "outward-looking" method. The family resemblance is reflected in work that takes seriously the specifics of one's place in the world, the circumstance of history in this hemisphere, and the awareness that one's language is inextricable from the economic and political policies that drive the uneven distribution of modernity. To speak only of the Brazilian writers we've published over the years, I believe this could be said of poets like Horácio Costa, Régis Bonvicino, Jussara Salazar, Sérgio Medeiros, Josely Vianna Baptista, and Virna Texeira.

It's this "inward-looking" and "outward-looking" method I read in the opening poem of *Mandorla*'s final issue, 16, "On the Monologic Archipelago," by the Brazilian poet Horácio Costa. It's important to know that in 1998, after more than a decade living in Mexico City, where we were close literary allies and friends, Horácio moved back to his native São Paulo, where he, like myself back in the United States, had to begin all over again. To Horácio the vast literary landscape of Brazil must have appeared, in part, a foreign soil, not exempt from possessive claims to the literary inheritance of its early twentieth- and mid-century modern movements.

There are dialogists who endeavor to save
one monologist after another. They're
the so-called 'unconscious' and, rarer

still, 'martyrs of monologism.'

Literary activity viewed only through the exceptional lens of locality, national language, or group formation, in the American hemisphere or elsewhere, runs the risk of devolving into a monologic archipelago.

Mandorla meant to serve as an alternate geography: welcoming to those for whom the poetic word is an attempt to resist the solipsistic seductions, and the enforced or self-imposed segregations, of the monologue . . .

Erin Belieu & Kevin Prufer

Erin Belieu is cofounder, with Cate Marvin, of VIDA: Women in the Literary Arts; professor of English at Florida State University; and author of four collections of poems, the most recent of which is Slant Six *(Copper Canyon, 2014). She is also coeditor, with Susan Aizenberg, of* The Extraordinary Tide: New Poetry by American Women *(Columbia University Press, 2001). This interview was conducted via e-mail in early 2015 by Kevin Prufer, one of the editors of this volume.*

LITERARY PUBLISHING: Why is VIDA necessary and how did it come about?

ERIN BELIEU: Now that VIDA has existed for five years, I think most recognize its necessity in that our mission was so quickly embraced and amplified by writers, journalists, booksellers, and readers from every part of literary culture, both at home and abroad.

The spark for VIDA happened when my cofounder Cate Marvin sent a handful of writers a particularly eloquent and dismayed e-mail asking what had happened to the feminist conversation in contemporary literature. That e-mail went viral on a large scale. The response to what she had written was astonishing to us. But Cate and I recognized the outpouring of frustration and enthusiasm for the opportunity it was. We'd been talking on and off for a few years about doing some kind of project together, one that focused on women in writing. It was clear that the project had presented itself and the right time for it had come.

I think Cate's missive landed just at the moment we'd

reached a cultural tipping point in America, with so many attacks on women's agency, autonomy, and abilities leading the news day after day. So many women writers and allies of women writers were feeling stymied, angry, lonely, just generally depressed about the business as usual of the publishing world.

VIDA gives people who believe in its mission a powerful political voice, actual data to point to, and a rallying point. One of the ways that gender bias typically works is to make women experiencing it feel deeply isolated with their concerns. They are sent the message that they are crazy, insecure, selfish, whiny, untalented, frivolous. Women are told over and over that they must be misreading the bias they encounter, that they're too sensitive and humorless, that they're scared of competition; that if they do put themselves out there they are unfeminine, bitchy, ridiculous; they will be unappealing to men. Patriarchal culture wants to make sure these messages are internalized as early as possible. Women are told explicitly and implicitly that some fundamental, genetic lack of goodness is the real reason women aren't being published at anywhere close to the same rate as their male counterparts. It's an ancient and effective tool for keeping any group of people down. "It's not us, it's YOU. In this case, it's "We, the *objective* gatekeepers of literary publishing, have decided your work does not qualify for serious consideration."

VIDA is now there to say, "Well, are we sure this is about the quality of the work overall? This HUGE, pervasive imbalance in the numbers of serious women's voices in print, the dearth of women publishing in the most influential literary outlets, is this really because women fundamentally aren't good enough writers? Or could such a regrettable imbalance reveal that the well-documented gender bias that infects pretty much every other part our culture is a problem in the writing world, too?"

Most thoughtful people see that the latter is a much more likely answer—though comment boxes on the Internet have a kind of sodium pentothal effect on a small percentage of people who are happy to tell you that they believe women are generally inferior thinkers and artists. That's where you see the unvarnished depths of the underlying misogyny still at work in American culture.

LITERARY PUBLISHING: You say that women writers "are sent the message that they are crazy, insecure, selfish, whiny." Do you have personal experience with this kind of bias? What form does it take (beyond the way it's reflected in the tables of contents of literary magazines) in your experience or the experience of women writers you work closely with?

BELIEU: I can't think of a woman writer I know who doesn't have stories about the disturbing things that were said or done to her because of her gender while pursuing her writing career. There are some women who'll say, "Oh, why make such a big deal out of it? Boys will be boys. Stop whining." But these women are vastly fewer in my experience, and are typically those women who either are in the inner circle which affords "special woman status," as Adrienne Rich called it, or are aspiring to the position and don't want to upend the boat they're attempting to float. In any case, some women will share their stories readily, and some are more reticent, as they believe speaking to this behavior will brand them as noncooperatives. But VIDA's presence has made a lot more women willing to take the risk.

We at VIDA aren't big fans of anecdote in discussing these issues. Anecdote is too easy to dismiss and, as much social science data indicates, typically supports those ideas a person wishes to be true for personal, gut-reactive reasons. Hence, the VIDA Count.

But I will tell you one personal experience I had that is illustrative of the kinds of often unconscious bias women encounter in the publishing world: back when I was an editor at *AGNI*, I received a phone call from a staff member at *Poetry* magazine. He was calling to ask me if I had any ideas about whom they should give their big-money, career-making prize to that year. He told me they were hearing a lot of "noise" about how very few women had received the prize in its long history. The trouble was, from their point of view, that they'd already given the prize to Adrienne Rich and they couldn't think of a single other woman poet who was "significant" or "deserving" enough to receive it.

Mind you, this person wasn't some mustachio-twirling, cartoon villain who tied women to the train tracks for fun in his off-hours. He was a man I knew professionally and socially, and had reason to think well of generally. He had no idea what the problem with his question was or how it was received on my end. I didn't feel malice coming from him. He was just presenting me with a problem that as a token woman writer he knew I might be in a position to help his magazine solve. I know my writer friends who are also people of color encounter this all the time, too. "We're going to get slammed by *them* for our lack of diversity in the table of contents. Who knows a brown writer to call who can recommend another brown writer whose work we've never read?"

So many people lead quite unconsciously by believing that when we talk about contemporary literature, the vast majority of the time that means work written by straight white men. That's the de facto position for our literary culture. Everyone else is an exception that proves a long-established rule. Most straight white men at this point in history haven't been raised to read across subject positions in the way that everyone who isn't a straight white man learned to do as a child. That is, for those of us who self-identified as

serious readers at an early age, the only way we could participate was by learning to appreciate and occupy subject positions other than our own. Through no particular personal
virtue, we were required to learn something I think of as
literary empathy.

To finish the story, when the fellow at *Poetry* magazine
asked me the question, I swallowed my shock at having the
bias I had begun to suspect laid out so tidily in front of me
and immediately rattled off a list of women poets who had
long, significant careers in poetry. But the fellow who'd
phoned me dismissed every woman I mentioned as "not
important enough." When the prize was announced a few
months later, they gave it to a straight white man.

I found it very revealing to be privy to the kind of insider
considerations that go into the awarding of literary prizes,
just exactly what the politics of the process often look like.
And having been in the writing world for many years since
that conversation, I am afraid this story isn't unusual. We
at VIDA have done the numbers and what you see is that
women in recent years start out going along fairly well in
their writing careers. But as the stakes for money and recognition get higher, the number of women receiving significant forms of recognition drops markedly.

LITERARY PUBLISHING: VIDA has generated some real
controversy. Critics have suggested, among other things,
that the VIDA Count oversimplifies data; that it reflects
the gender disparity in the number of writers submitting to
journals; that it seems to promote a kind of needless affirmative action. I know you're certainly very familiar with
these sorts of objections. How do you respond to them?

BELIEU: Critics of VIDA's Count offer a lot of anecdotal
responses for which they offer no evidence—such as the idea

that women don't submit as often to journals and presses. They appear to have emotional reactions to information that makes them feel anxious that their privilege or possibilities for privilege are being threatened by our work.

VIDA, on the other hand, has gathered hard data and simply presented it to the literary community for discussion. VIDA's motto on all of our materials is "Welcome To The Conversation." We have said from day one that the Count brings up complex issues that should be explored in depth. We'd like to discuss those issues and what best next steps would be for understanding the factors that result in the significant to drastic gender imbalance the Count reveals in the selection of writers for serious publications and prizes. We believe it's salutary to drag these irritable issues to the surface. Unpleasant things typically benefit from a little wholesome light and air. But as someone said recently, VIDA's microphone can pick up a lot of noise, overly simplified messages that aren't our own. We have never said, "The Count reveals THIS." We say, "It appears that these numbers reveal a problem in that having such a lack of women's voices represented within the literary universe isn't a good thing for our art." That's the one assumption we make at VIDA: that having the intellectual and artistic leadership of significantly more women in print would be a good thing for the world at large. It's the only assumption with which we're comfortable. Call it a well-founded hypothesis we'd like to have the chance to prove.

But let's be clear: if by affirmative action we mean the preferential promotion of some members within a group based in part on their gender, ethnicity/race, or sexual preference, then straight white men writing in English have benefited massively from their own affirmative action program for hundreds of years. It's called patriarchal culture. You expand beyond writing in English and you can say the program has been going on since time immemorial.

This myth of a purely artistic meritocracy in the writing world is exactly that—a myth perpetuated by people who want to believe their good fortune has nothing to do with certain key advantages they were given as accidents of birth. I call it Mitt Romney Syndrome.

This is not to say there aren't lots of gifted, admirable, dedicated men who've worked very hard to get where they've wanted to go with their art. Or that being a straight white man immediately gives you everything you want for your writing career. But the illusion that the writing world is somehow a fair playing field and everyone has a reasonable chance to have their work recognized is absurd. Those of us who've worked in literary publishing for years know that some pigs are definitely more equal than others. You add class into it and you see that the literary world at the highest levels is a group of tastemakers comprised by a majority of male writers and editors who frequently hand publications, prizes, and other essential forms of recognition back and forth to one another. I can't say this is an entirely conscious behavior on their part. They don't see themselves as actively suppressing other people's ambitions. They are often very wounded to be perceived as such. Some are men who've actually published many of us associated with VIDA's leadership. But they unfortunately often trot out their token list of women writers they've published to show that ALL they care about is the work. Is it their fault that the BEST work happens the vast majority of the time to be written by other straight white men? It doesn't occur to them to genuinely question what exactly constitutes their construct of "the best." It is clear that these editors and publishers often want stories, essays and poems that are written from the subject position with which they already identify. That seems to be a big part of what "the best" means to them. Which is sad as they miss so many pleasures by not opening themselves to writing that doesn't automatically reflect what they already know and with which they're comfortable.

But to put a point on it, VIDA has never called for publication quotas and we never will. That's not how art gets made. We want the conversation we've started to help people in positions to do something about this imbalance think about their reading habits and how and why they're constructed as they are. And if you're an editor having trouble getting more women writers to submit to your magazine or prize, you can actually seek out women writers. You can identify and mentor them in the same way you do emerging male writers. Because if it were true that women overall submitted to publications less frequently than men, I wouldn't be entirely shocked. Some people have this idea that women should all be like the plucky, single-minded heroes in made-for-television movies, little Horatio Algers bloodying themselves against the wall over and over. This bootstrap mentality is a punitive one and is designed to make sure people don't succeed—and blame themselves for it. If you're a woman who's been slamming into these walls for years, decades, maybe you might become a little disheartened by what you find (or don't) over and over and over in the table of contents of places like the *New Yorker* and *Harper's* and the *Atlantic*. Maybe that's a normal human response to being told you're not quite good enough for your entire professional life. Again, editors have a great amount of control over this, as evidenced by *Tin House* and the *Paris Review*. Their editors said, "Yep. VIDA makes a good point. Let's fix this." And they did. No drama. No diminishment in the quality of their publication's work. They decided that what VIDA is saying matters and they fixed it without much trouble. It's having the will to recognize what VIDA is talking about that seems to be the hard part.

LITERARY PUBLISHING: VIDA focuses primarily on prestigious, high-visibility publications and awards. That's understandable, since these are the sorts of places that tend to make the biggest careers happen. At the same time, we're at a moment in literary publishing of widespread diffusion and proliferation of smaller publishing venues. New literary journals pop up every day, both online and on paper, and there are many new smaller-scale book presses. What's more, non-NYC, nonprofit presses like Graywolf have been winning major national awards for their books— awards that used to be reserved almost exclusively for the big NYC presses. How have these shifts in publishing affected women, LGBTQ, and other marginalized writers? Have they offered more access? How involved have women/ LGBTQ/etc. writers been in start-up journals and presses? If that participation is widespread, has one possible effect been to steer these writers away from larger, more prestigious venues?

BELIEU: Yes, the "grey ladies" don't have the kind of singular sway culturally as they did in the past. But let's not kid ourselves; they still have an enormous amount, conferring the kind of attention and prestige that any writer generally needs to make a long life in writing. And I'm not sure how much it helps women writers to go off into their own corner and publish for people who already believe what VIDA is getting at. I don't think we address gender bias by taking our ball and going off to make our own game. Why should women writers want anything less than their male counterparts have? And many, many writers make their living inside academia. Academia still doesn't acknowledge much of what is vital and lively on the Internet. Add to this that online content still doesn't pay at the rates many of the prestigious print journals do and I think it's clear we shouldn't look to the Internet to solve these problems. There will always be gatekeepers. There will always be prestige publications. Human beings seem to want these hierarchical categories in most things. I don't see that changing soon.

LITERARY PUBLISHING: Junot Díaz has gotten some attention for voicing his concerns about MFA programs and the ways in which they can be problematic for writers of color. I'm wondering how the rise of MFA programs has affected women writers (and/or LGBTQ writers)?

BELIEU: I can give general remarks, because I don't have recent data to support more detailed observations. But one of the truisms is that the majority of people in MFA programs is women. But the majority of faculty in MFA programs is men. I think that is starting to change a little, but as someone who knows well the faculty makeup at MFA programs all over the country, it seems it's not changing quickly. It's also worth looking at how various faculty members are rewarded within their programs. From what I can tell, pretty much across the board, women faculty make significantly less money than their male colleagues nationally. Why is that? Well, beyond the wage gap that has existed forever in American culture, one reason may be that academics are financially rewarded for prestigious publications and prizes. They also earn more time off from their teaching duties to pursue their writing the more prestigious their careers become, the more marquee value they bring to their departments. So we can say that the VIDA Count points to the practical ways in which the gender disparity in publications has a damaging effect on women's livelihoods. It's also pretty common for women in academia to do the majority of grunt work within their departments. I don't have data

to support why this appears to be the case. But it's a phenomenon I see over and over in departments. It could be
that this is a general expectation—that women will do the
organizing and bean counting, men will be the visionaries
who handle the larger issues. Men are bosses; women are
support staff. So if you're a woman on the tenure track sens-
ing this expectation, knowing how you will be perceived if
you say no to the grunt work, maybe you put a lot of your
effort there. You're kind of damned if you do and damned
if you don't. Because service isn't typically valued the way
publications are. But you spend so much time doing service
for the department that it impacts the space and time you
have for your work.

LITERARY PUBLISHING: VIDA's been around for a while
now and, as you say, its influence has in some ways already
changed the publishing landscape. But how has VIDA itself
changed over the years? How has it evolved?

BELIEU: VIDA started out as Cate Marvin, Ann Townsend,
and me in our houses rabble-rousing between teaching
classes, childcare, scrambling around between bouts of our
daily quotidian. In these five years it's become an international presence with many volunteers, an executive committee to lead us, a board of directors, etc. Our infrastructure
hasn't grown as quickly as our name recognition, so we're
working to make VIDA something stable for the future—
fundraising, developing programs beyond the Count. The
idea is that someday we original founders can hand it over
to other women who are ready to celebrate and advocate for
the work of women writers in all genres.

LITERARY PUBLISHING: If, say, ten or twenty or fifty years
from now VIDA has influenced publishing in the direction it

would like to—and, thus, has achieved a good number of the successes it aims for—what will the literary-publishing landscape look like? How will it have changed? Which changes will have been the most important?

BELIEU: The most important change will be turning more people into readers who won't think twice about reading a book that has a woman author's name on the cover, or reading from the positions of main characters who don't come from their same experience. Another significant change will be that women writers won't feel hemmed into certain subject matters and approaches. They'll feel they have the authority and confidence to speak to whatever they want to speak to. What a beautiful world that will be.

APPENDIX

Cate Marvin's original founding e-mail:

From: Cate Marvin
Subject: As I Stood Folding Laundry: Women's Writing Now
Date: Monday, August 3, 2009, 11:07 a.m.

Dear Female Writer,
Greetings. The following text is an email I wrote the other night whilst in a fit of frustration (not rage, though there may not be much of a difference) about the situation of women writers in our country. In this letter, I propose we start an association of American women writers, which would sponsor a yearly conference at which we could talk about our

concerns—literary, aesthetic, historic, practical—you
name it—a forum which would unite us, as well
as enlighten us as writers and readers of women's
work. If you are interested in taking part, please let
me know by emailing me. Also, please feel free to
forward this email to any and all female writers you
think might be interested in this project.

Here's the original email I sent out:

Dear Friend,
I just experienced a moment of vicious self-mock-
ery, in which I imagined myself in the same pose of
concentration over the laundry I had spread over
my bed as the narrator of Tillie Olsen's legendary
piece in which a mother considers the circumstances of her gender as manifested in her daughter's (lack of) self-confidence . . . I was dwelling on
a thought not entirely different. You see, I had an
AWP panel proposal rejected today. Big deal, right?
Everyone has their proposals rejected. Yet, this
rejection really nagged at me. I proposed on a topic
concerning the narrow field (sarcasm intended) of
contemporary American women's poetry . . . I've
had a lot of panels accepted over the years. Last
year, one on Wallace Stevens. The year before that
on the elegy; before that, the crafting of an anthology. Then transgression in poetry. Ahah! This
was the first panel I ever proposed that concerned
women's work exclusively.

It was an excellent proposal. Because it was interesting.
I just honestly can't see HOW it could be turned down.
Here it is:

Title: Arsenic Icing: Sentiment as Threat in
Contemporary American Women's Poetry

Description: Six contemporary female American
poets explore how sentimentality is deployed in
twenty-first century women's poetry, with regard
to both content and rhetoric, as a means to counter
traditional assumptions regarding female desire
and identity. What personal and political alchemies
occur when the affectionate address verges on acer-
bic? What transformations are sought when a female
speaker, once familiar as mother, daughter, sister,
wife, or lover, employs sentiment to reveal herself as
Other?

Rationale: The first female American poets to be
respected for their intellect, Marianne Moore and
her protégé, Elizabeth Bishop, were careful not to
express an excess of sentiment; poets Anne Sexton
and Sylvia Plath would make a stark departure from
this mode by channeling emotional
extremity. It is now important to explore how twenty-first century American women poets understand
and reinvent these opposing traditions in their work.

By the way: I had a stellar group of panelists
(VARIED and FAMOUS) lined up for this.

*

As I stood rolling my socks into balls and shoving
folded shirts into drawers (warning: dangerously
clumsy use of heavily figurative language in use:
the women are the clothes, get it?? Being shoved

into drawers, i.e. repressed!), I considered how
another panel proposal I was on was accepted.
It concerns the uses of criticism, harkening back
to the New Critics, Eliot in particular. Nothing
WRONG with that . . . but hasn't it been done?

And I thought, too, of how often I see more men's
names in prominent magazines than women's, how
I see men getting prizes more often than women,
how even though female students would love to
read newer work by female writers, they are rarely
taught the work of women—except for the usual
suspects.

And I thought about how a male poet friend of
mine discouraged me from getting involved with
editing a book of feminist poets/poems from the
past two decades because it would be "dangerous"
and "divisive."

And I thought about how one male poet friend of
mine only refers to Ellen Bryant Voigt and Louise
Glück when he speaks of female poets. Not that I
don't love these two poets—but I am sure these two
women would be none too happy that they are the
sole representatives of where women's poetry has
arrived (and, practically, to this male-poet's mind,
where it comes from).

I am, in short, irritated, and it's not just because
I'm on the rag.

Here's the thing: why can't we have an organization
of female writers (poets and fiction writers) that

has a conference every year? Where we writers of women's lit can get together and talk about issues that affect our work as women? An organization that would be very open aesthetically, one that would really be a forum for discussion along any lines of the female writer's experience? An opportunity for women writers to be exposed to everything (or almost everything) that's going on in our country with regard to women's literature? Like AWP, it could be an organization for writers, not scholars. And in that way different from some organizations that no doubt already exist.

Perhaps this organization could also produce a literary journal to present women's writing (prose) on what it means to be a woman writer in our time? An overview of some of the presentations from the conference itself?

Perhaps we could have a retreat at which established female authors MENTOR younger women writers? (Like Cave Canem does for younger African American poets.)

We'd have to start out small, and we'd necessarily become big (there are lots of women writers!). We'd need grants and the help of our affiliate universities. We'd have to be national, with representatives from all over the country. And our organization would have to be DISTINCTLY different than those of the past that have the lingering smell of post-feminism and the eighties hanging over them.

We need not even announce ourselves as a feminist project. The very definition of feminism in women's work could be discussed at our conference. (By a panel, naturally.)

Eventually, we might think of creating a press or an imprint of female writers.

But, first things first . . . are any of you as "concerned" as I am? I really do think we need unity as females more now than we have for some time.

You are welcome to tell me I'm crazy. Or offer ideas. Am I crazy? Am I?????

Your friend,
Cate

Examples of 2014 VIDA Count Tables:

VIDA Count™
www.vidaweb.org

THE NEW YORKER

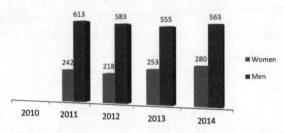

Overall
Five Year Comparison

"VIDA has put a spotlight on the editorial staff of these publications—insisting that they either demonstrate a commitment to achieving gender parity or reveal their steadfast commitment to preserving patriarchy by default." —*Syreeta McFadden*

VIDA Count™
www.vidaweb.org

THE TIMES LITERARY
SUPPLEMENT **TLS**

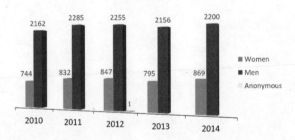

Overall
Five Year Comparison

"The VIDA count draws attention to the gap between the ostensible values of an institution ('best writing'!) and the reality of how freelance dollars are spent and bylines are distributed." —*Alison Hallett*

VIDA Count™
www.vidaweb.org

TinHouse

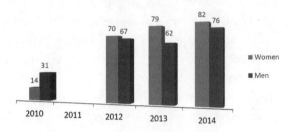

Overall
Five Year Comparison

"Why are literary journals and book reviews important? Because these things make our culture. The voices we broadcast determine the culture we live in, celebrate, see, miss entirely, or ignore. The media we create and give to others to consume matters." —*Lex Schroeder*

VIDA Count™
www.vidaweb.org

the PARIS
REVIEW

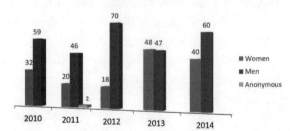

Overall
Five Year Comparison

"Despite these findings and the positive changes that have been made so far, it is apparent that we still have a long way to go." —*Maddie Crum*

19 THINGS: MORE THOUGHTS ON THE FUTURE OF FICTION

John O'Brien

John O'Brien founded the Review of Contemporary Fiction *in 1981, Dalkey Archive Press in 1984, and* CONTEXT *magazine in 1999. His essay "31 Questions and Statements about the Future of Literary Publishing, Bookstores, Writers, Readers, and Other Matters" appeared in the* Review of Contemporary Fiction *in 1996. Since the following essay was written, Dalkey Archive Press has found a permanent home at University of Houston-Victoria.*

When I first wrote my essay on the future of fiction about twenty-five years ago, I had much to say on several topics. In rereading that essay that appeared in the *Review of Contemporary Fiction*, an issue coedited by myself and a newly arrived faculty member, David Foster Wallace, I was surprised by the accuracy of the predictions. But now in old age, one does not worry, or even think about, the future: the future belongs to others to worry about and to speculate on. And so I have far less to say, just a few odds-and-ends comments that may be more about the present than the future.

I

Let's start with Amazon. At the time of my first essay, Amazon was cause for laughter: who would buy books without being able to browse? But Amazon has succeeded, though at the expense of a number of independent and chain bookstores across America. Driving other stores out of business was not an unfortunate byproduct of the service and discounts Amazon offers, but part of a business plan to take over bookselling in America and become the near-sole source for books. And Amazon has now set its eyes on publishing. Will it succeed? Quite possibly, or at least cause enough damage that only very small publishers doing books out of their basements and garages with little overhead will be left; even these will barely survive because the means for distribution will be Amazon.

And now Amazon—depending upon what it needs to be on any particular day—is a distributor, a bookstore, and a publisher, both a producer and supplier, competing on terms that no one else can match (United States anti-trust laws don't seem to apply to Amazon). One wonders why Amazon hasn't completed the circle and bought or merged with Barnes & Noble, even if the ultimate plan would be to close down the retail stores and do all business online.

It's still too early to tell whether Amazon, in building its empire, should have become a publisher before wrapping up the supply side by consuming Barnes & Noble. Rather than starting its own publishing arms, it could have consumed Penguin Random House. And since the Obama administration has apparently suspended all antitrust laws for Amazon's sake, what would stop this lockstep method of controlling books in America and beyond?

2

At the same time, Amazon has also become a philanthropist to various literary organizations and publishers, thus effectively silencing them concerning the intentions and practices of this Goliath. PEN, for instance, should be very concerned about "free speech" when a corporation such as Amazon threatens to control what's published and what's made available in the marketplace of ideas and expression. Others that pride themselves on being watchdogs of publishing and book reviewing remain silent as they benefit from Amazon's largesse. Their moral indignation, which characterizes much of what they have to say, bypasses Amazon's door. Can the do-gooders be bought off at so cheap a price?

3

Funding for literary translators has increased in recent years, as well it should. Ignored in all of the attention paid both to translators and the never-ceasing conferences and roundtable discussions concerning translations are those who take all of the financial risk and make the final decisions about whether translations will make their way into the world: the publishers. Translators have fought hard for their rights and increased compensation, but publishers as a group have not, perhaps because there are so few of them who are even interested.

4

The intensity and frequency of discussions about translations have led to a false assumption that the number of translations has appreciably increased over the past five to ten years. I will here just point to numbers that concern adult fiction and poetry published in the United States and (selectively) in the United Kingdom. The best guess is that there has been a modest increase of perhaps thirty to forty titles, and this increase occurs amid the reality that the total number wavers between three hundred and four hundred. Quite typically one finds some very brave but very small publishers pushing the numbers upward, though these presses are usually publishing as few as two to ten translations per year and can hardly be thought to be making much of an impact despite the impression that some few of them make that they are fighting a Holy War (and perhaps they are, but with a slingshot). My point here is that publishers are usually not asked to sit on panels, nor asked the inevitable question: "What would cause you to publish more translations?"

5

If philanthropy and government in the United States do not see the value of bringing the literary art of other cultures into the English-speaking world, then how do small presses carry the burden? Let MacArthur, PEW, Ford, Mellon, and Rockefeller assume responsibility. The last time I met with Rockefeller, at the request of the head of the translation program of Arts Council England, who had come to the States to try to form a worldwide coalition of funders for translations, Rockefeller began the meeting by saying, "I have no idea why I agreed to this meeting." Welcome to America!

6

Universities and nonprofit literary publishers would seem to have much to offer each other. But . . . Robert Creeley said to me one night as Dalkey Archive Press was about to move to a university: "Get everything you can going in because once you're there, all that they will do is take away." Strangely, some years later, I saw him again at a dinner party the night before meeting administrators at another university to discuss Dalkey Archive moving to their campus. He pulled me aside and said, "I hear you're meeting with the provost tomorrow. If they ask you to tell them how they will benefit from bringing Dalkey here, walk out." The next day, that is exactly what the provost asked me. The provost was one of those awful creatures whose ambition was to keep moving up the administrative ladder, from one school to another, inflicting damage at one place, using that damage to sell themselves on the basis of how deeply they cut expenses at the previous school while initiating four new campus-wide physical fitness programs.

7

Academics are the laziest people in the world. And they dress badly.

8

My advice to young people: I have none. I once did, but no more. The older you get, the less you know. Plato was right.

9

American publishing is on the verge of collapse. It's based on an economic model that cannot sustain itself.

10

The literary presses in Minneapolis have always had a different model for surviving, central to which are the foundations in Minneapolis that created and sustain a literary scene there by funding literary presses, and, as a consequence, causing presses to relocate there. This model of financing could have existed in other American cities, but the foundations said no. On a few occasions, I made my best effort to persuade the MacArthur Foundation to support literary presses—and not just Dalkey—to create a scene that could cause magazines and presses to stay in Chicago or to move there. MacArthur said no. One year, the head of culture, after I described what had happened in Minneapolis, suggested that I move Dalkey Archive there. I said that Dalkey had started in Chicago, that it was my hometown, that I wanted this for Chicago, and that MacArthur should move to Minneapolis.

11

The United States is a third-world country in relation to supporting its literature and bringing literature to the United States. Some of the smallest countries in Europe, and some of the poorest, spend more money to support their literary culture than does the United States.

12

Commercial publishing is doomed—and that leaves the small presses, forever on the verge of going out of business. But the very small presses, those doing fewer than ten books per year, have a chance to survive because they have one or two or no paid employees. They do short print runs, and don't have the money to properly support their books. And yet this lack of money is also what makes the model work financially: their problems begin when they have enough money to hire a third person (the other two are founders). But will these presses survive their founders? Most likely not.

13

Again: Who has consistently been left out of the discussions concerning translations? Editors and publishers. Which would seem to be an odd omission. These two figures—oftentimes one and the same person—are the ones who put up all or most of the money. Editors tend to be perceived as people who have an "opinion" (not to be taken too seriously) about such matters as word choice, syntax, and readability. Oftentimes, the Ministry of Culture or a book office will reserve the right to approve the translation, or even to appoint the translator, after which the translator has the right to accept or reject an editor's "suggestions." And the publisher? The publisher is hardly thought of at all once the decision has been made to have a book translated and published. And if a translator is late in submitting the translation and the deadline is past for when the book had to be issued according to the funding agreement . . . well, in that case, the publisher must then absorb the full cost of the translation. And all of this is quite the opposite for a book written in the "home language." The publisher and editor make a final decision as to whether a book is in acceptable form, whether changes need to be made, and whether to proceed with publication:

this power is granted to the publisher because it is the publisher who must make the decision to have the company's name on the book's spine and take the financial risks. PEN has taken the lead in creating discord between translators and publishers.

14

How is it that editors and publishers do not at least have a place at the table or on the panel when funders call for a meeting to address issues of translation? In all the years that I have been publishing translations, there has been only one meeting to which I was invited to tell a funder what the problems were in doing translations, and what would cause both myself and other publishers to increase the number of translations. One!

15

What I think most about these days is who will become the next generation of Dalkey when I am gone. If Dalkey came into existence to publish books that would stay in print regardless of sales and be the protector of those books (now over 750 in print), who will protect the protector? The United States does not have a record of success in keeping a publishing house intact after the founder is gone. The names may continue, but not the values. Of the nonprofit publishers, Graywolf, Copper Canyon, Milkweed, and BOA have successfully gone into a second generation. These are not encouraging statistics: four out of so many.

In brief, I've no idea what Dalkey's future will be.

16

The National Endowment for the Arts is responsible for the existence of many small presses in the United States. Had literature not been included as a fundable art form in the 1960s, many small presses would not have survived those difficult early years. The founders had no experience either in publishing or running a nonprofit organization. They had a vision of change, and here was government money to support what they did, as long as the "organization" (these were not organizations) would be nonprofit. Graywolf, Coffee House, and Milkweed were among the first on the scene. When the Mellon Foundation in 1990 or thereabouts became interested in funding nonprofit literary presses, they could find only nine that fit the minimal criteria of: (1) nonprofit status and (2) a budget of at least $100,000. Dalkey had just reached $100,000 in grants and sales.

Move this up nearly twenty-five years, and these presses have become much larger, while two have ceased to exist. Leaving aside the Minneapolis presses with foundations providing ongoing support, the others still hang on a shoestring. And yet, regardless of their status as "organizations" even to this day, they exercise an impact on literature in this country far beyond their organizational capacities.

Back in the early nineties, many of them would even would describe their roles as being "farm teams" that found and cultivated young talent that would then move on to commercial houses. Though I objected to this description and thought the opposite (that the commercial houses found the authors, paid them fairly well, and then would dump them when they weren't making enough money), we certainly could not compete with the large publishers in the marketplace. The situation has now changed: these presses, and many others like them, are responsible for almost all the poetry that's published in the United States and much of the nonmainstream fiction, and of course about 98 percent of the translations. And yet almost all of these presses are endangered species. Who in American philanthropy is thinking in terms of how these presses will survive and become permanent and continue into the future?

I can imagine that the National Endowment for the Arts would not welcome the following suggestion—but who else is there on a national scale to undertake this as an issue?—but here it is: there should be a fund, a sustainability fund, that provides multiyear operational grants for these presses, ones that have survived, let's say, twenty or more years, have produced a certain number of literary books, and now have overhead expenses they could not have imagined twenty or thirty years ago: insurance and retirement plans for employees; warehousing; audits; professional bookkeeper; rented space; updated equipment; a human resources manager; business plans; office managers: need I go on? All of those expenses that have nothing to do with the core mission but eat away at the money intended for that mission.

And let us say that right now in America there are about ten to fifteen presses that fit this profile.

17

At one point, all roads seemed as though they would lead to Minneapolis. A scene was being created there, in large part because Minneapolis foundations were funding nonprofit literary publishing, and nothing like this existed in the United States. Publishing in the United States was being defined by two cities: New York and Minneapolis. (As previously mentioned, Dalkey Archive came very close to locating there.) Bringing in a few more presses and literary magazines from other parts of the country would have made Minneapolis the city to be in, and the city to go to. But something stopped this migration, and I have yet to figure out what this was.

18

The time has come to wrap things up. Dalkey Archive is on the verge of seeing whether there is life beyond its founder. Which reminds me: Douglas Messerli of Sun and Moon Press (now renamed as Green Integer) and I used to have arguments when visiting Minneapolis for meetings with the Mellon Foundation (a New York foundation that held its meetings in Minneapolis!). Douglas would argue that a press had its "moment," that after a while it starts to parody itself, and should end when the founder does; I'd argue the opposite, that there was no good reason to have spent thirty to forty years creating and running a press, only to have it end, something akin to constructing a building with a plan to tear it down in thirty years (this, in fact, is Chicago's general building plan). We've yet to see who was right, and perhaps we will end up in the same place regardless of the difference in our views.

19

After one attempt to exit this random series of observations, it is indeed time to turn off the lights and send it on to Milkweed Editions. There will be no further updates.

Megan M. Garr

Megan M. Garr is a poet and the editor of the literary and arts journal Versal. *She is the author of* Terrane *(MIEL, 2015) and* The Preservationist Documents *(Pilot Books, 2012). Garr grew up in Nashville, Tennessee, and has lived in Amsterdam, the Netherlands, since 2001.*

"Printing magazines requires actual cash and the printer does not take idealism as currency, nor does the postal service."
—ROXANE GAY, EDITOR OF *PANK*, IN AN INTERVIEW IN 2013

"If you get through the door, hold the damn door open for those behind you."
—SAEED JONES, DURING THE "PARIS IS STILL BURNING" OFFSITE AT AWP 2015

When *Versal* started in 2002, we did not set out to make our literary magazine economically viable. We did not even consider it a possibility. We started where most start: our own pockets, donations from friends and family. The following year, we applied for a grant from a Dutch cultural foundation, received a small sum, and made another issue. We built a community around it, workshops and writing groups, literary series and readings—selling copies and piecemealing programming revenues until we went to print and went broke again.

While I may have started a literary magazine with a

defeatist attitude towards its economics, that did not stop me (as my early editorials confirm) from questioning how *Versal* could survive the forces of its circumstances. It could be said that a literary magazine exists in two economies. One is capitalism, where cash is traded for services rendered: the press pays the printer, the press pays the postal service, the reader pays the press. The second economy is often called the gift economy: the currency of recognition, the barter between a writer's work and the press's ability to "get it out there," the philanthropy from editors (and others) to make this possible. And it is the push and pull between these two economic forces that is, at least in part, behind the stresses in our community.

These notes from the field are both empirical and factual in nature. My conclusions are not watertight, nor are they intended to be. But in the halls of the Internet and our gatherings at conferences, in our acute discourses over submission fees and contributor payments, in all that back and forth, important details, data, facts are missing. What does our economy really look like? How does the money circulate? Why aren't we selling? And most importantly: who is the economy leaving out?

What follows is a start towards formulating a view of the literary magazine economy from the U.S. perspective—an attempt to take the discourses we're having to a next level, to a place where conversation can lead to cooperation, a shared project of the many to fix our foundations, solve our shared problems, and make it possible to hold our doors open.

The Lit-Mag Economy is Not Nothing

While some may consider that the literary magazine operates in an economic vacuum, that is to say a "null economy," I prefer to think of it as caught between the two strong and contradictory forces of pay-to-play and donation, whether in terms of printing, shipping, content, or time. The reason I prefer this description is that the dynamics between these two forces are the cause of much of the stress in the community. Honing in on our various currencies helps uncover these dynamics, and why, and who, the economy is failing. This viewpoint is also more actionable—we can do something with it, it can be a tool for change. In a vacuum, we are blameless; in a vacuum, our community's financial failures are out of our hands.

Most cash (which is to say, the U.S. dollar) in the lit-mag economy flows in one direction: from the press outwards. What's more, the majority of this cash leaves the lit-mag economy, never to return: it goes to printers and postal services, neither of which have direct or indirect interest in the literary magazine. There is a relatively minor cash flow *towards* the lit mag from writers and readers via copy sales (and now, to some extent, via submission fees). But sales and submission fees alone do not make up the cash to support a lit mag's liquidity, which must cover print runs, postage, advertising, conference fees, and, in rare cases, paid contributors and staff. No, that liquidity depends, in whole or in significant part, on outside sources, what I call external funding: from universities, arts councils, grants, endowments, donations, Kickstarters, and editors' own pockets (namely, MasterCard and Visa). It is "external" funding because it does not come from the inner workings of the magazine itself, from its own efforts and production processes. There is a long tradition of this type of funding for the arts, of course, and for arguably good reasons.

On the gift side of the lit-mag economy, lit mags are not lit mags without editors or writers, and here the currencies of time, content, and recognition are at play. On the Best American Poetry blog, *Rattle* editor Timothy Green refers to lit mags as "social benefit organizations," which asserts a common belief that editors should give their time—and money—for the good of literary society, for the good of *writers*, without expecting recompense. And since few magazines can pay a writer what their work is worth, if anything at all, the lit-mag editor's often volunteer task for the writer is one of reputation. This is the economy of publication credits, which writers build (in some cases, must build) over time. Rather than to "make a living" with their writing, writers enter this economy to make their careers, developing their names and their works, their relationships with editors and magazines, in order to reach readers—and, ultimately, reach those readers through novels and collections. It is generally accepted that neither the lit mag nor the writer has any liquid capital, and so the trade is made between work (what the writer has written) and recognition (what the magazine can give the writer). In this sense, the term "publication credit" is perfectly apropos. It is simultaneously public acknowledgment and a promise of future returns.

These two forces of the lit-mag economy collide every single day. To put it simply: the cash that flows in flows right back out to pay the printer and the post office, largely, if not entirely, bypassing the makers of the art (be that the art of writing or the art of publishing). Meanwhile, the reliance on gifts to make the art *the art*, the trade of time for masthead, work for reputation, circumvents the fact that *to publish* requires money. To write a poem takes talent and effort and time. To keep a magazine afloat requires time and financial credit, or grant-writing skills, or both. For far too many of us, the lack of hard currency means that *some of us cannot make the art*. Money does not flow into the community itself; our art's currency is in kind, and *to give* is an economic luxury. And so the strongholds of the community remain where they always have, with the straight, white, male population.

And though literary magazines do not consider themselves

corporations exploiting the hard work of writers and editors, we are in fact doing just that. Relying, by and large, on donated funds *and* content, and siphoning those liquid funds and sales margins into the printing and postal sectors, the lit-mag economy is either a capitalist failure or a pretty impressive achievement. Viewed as achievement, in fact, the lit-mag community can be reductively relabeled as a conduit for capital, moving it from philanthropic sources into two struggling, predigital sectors: printing and snail mail. Until it can be said that the lit-mag community can cover a living wage for its editors and writers, then we must admit the exploitative and exclusionary natures of our economy.

FROM ONE LIT MAG'S BOTTOM LINE TO AN ENTIRE ECONOMY'S TOP LINE

Like many others, *Versal* is not just a literary magazine. It is also a literary programmer, running monthly readings, workshops, and other community events throughout its now nearly fourteen years. Somewhat ignorantly, I used to call this our circular business model. Profits from readings and workshops, in addition to magazine sales, paid (just) for the magazine's printing and shipping costs in our first decade.

In 2010, I realized this business model had all but broken down. The canary, for us, was the price of paper, which shot up that year—due, at least in part, to rising raw material prices in the wake of several supply disruptions. Faced with our additionally unique circumstance of having to ship at least half of our print run abroad, we were struggling to maintain cash flow to cover *Versal*'s rising costs.

Thanks to my professional work as editor and translator in the corporate sector, I was able to solicit advice from one of my clients, a global top-five management consultancy. They crunched our numbers, challenged my assumptions, and suggested we do two things. The first was to slow down our local activities to focus on the magazine. There was much optimism at this time, from the consultants especially, that with the right focus the magazine would secure the sales it needed to continue to grow. We had a good product, they said. A beautiful book that anyone would want on their coffee table or bookshelf, even "nonwriters." All we had to do was focus our attention, achieve a bit more scale, and we would reach our readers.

But in order to be able to focus, we needed cash to come in from somewhere besides sales, cash that would replace any profits we once made from local activities. We considered raising our copy price, but it would reach a level three or four times higher than most literary magazines simply due to shipping. And at least 50 percent of a *Versal* print run must be shipped overseas, the rates for which approach two times our cost price.

Here the consultants brought their second suggestion. According to their calculations, profits from a two-dollar submission fee would be enough to replace what we made in a year's worth of local programming. After much debate, which extended beyond our own team into the wider lit community online, we implemented the submission fee for issue 10. We paid the printing and shipping bills, and were even able to offer a small (very small) contributor payment for the first time. Things seemed to be going in the right direction.

But over the course of 2012–2013, and despite our renewed "focus," the magazine was still just scraping along. We were working on our eleventh issue, and sales of *Versal* 10 were surprisingly sluggish. Printing *Versal* 11 was not only going to completely empty our coffers, it was going to put us in debt.

I went back to the consultancy, hoping to find an answer. This time, the consultants and I decided to look at the U.S. market to get a snapshot of the economy. We analyzed fifty American literary magazines, big and small, using data supplied by the magazines themselves on CLMP's directory and their websites. Twenty-nine of these magazines relied to some extent on a university, nearly all on some form of outside funding. At the time of data collection, these magazines printed a total of 264,750 copies a year. We estimated that 731 people worked for them, but that only 99 of them were paid for that work. Twenty of the magazines had only one form of payment, and that was in copies.

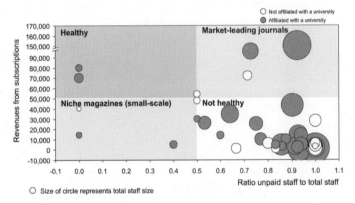

FIGURE 1. Only a small number of lit mags appear to be financially healthy, and most of them are affiliated with a university.

When we looked at the potential revenue in this sample in a single year—which we did by taking subscriptions and 50 percent of remaining single copies sold at the full retail price (assuming that a literary magazine would sell half of its available stock and give the other half away to contributors, reviewers, other magazines, etc.), adjusted for the number of issues per year and the print run—we came up with an estimate between $1.7 million and $2.7 million.

At first I thought this was a lot of money. It seemed that way, coming from an economy of next to nothing. My friend at the consultancy, though, wasn't impressed. He said that there was something wrong if fifty magazines were only able to make a combined total of $2.7 million maximum. After printing and shipping and other overhead, that certainly was not enough to pay the 731 staff members, much less the contributors who offered up the work that made the magazine a magazine in the first place. He called the market "fragmented." If just this small sampling was any indication, then the total economy was nothing short of flooded.

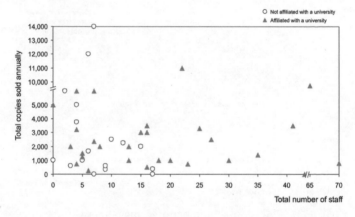

FIGURE 2. The audience and number of staff seem almost negatively correlated. Many people work for small audiences.

To solve this fragmentation, my friend suggested, magazines should consolidate. The simplest way to explain this logic is to look at it in terms of market share. There are different ways to measure market share, but usually it is measured in terms of either products sold or revenue as a percentage of the total market. In a fragmented sector, many small players have tiny shares of the market—which makes it hard to reach consumers. Basically, the more choice there is out there, the more sales are dispersed, and the less each individual magazine can make. This is why we see so many editors plead for sales that are more in line with submissions: the "if everyone who submitted bought a copy" logic. While it's arguably affordable for a writer to submit to a hundred literary magazines a year, buying those same hundred literary magazines would cost a writer at least $1,000—a hefty sum.

Consolidation, on the other hand, would mean fewer magazines with greater shares of the market; the new, larger scale of these bigger magazines would allow them to pool resources on both the procurement (printing, shipping) and sales (marketing, footprint) sides. This is called economies of scale. While indeed, in this "new economy," fewer human resources would be needed, those who would work at the presses would presumably be taking home a paycheck. And from the "consumer" angle, there would be less to choose from; sales would be more concentrated and top lines healthier. Richard Nash alludes to this in his insightful "What Is the Business of Literature?" article published in the *Virginia Quarterly Review* in spring 2013: "The most profitable print-publishing business of all would be in a society where everyone reads the same book."

This wasn't the answer I was looking for. Rather than discovering a new business model that would take *Versal* to new heights, I was face to face with the hard numbers of an inherently broken economic system, money funneling in from outside, continuously, to keep an ever-growing number of lit mags afloat. A system that, while largely avoiding many basic business practices, is still bound by and indebted to capitalism's mechanisms. In other words, the problem is systemic. A single magazine cannot change it from within, and no amount of economic logic will slow down the trend to start your own magazine. Even with systemic dynamics forcing university magazines into smaller budgets, or worse, out the door, these dynamics are usually viewed in isolation, a problem of university board priorities, and not the dynamics indicative of a larger problem that affects us all.

THE ANXIETY OF OVERSUPPLY

Across the conversations we're having with each other about these issues spans an underlying anxiety of oversupply: too many lit mags, too many presses, too many writers. But it's difficult to criticize our vibrant, highly engaged society. A literary magazine is a community, one many of us may miss after our MFAs are complete (or miss because we are not in an MFA program). The editorial team is a place to hone aesthetics, and therefore our own writing. Today's dialogues around literary citizenship reflect, as well, the activist habits that many of us seem to share: "giving back," "bettering our community," "extending access"—these are some of the (very valid) motivations underlying our small-press work. Mine as well.

But nowhere in this is the economic problem solved, or even forgiven. In fact, as the literary-citizenship dialogues have intensified, so have calls for healthier economics. I believe this has something to do with the immensity of the situation at hand. If we reduce the lit-mag economy down to its most simplified parts, then our oversupply, our overproduction, is indeed a capitalist triumph. Large swaths of free labor acting, in sum, as a middleman between external funding sources (government, arts foundations, Kickstarter, Visa) and the printing and postal sectors. Unless something drastically, systematically changes, this hemorrhaging of cash will continue.

There is another, more subtle logic circulating around the question of magazine overpopulation. A 2014 *Ploughshares* blog post argues that to rise above the "crowded literary magazine landscape" a magazine must "challenge the notion of the online and print magazine itself . . . own and celebrate truly fresh aesthetics, and . . . remind us of the power of the work, collected and distributed with desired effect, with consistent and often powerful aim." The magazines listed are by and large praised for their innovative presentations of content; neither sales data nor distribution figures are given as proof of their success. *Ploughshares'* list suffers the false logic many of us fall prone to: that the "cool factor" of our efforts is our success, and is how we will "rise above"—essentially, that our finances depend on the forces of meritocracy.

But the economic fact of today's lit-mag economy is that no matter how good a magazine's "unique selling point" (USP), a combination of poor sector dynamics and skewed business models will keep it—will keep most of us—in a constant battle with funding, bills, and insufficient sales. The large majority of presses have neither the footprint nor the scale to reach an adequate number of buyers to counteract the fragmented economy, much less to compensate the core costs of publishing. And publishing is what we do. If we cannot pay for it, for the printers and post offices but also for the writers and editors, then we are failing our craft.

THE LIT-MAG "BUSINESS" MODEL

In the lit-mag economy, while market success may be measured by our USP, business success seems to be measured by the size of our external funding. Today, this is the only "business model" that appears to be truly working, though by no means is this what most outside of our field would consider a successful business model.

A business model is how money, or better stated, value,

is created in pursuit of an organization's aims. It is what makes those aims achievable. On one side, there's a literary magazine. On the other side are the readers (the so-called consumers). The business model is the structure that gets the magazine to those readers, takes those readers' money, and then turns that trade of product for cash into value for the magazine—for example, by balancing revenues and costs so that they lead to profits and so that, in turn, the magazine can continue—or even grow.

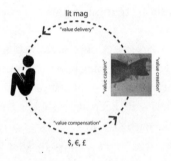

FIGURE 3. The business model can be simplified by looking at how value moves from an organization to its customers and back. Value is delivered, compensated, and captured by this system.

In the corporate world, sound business models are the *sine qua non* for success. If any part of the scaffolding of this architecture is weak or breaks down, the entire business can collapse. Allow me to illustrate with an overly simplified example. Let's say the *World Review* was started in the 1950s in the United States. It subsisted off of a loyal subscription base that it communicated with via post. Subscriptions were also renewed via bank checks sent in the post. In the late 1990s and early 2000s, online payment systems started to take off, and by 2010 these systems had become the primary payment method for subscriptions. But (humor me here) the *World Review* was only able to process checks and would not open a PayPal account. It started to lose subscribers as e-mail and websites replaced post as the primary means of both communication and payments. Over the first decade of the 2000s, the *World Review*'s income steadily declined. By 2015, it could no longer sustain itself, and the magazine folded.

The obvious failure in this example was the *World Review*'s inability (or refusal) to keep up with "the times" in terms of payment systems. The *World Review*'s compensation structure was no longer aligned with its readers, who increasingly expected digital communication and payment means. This put too much pressure on the other structures of the business model, and ultimately the entire system broke down.

In simple terms, the ideal business model for a literary magazine would be that copy sales thoroughly compensate the costs that go into making those copies, and that there would be adequate distribution infrastructures that make this exchange possible. But even for large publishers, which do have scale and footprint, this 1:1 ratio is rarely achieved, if my 2013 study is any indication. The literary magazine seems doomed to need something outside of itself in order to survive.

One of the problems might be the average recommended retail price (RRP) accepted in the lit-mag economy. In my survey in 2013, the average retail price of a single copy of a literary magazine was $10.30. In that analysis, only ten of the magazines would be able to pay two full-time staff if they sold half of their print runs (keeping in mind that our assumption was that half was given away, the other half sold). In other words, the compensation of value in our business models is not an equal compensation for its delivery. In still other words: we're not charging enough for our magazines.

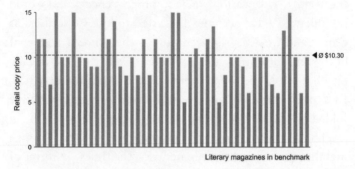

FIGURE 4. The average retail price of lit mags in the 2013 study was $10.30.

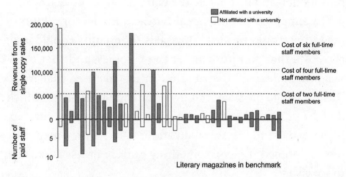

FIGURE 5. Assuming lit mags sold half of their available print run, only a handful would be able to pay two staff members full-time salaries.

Another problem could also be found in the value delivery. Distribution companies will carry a literary magazine—if it's big enough. For most smaller, noninstitutional literary magazines, however, distribution is a time-consuming, manual task, a web of precarious consignment agreements with bookstores that often remain unfulfilled. Shipping costs are on the magazine's account, as are unsold copies. In the eleven years we worked to distribute *Versal* to bookstores, we never made a profit from any consignment agreement. In many cases, we never saw any sales revenue at all; follow-up over borders, despite e-mail's ease, seemed a major obstacle to securing those relationships. Consignment, however beneficial to bookstores, may in fact be a waste of money and time for the smaller literary magazine. But that is how we get our lit mags on shelves—most of the time, that is the only way.

Of course the printing bill isn't helping here either. This is what is called the value-capturing system of the business model, where a magazine would make sure its costs align with what it can achieve in the market so that it can make a profit. In my survey, print runs ranged from three hundred to seven thousand, with about half of the magazines at or around two thousand and the other half significantly below. Unfortunately, even a print run of seven thousand doesn't go that far for a printer's profit margins, so a single lit mag would have very little leverage with an average printer's pricing. The choice then is to keep things as simple and cheap as possible, which is why many larger-run literary magazines are digitally printed on slightly slick white paper, with black and white art (if any), perfect binds, etc. Consolidation would do the eco-nomics of the bigger magazines a lot of good.

For those magazines that have print runs under two thou-sand (more like under one thousand), costs are simply higher. A lot of these magazines are printing offset, or using older—and more manual—printing techniques like letterpress. This is perhaps where the margins are the least aligned, because while the printing itself is higher quality, even in some cases hand-made, the RRP of these magazines stays within range of their larger-print-run counterparts. The aesthetic value they deliver is likely not even halfway compensated by the prices they charge. And this goes back to the RRP problem in general: we cannot charge much more than ten dollars for our magazines.

In the current lit-mag economy, we are all in the same game, from *Poetry* to *Parcel*, charging about the same for our products, vying for the same readership. This playing field, as it were, is not a balanced one—because of the large range of printing techniques but narrow choices for copy prices, because of the poor distribution channels, but also because many magazines are structurally funded: by universities, by large public grants, and, in some cases, by considerable endowments. These magazines, in a sense, do not need to worry about the economics. They can give away free copies, they can lit-mag swap, ship anywhere, because at the end of the day they will still have the money to go to print again. But magazines that receive no structural external funding do have to worry. They must reach the same readers as the magazines with strong financial backing. They must charge about the same for their issues. No matter the magazine, no matter how innovative it is, no matter how small, it is by and large beholden to the same dynamics as any other magazine, no matter how traditional, no matter how big, no matter how backed. And this is why it is so hard to break out of the old economic patterns. That Kickstarter and Indiegogo have become major sources of funding for many independent magazines may seem to herald a new era in the lit-mag economy, a new, innovative way to fund it. But the fact is, Kickstarter is no more than philanthropy 2.0; it is still external funding, feeding the broken literary-magazine business model in the broken literary-magazine economy.

OUR ECONOMIC OXYMORON

1. Literature transcends economy.
2. We should be paid for our work.

My guess is that many of us agree with both of these statements. I know I do. But when I first wrote them down I
thought, "We want to have our cake and eat it too." And
indeed, much of the dialogue out there implies that we
deserve to be paid, but that we're too important to be both-
ered with the real economy of it all.

But this is not where the contradiction is at its most
poignant. In believing in these two statements simultaneously, we are simply adhering to a learned tradition, passed
down to us through the poems and stories we read, mimic,
and rewrite: a classicist (and, I would argue, classist, patriarchal, and racist) model of the writer-artist, supported by
the nation-state for the good of society. In this model, literature is not subject to the demands of economies. Supply
and demand, gross domestic product, business models,
sales figures, key performance indicators—these things
have nothing to do with the writing on the page.

The poignancy of this contradiction—a contradiction
that underpins the entire small-press sector—originates in
the dissemination of the writing itself. To print a book or lit
mag, you must enter the capitalist economy. Even if you own
your own printing press, you'll have to source ink, paper, or
both. You still have to go to the post office to mail a copy
to a reader. To get your work out there, there are inevitably
bills (in hard currency) to pay.

Since we're not being paid to pay those bills, we have to
take on other jobs. We help presses market our books. We
set up our own reading tours and hire our own venues and
buy the wine to serve there. We donate to Kickstarters and
we commit to buying x many lit-mag subscriptions each year.
All of this to keep (our) writing in circulation.

The Wisdom to Know the Difference

I grew up in an activist Catholic family, which for some might sound like a contradiction. But for me in my small church in one of Nashville's old farming neighborhoods, watching my parents, whose activism grew up alongside their faith, it was one and the same. Even after leaving the church, the Serenity Prayer is still in my head so many years later: *Lord, grant me the serenity to accept the things I cannot change, the courage to change the things I can, and the wisdom to know the difference.* I saw my parents work, often through the church, to change things that others seemed to accept: homelessness, poverty, access to health care. So I grew up thinking I could change just about everything.

To publish *Versal*, I have to accept that the literary magazine straddles two economic forces: one being capitalism, the other a dissatisfied barter between work and recognition, time and mastheads. And I have to accept that changing this, the lit-mag economy, is a long game, but also that change is possible. The insufficient distribution channels, unlevel playing field, negative sales margins, all the free labor—all of this can change. My research may have yet to find an answer for the lit-mag economy, but I have seen the immense value in having a deeper understanding of the simultaneity that it occupies, and in seeing those dynamics in hard numbers.

An annual report on our sector, a benchmark, would track the health of our economy and help us all navigate its dynamics in more informed, more conscious ways. It would ideally take a representative sample of literary magazines, maybe one hundred or more. Like the survey I conducted in 2013, the sample would comprise both larger and smaller magazines (e.g., measured in terms of print run as indication of market share), and would distinguish them as such so that the benchmark could be useable across the sector, from the smallest handmade magazine to the larger, heavily funded nonprofit publications. Similarly, the sample would make sure to account for magazines across funding mechanisms, from university budgets to arts grants, self-supporting finance cycles to Kickstarter dependencies. Collected data would include:

- Source(s) of funding
- Annual revenues, costs, and profits
- Number of staff, paid and unpaid
- Cost items and amounts (annual printing costs, annual postage costs, salaries, overhead)
- Number of books/magazines per year and print runs
- Circulation estimates
- Number of copies in each print run given away
- Number of copies in each print run sold
- Price per copy
- Price per subscription
- Types and amounts of author payments
- Submission-fee level and revenues
- Number of grants applied for vs. received
- Number of crowdfunding campaigns and success rate
- Etc.

Not only would the benchmark collect data on each press, it would also collate this data into meaningful relationships, like:

- Financial health: revenues vs. ratio of paid staff to total staff
- Cash flow: printing and postage costs as percent of total budget
- Human-resource health: total copies sold vs. total number of staff

- Price elasticity: price per single copy vs. total copy circulation
- Scale: external financial dependency vs. circulation, paid staff, author payment
- Degree of professionalization: size of budget vs. total annual circulation

The benchmark could also address key issues in our community, such as what types of presses successfully receive external funding from grants or crowdfunding, information which could then be linked to who runs these presses (men, women, people of color, LGBTQ)—thus revealing exclusions that our current economy helps cause. The submission-fee debate could progress out of its current stalemate thanks to numbers that reveal the contribution (or lack thereof) of a fee to a magazine's bottom line, and distinctions could be more clearly made between structurally funded mags that have the fee and independent ones that, one could argue, need it to survive.

Once the first and then second benchmarks are made, a picture of the health of our economy will start to form. This picture will finally give a lit mag the hard data it needs to make decisions that affect its bottom line. It will be able to map itself on this benchmark and find out where it falls on certain metrics, asking questions like "Are we more financially sound than our peers?" A magazine can take this kind of data to its board, if it has one, or use the benchmark to reinforce *raison d'être* arguments when university budgets are being slashed. Lit mags that receive external funding could use such data to make sure that funding works towards a more sustainable future, rather than the short-term bills. Those that have found success in the current economy could use this to build further—in other words, focus on their top lines. New magazines could use it to see where they want to position themselves, establishing their business models accordingly.

Writers could also make good use of this kind of data. Not only would the benchmark chart the sector's ability to pay its editors and writers over time, it would also reveal how healthy certain types of presses are compared to others. As we've seen with the VIDA and Duotrope data, writers can use this information to better target their submissions *and* subscriptions. Jessica Piazza's work through poetryhasvalue.com further underlines the fact that there is a community out there looking for data: insight into magazines that goes beyond back-cover contributor lists. Our literary activism, citizenship, commitments, and communities would, importantly, be better informed.

The potential of this kind of benchmark would also extend towards a real conversation, in numbers, about what writing is worth. Dan Brady of *Barrelhouse* writes, "Resources are scarce no matter what poetry publishing model a magazine or small press follows. When we decided that we were financially sound enough to consistently pay writers, we settled on the amount of fifty dollars per contributor. We had a long conversation around if that was enough." What is enough? To evolve this conversation, we need hard data on what is already being done and what is actually feasible, given our community's economic circumstances.

HOLD THE DAMN DOOR OPEN

To quote Richard Nash again, "the business of literature is the business of making culture, not just the business of manufacturing bound books." Alongside collating data in meaningful ways and improving our understanding of our financial actuality—a task which will yield concrete answers

and provide a clearer sense of the possible ways forward—
literary magazines, the literary community as a whole, can
already take steps to shift the chains of value. These steps,
in general, involve activities, experiments, and dialogues in
the following four areas:

- Cultivating our local microclimates and communities, however that may be defined
- Finding ways to make external funding work forward towards our magazines' long-term sustainability, and sharing that "wealth"
- Encouraging healthier submission practices to
close the gap between submission and subscriber
numbers
- Rethinking the role of the editor beyond her traditional civic obligations

At the "Literary Production and the Gift Economy" panel at
AWP 2015, it was suggested that we change how we position
money in our economy. Annie Guthrie of the University of
Arizona Poetry Center said, "Money has no inherent character." TC Tolbert argued that spending money could be
made a creative act, one that builds relationships.

Chaun Webster of Minneapolis's former Ancestry
Books was in the audience. When the panel opened for
questions, Webster confronted the panelists with money's
larger implications and dangers. It goes to some, and does
not go to many. People of color, women, queers—these are
some of the many left out of our literary-magazine economy,
in substantial, material ways.

I want to believe that we can change this, and that money
can be a tool for this. A tool, like *Versal*, for my activism. But
I first have to find the money, where it comes from, how it
circulates, where it goes.

I want to believe that if we use our money better, if we spend more wisely, if we spend consciously, our community can reach into the margins that our current economy excludes.

I want to believe that our value chain, the one that gets writing to readers, can be disrupted and redistributed.

I want to believe that *it can happen on paper.*

That literary magazines can continue to open doors for our community, take us into rooms we have not seen before, and find the writers who reside there.

DIVERSITY IS NOT ENOUGH: RACE, POWER, PUBLISHING

Daniel José Older

Daniel José Older is the author of the young adult novel Shadowshaper *(Arthur A. Levine Books, 2015), the* Bone Street Rumba *urban fantasy series (Roc/Penguin Group, 2016), and the ghost noir collection* Salsa Nocturna *(Crossed Genres Publications, 2012). He coedited* Long Hidden: Speculative Fiction from the Margins of History *(Crossed Genres Publications, 2014), which was nominated for both the Locus and World Fantasy awards for best anthology. Older lives in Brooklyn, where he worked for ten years as a paramedic. "Diversity Is Not Enough" was first published on April 18, 2014, on the website Buzzfeed Books.*

"Cuando el EZLN logre lo que busca, entonces ya no será necesario el EZLN, por eso decimos que luchamos por desaparecer."
"When the Zapatista Army of National Liberation achieves what it seeks, it will cease to be necessary, and so we say that we fight in order to disappear."
—SUBCOMANDANTE MARCOS, EZLN
FEBRUARY 2001

A few years ago, someone in the publishing industry crossed out a line I wrote in a novel. I'm pretty good at taking criticism; I don't usually get gooey over the words I write, even if the stories are close to my heart. This line, however, had to do with a Latina character feeling uncomfortable in a shnitzy part of Brooklyn because all the other women of color had little white babies and all the white people were looking at her sideways. The

154

note beside the crossout said: "Doesn't happen in this day and age."

Now.

Let me skip over the outrage I felt and then the internal gymnastics I did trying to fit that outrage into some sentences I thought this person might understand. Another essay, perhaps. . . . Suffice it to say, we don't work together anymore. Instead, I want to take a moment to recognize a more unspoken consequence of having a mostly white industry dictate mostly white standards to a mostly white author-base: the stories that won't get told.

These are the moments we self-censor, we sidestep, pirouette, tiptoe, softspeak, do whatever it takes to not get too deep into the tricky race and racism quagmire. We do it because we want to be published, and even if we haven't seen the X scratched through a line on the page, we've felt it in conversations, heard it happen to friends, internalized the truth of it from so many whitewashed covers, trollish comments sections from industry folks, micro- and mega-aggressions at cons. I still catch myself self-censoring, and I spent most of my twenties speaking to people about racism, engaging in these very conversations in intensive workshop settings, organizing, thinking, overthinking, doubting, rewinding, engaging, getting enraged, falling apart, tearing into my own racial history, privileges, fears, wishes.

Still, I want to be heard. I know who the gatekeepers are. Writing and, more so, publishing are always negotiations between what you want to say, what you can say, and what society will allow you to say. The censorship happens on many levels, at every step of the game. It doesn't have to be so obvious as *that doesn't happen*, because the insidiousness of race in America reaches deep inside each of us, keeps us second-guessing and analyzing, wondering if we've gone crazy.

Be courageous, they say. It's your job as a writer. Yes,

and we are, we are. And still we struggle, stifle, collapse, recuperate. There are no guidelines or dos and don'ts for writing about what three hundred years of euphemisms and a whole academic/political machinery still can't quite figure out how to face head-on. We know this: the publishing world is overwhelmingly white. Writers of color puzzle over rejection letters that say things like, "Great writing and story but I didn't identify with the main character." What are we to do with such a comment? *Write more universal characters,* some will say. "Universal" has become an empty word; it *generally* indicates a false neutral that more or less resembles whiteness. Do we then write the character as we imagine the white imagination imagines people of color? How many layers of fantasy and identity must get breached to walk that delicate line between truth telling and pacifying?

There are no easy answers. These impossible negotiations fall somewhere on the matrix of literary success and failure, privilege and empowerment. Writers of color face the dual challenge of succeeding in an industry that still hasn't reconciled its racism and allowing our true voices onto the page. And while it's daunting, the problem demands we step back from traditional understandings of "making it" and redraw those lines for ourselves; sometimes with tears, sometimes fire. There is no map; there is no path—we make it by walking, as the poem asks of us. And we can't do it alone.

.   .   .

IN THE *NEW YORK TIMES* LAST MONTH, children's book illustrator Christopher Myers wrote about "the apartheid of literature—in which characters of color are limited to the townships of occasional historical books that concern themselves with the legacies of civil rights and slavery but are never given a pass card to traverse the lands of adventure, curiosity, imagination or personal growth."

Myers's father, author Walter Dean Myers, wrote about growing up a bibliophile in Harlem, falling out of love with books when they offered up no characters he could relate to, and the revelation of reading *Sonny's Blues* by James Baldwin: "I was lifted by it, for it took place in Harlem, and it was a story concerned with black people like those I knew. By humanizing the people who were like me, Baldwin's story also humanized me. The story gave me a permission that I didn't know I needed, the permission to write about my own landscape, my own map."

These two essays perfectly frame the emotional and social debacle of publishing and diversity today. They begin with this stat: "Of 3,200 children's books published in 2013, just 93 were about black people," according to a study by the Cooperative Children's Book Center at the University of Wisconsin. The wide world of literature in general, and by no coincidence, the publishing industry itself, suffer from similarly disastrous numbers.

When Christopher Myers asked his uncomfortable questions about the apartheid in children's lit, the industry hid behind The Market. The publishing industry, people often say, as if it's a gigantic revelation, needs to make money and, as such, it responds to The Market—and people don't buy books about characters of color. This is updated marketing code for "you people don't read," and it's used to justify any number of inexcusable problems in literature. "The Market is so comfortably intangible," Myers writes, "that no one is worried I will go knocking down any doors. The Market, I am told, just doesn't demand this kind of book . . . because white kids won't buy a book with a black kid on the cover— or so The Market says, despite millions of music albums that are sold in just that way."

By blaming an intangible force, the publishing industry absolves itself of any responsibility, when in fact it is very much in the business of manipulating The Market to its ends. "Those conversations happen without acknowledging that there's a huge disparity in how books are marketed and publicized," Saray McCarry tells me. McCarry worked in publishing on and off for a decade, most recently at a New York literary agency. "That money and attention overwhelmingly goes to what the industry has already decided is 'marketable'—heterosexual narratives featuring white characters. A book has very little chance of doing well if there's no marketing push behind it."

Lee and Low Publishers convened a panel last year and asked agents what they could do to help shift the troubling lack of diversity in publishing. "I think the change is going to have to come from within those who are affected," one agent responded, "just like any underrepresented group in any profession. But since the return on the investment for the author is so low, I don't know how many people of color are going to have the desire to climb the mountain to publication that every new author faces, or have the luxury of dedicating the time it takes to master the craft."

Another agent, when asked why less than 1 percent of her submissions were from people of color, captured what seems to be the publishing industry's general attitude in just ten words: "This seems like a question for an author to answer."

This is the language of privilege—the audacity of standing at the top of a mountain you made on the backs of others and then yelling at people for being at the bottom. If it's not the intangible Market that's to blame, it's the writers of color, who maybe don't have what it takes and don't submit enough anyway. Read the subtextual coding here—the agent first places the onus of change on the folks with the least institutional power to effect it, then suggests we probably won't be able to find the time (i.e., lazy) to master the craft.

Of course, we have climbed many mountains, and mastery of craft is not a luxury for writers of color, it is a necessity. But many of our gifts and challenges won't be seen or recognized within a white cultural context. Nuances of code-switching, racial microaggressions, the emotional reality of surviving white supremacy, self-translation—these are all layers of the nonwhite experience that rarely make it into mainstream literature, even when the characters look like us.

The disproportionally white publishing industry matters because agents and editors stand between writers and readers. Anika Noni Rose put it perfectly in *Vanity Fair* this month: "There are so many writers of color out there, and often what they get when they bring their books to their editors, they say, 'We don't relate to the character.' Well it's not for you to relate to! And why can't you expand yourself so you can relate to the humanity of a character as opposed to the color of what they are?"

So we are wary. The publishing industry looks a lot like one of these best-selling teenage dystopias: white and full of people destroying each other to survive.

But let's go back to this: "It's not for you to relate to!" Write that in the sky. And it's true—often, as writers of color, to portray our stories in all their vibrant authenticity, all their difficult truth means we're not writing for editors and agents, we're writing past them. We're writing for us, for each other. And it's not just a question of characters of color, it's not a numbers game. It's about voice, about narrative flow. Because of who we are and what we've lived, our stories often contain implicit critiques of white supremacy, critiques that we know stand little chance of surviving the gauntlet of the majority-white publishing industry. We see diverse futures, laden with the tangled past of oppression and we reenvision models of empowerment and survival. But only a few of us make it through. There is a filter and the filter is white culture.

Ultimately, editors and agents hold exactly the same amount of responsibility that writers do in making literature more diverse. The difference is, editors and agents have inordinately more power and access in the industry than writers do. As Arthur A. Levine's executive editor, Cheryl Klein, said in a July 2014 CNN interview: "It's important to have advocates at every stage, from editing to marketing, from librarians to authors, so it's an industry-wide effort." Klein cofounded the Children's Book Council Diversity Committee, a group of editors "dedicated to increasing the diversity of voices and experiences contributing to children's and young adult literature." And that's what I'm talking about.

The question industry professionals need to ask themselves is: "How can I use my position to help create a literary world that is diverse, equitable, and doesn't just represent the same segment of society it always has since its inception? What concrete actions can I take to make actual change and move beyond the tired conversation we've been having for decades?"

"As I discovered who I was, a black teenager in a white-dominated world," Walter Dean Myers writes, "I saw that these characters, these lives, were not mine. I didn't want to become the 'black' representative, or some shining example of diversity. What I wanted, needed really, was to become an integral and valued part of the mosaic that I saw around me."

And the "shining example" Myers speaks of is exactly what the industry responds with when we raise the question of diversity. No one is demanding more tokens though. We're talking about systemic upheaval.

. . .

HERE'S WHERE THE CRITIQUE IS met with deafen-
ing silence. CNN recently published an article on diversity in young
adult literature that asked, "Where is the Mexican Katniss?"
In the *Hunger Games* novels, Katniss isn't white, so let's also ask:
Where are the publishing-industry players who will take a stand
to make sure literary characters of color become big-screen
characters of color? And let's go back even further. Octavia
Butler gave us Lauren Olamina in 1993. Nalo Hopkinson gave
us Ti-Jeanne in 1998 and Tan Tan in 2000. Where were the
mass-marketing resources, multimillion-dollar ad campaigns
and spin machines when *Parable of the Sower, Brown Girl in the
Ring,* and (my favorite) *Midnight Robber* dropped?

Nancy Larrick begins her essay "The All White World of
Children's Books" with essentially the same question: "Why
are they always white children?" That was written in 1965.
The CNN article from this month refuses to make a cohe-
sive statement about race and publishing that isn't tempered
with phrases like "Some writers feel." It ends with the hope
that a nonexistent contest with five winners could be "the
beginning of real change in young adult fiction." The 1965
article, on the other hand, concludes with a reminder to editors that "what is good for the Ku Klux Klan is not necessarily good for America—or for the book business. White
supremacy in children's literature," Larrick writes, "will be
abolished when authors, editors, publishers, and booksellers
decide that they need not submit to bigots."

. . .

A YOUNG WRITER THAT I MENTOR reached out to
me last week. "None of these agents look like me," she said,

"and they don't represent anyone that looks like me." She's wrapping up a final draft of her first novel and I'd told her to research literary agencies to get a feel for what's out there. "What if they don't get what I'm doing?"

I thought back over the many interactions I'd had with agents—all but two of them white—before I landed with mine. The ones who said they loved my writing but didn't connect with the character, the ones that didn't think my book would be marketable even though it was already accepted at a major publishing house. Thought about the ones who wanted me to delete moments when a character of color gets mean looks from white people because "that doesn't happen anymore" and the white magazine editor who lectured me on how I'd gotten my own culture wrong. My friends all have the same stories of whitewashed covers and constant sparring with the many micro- and mega-aggressions of the publishing industry.

"I don't know," I said. Useless words, but they were all I had in that moment. I don't. There are so many paths to success, so many meanings of the concept, and race and power complicate the equation infinitely. It's not enough for writers of color to learn craft, we need to navigate the impossible waters of an unwelcoming industry. I flailed for words that would prepare her for all that lay ahead; none came.

"What happens," she asked, "if none of them want a book about a black girl and I never find an agent?"

Writing—becoming a writer—is the greatest thing that's ever happened to me, and the only thing comparable is seeing that love of craft blossom in someone else. But navigating the complexities of industry that still hasn't dealt with its own institutional racism is a struggle I wouldn't wish on anyone.

I closed my eyes, tossed up a tiny prayer, almost without meaning to—that she'd find good people like I have, people who would cultivate her voice instead of mangling or silencing it. I'd had this conversation before, years ago, when I was starting out and I didn't know what lay ahead. My mentors shook their heads, and, I imagine, sent up their own tiny prayers. The faces they made probably looked much like mine as I said, "You just have to find the right folks." I cringed when I said it—tepid words for such a devastating labyrinth.

Diversity is not enough.

We're right to push for diversity. We have to. But it is only step one of a long journey. Lack of racial diversity is a symptom. The underlying illness is institutional racism. It walks hand in hand with sexism, cissexism, homophobia, and classism. To go beyond this same conversation we keep having, again and again, beyond tokens and quick fixes, requires us to look the illness in the face and destroy it. This is work for white people and people of color to do, sometimes together, sometimes apart. It's work for writers, agents, editors, artists, fans, executives, interns, directors, and publicists. It's work for reviewers, educators, administrators. It means taking courageous, real-world steps, not just changing mission statements or submissions guidelines.

Maybe the word hasn't been invented yet—that thing beyond diversity. We often define movements by what they're against, but the final goal is greater than the powers it dismantles, deeper than any statistic. It's something like equity—a commitment to harvesting a narrative language so broad it has no face, no name.

We can love a thing and still critique it. In fact, that's the only way to really love a thing. Let's be critical lovers and loving critics and open ourselves to the truth about where we are and where we've been. Instead of holding tight to the same old, failed patriarchies, let's walk a new road, speak new languages. Today, let's imagine a literature, a literary world, that carries this struggle for equity in its very essence, so that tomorrow it can cease to be necessary, and disappear.

Douglas Wolk

Douglas Wolk is the author of two books: James Brown's
Live at the Apollo *(Bloomsbury Academic, 2004) and*
Reading Comics: How Graphic Novels Work
and What They Mean *(Da Capo Press, 2008), which
won the 2008 Eisner Award for Best Comics-Related
Book and the 2008 Harvey Award for Best Biographical,
Historical, or Journalist Presentation. Wolk's essays on
comics and popular music have appeared in the* New York
Times, Rolling Stone, *the* Washington Post, *and
elsewhere.*

T he first four or five times you think you know how
comics publishing works, you're wrong. The initial mistake that people from the book-publishing world tend to make is imagining that comics are pretty
much the same sort of thing as prose books, just with illustrations on each page in addition to text. I use the word
"illustrations" advisedly, because it gets to the heart of the
problem. If you're thinking of comics as a kind of writing
that happens to be augmented by pictures, you're missing
the point. The publishing business has taught us to think of
writers as the creators of books, and that's more or less true
for most books.

Comics, though, are a totally different medium, disseminated in a similar physical form and through similar
channels. They're made of ink and paper and glue; they have
words in them. But they're not the same thing. Comics are
a *visual* medium. More specifically, they're a *drawn* medium.
The specific visual idioms and styles of the particular artists

who draw them have nearly everything to do with whether particular projects sink or swim.

If there is a single "author" of a graphic novel, that person has written and drawn it. (That is the practice, pretty much universally, for the artier wing of American comics.) If there are multiple names listed on the cover of a graphic novel, they (usually) include a writer and one or more artists—and they generally get equal billing. Ideally, they have been working very closely together since the beginning of the project, because otherwise there's somebody who thinks that he or she is the creative visionary and somebody else whose vision is the one actually visible on most of the page, and that's never a good combination. When an artist's name is smaller than a writer's on a graphic novel's cover, that generally means that somebody's got an outsized ego. When an artist's name does not appear at all on a graphic novel's cover, that inevitably means that the book is an embarrassment. Again: in comics, artwork *is* primary authorship.

(Oh, there's that phrase "graphic novel." Let's deal with it right up front. It was initially intended, more or less, to mean a fictional comics work of substantial length. Almost immediately, it became a commercial term, meaning a squarebound volume of comics, whether it's fiction or nonfiction, a single piece or a collection of shorter pieces. It does not, however, mean exactly the same thing as "comics"—that's the name of the medium, sorry if you don't like it—and it is no more correct to refer to an eleven-page webcomic about the history of a corporation as a "graphic novel" than it would be to call a five-hundred-word newspaper article about farm conditions a "cookbook.")

The question I hear most often from people who say they're interested in creating or publishing comics is how they can find somebody to draw their project. My answer is usually a harsh but realistic one: don't. First, if it's "your project" being drawn by somebody else, it's going to turn out badly, because it's going to require the creative devotion of somebody with no horse in the race. Second, if you need a collaborator, you're going to do well to work with the people you already know. Third, if you intend to write or publish comics and you don't already know comics artists, maybe you should start hanging out with some, just so you don't come off like, say, a playwright who doesn't know any actors or directors. (It's also worth noting that cartoonists who have put in the years of sweat required to get good at drawing comics very rarely wonder aloud how they can find someone to write a script for them.)

So what exactly does American comics publishing look like right now? Again, if you're looking at any one part of it, you're missing some very different parts. The last time "American comics publishing" was a single entity was probably the early seventies, when it meant thirty-two-page pamphlets printed on newsprint, sold on newsstands, and published by a few companies, with a few outlying oddities, like the West Coast artists making their own underground "comix." Now "comics publishing"—and readership—are a host of different economies that just barely overlap.

The biggest of those economies is still mainstream comics, the thing you think of when people say "comic books": saddle-stitched pamphlets, 6.75 inches by 10.25 inches, published periodically (monthly, most often). They're usually in color on glossy stock, and they usually have twenty or twenty-two pages of story content and thirty-two or thirty-six pages in all. They are almost always created by teams—a writer, a line artist or two, a colorist, a letterer—a practice that dates back roughly seventy-five years, to when publishers learned that it took an assembly line to crank out a new issue every month. The "big two" publishers are Marvel Comics (owned by Disney) and DC Comics (owned by Time Warner), who

between them currently control about 70 percent of what's
called the "direct market" of comics.

That "direct market," though, is very different from
most book publishing. It consists of several thousand independent stores in the United States, which order comics several months in advance from a single distributor, Diamond
Comic Distributors, almost always on a nonreturnable
basis. Those stores survive by cultivating devoted customers and knowing *exactly* what they want: if a store orders too
many copies of something, it'll be stuck with them, and if
it orders too few, its customers won't be able to find what
they're looking for. (The book market generally still gets to
order graphic novels on a returnable basis, but direct-market stores are where readers go to buy periodicals on the
Wednesday they're released, or to stock up on half a dozen
graphic novels every couple of months.)

The advantage of nonreturnability is that it makes certain kinds of publishing much less risky. If you're publishing a
returnable magazine that goes out to newsstands and ends up
selling twenty thousand copies, you're doomed. But if stores
order twenty thousand copies of your comic book through
Diamond, that means you can print *exactly* that many copies
and get paid for all of them, and whatever remains of that
sum after printing and editorial costs is profit. The disadvan-
tage of non-returnability, on the other hand, is that there had
better be a very good reason for direct-market stores to take a
risk on ordering a given project at all. No-Name Comics #1
by a couple of unknowns? *Forget it.*

The things that do well in the direct market are big
franchises and big (creative) names, and it's also worth
noting what *do well* means right now for periodical comics. As of 2014, sales of over one hundred thousand copies
of a single issue always set a comic at or near the top of
Diamond's monthly charts. Fifty thousand means a solid

success. A Marvel or DC series that sells under twenty thousand an issue is probably not long for this world. For smaller publishers, cut those figures in half or so. DC's creator-driven imprint Vertigo also generally treats its trades as the real moneymakers. (Trades? Hold on, we'll get there.) First issues are almost always the best-selling ones, with attrition fast or slow setting in thereafter; these days, the arrival of popular creators often means a relaunch with a new #1.

What DC and Marvel's main lines publish is almost exclusively in the superhero genre, and has been for several decades; that's probably why people sometimes get that weird little genre and the medium confused. (And what those two publishers are selling most of the time is, more specifically, stories that belong to huge, shared fictional universes with seventy-five-year histories.) Both companies are also still selling the long-broken promise of "collectibility," with rare alternate covers and so forth: *invest now, because your old issues may someday be worth astronomically more than their cover price!* That hope is only true of comics that are astronomically more interesting in retrospect than they seemed to be when they were published—which is very rare for issues first published after, say, the mid-1960s.

All mainstream comics publishers that aren't Marvel or DC are considered "independents": Dark Horse, Dynamite, IDW, Image, and a host of others. Some of them make most of their money from licensed properties; others specialize in "creator-owned" work, which in the comics business can mean nearly any financial arrangement other than work made for hire. Image is the biggest of the independents in the book market, and it's a special case. It's technically a vanity press: creators pay for the printing of their work, plus a flat fee for every publication they release, and keep whatever further profit comes in.

That sort of arrangement is anathema to the conventional book world, but comics have a long-standing tradition of successful self-publishing in a way that book publishing doesn't. (*Bone* and *Teenage Mutant Ninja Turtles*, for instance, began as self-published projects.)

The founders of Image were a group of big-name Marvel artists who decided in the early nineties that they could do better if they pooled their resources and owned their own work, and that's generally what happened. The company's first big hit was *Spawn*, and its big hit of the past few years is *The Walking Dead*, whose Bookscan figures in 2013 were in the mid-six digits. Image still publishes some relatively low-selling labors of love that serve as their creators' proof of concept or proof of competence, funded out of those creators' pockets; it also publishes major successes by huge stars, and some of the former group (like *The Walking Dead*'s writer Robert Kirkman) have turned into the latter.

Even so, brand loyalty is bizarrely huge in mainstream comics. If it's not published by one of the Big Two or isn't connected to a familiar franchise, many direct-market customers simply don't want to know. Grant Morrison and Frazer Irving's *Batman* comics for DC, for instance, were mammoth chart-topping hits. Their next collaboration, *Annihilator*, from the independent publisher Legendary, barely scraped the bottom of Diamond's monthly Top 300 chart.

The mainstream comics economy also relies on selling everything it publishes in at least two forms. As late as the early nineties, once a given month's issue was gone, it was assumed to be gone forever; occasionally, there would be a paperback collecting a particularly high-selling miniseries or sequence (Neil Gaiman's second *Sandman* storyline was actually collected before the first!), but otherwise you had to haunt those "direct market" stores in hopes of finding a secondhand copy.

Then it dawned on comics publishers that if they routinely collected serial comics as books, they had readymade content that wouldn't have to be commissioned, and they could keep it in print as long as it sold. Trades, as they're called—short for "trade paperback," although there's not a mass-market equivalent—generally collect somewhere between four and eight serial issues. (Yes, the practice has affected the rhythms of serial comics.) Particularly successful series are sometimes collected first (or later) as hardcovers, and sometimes later again as "omnibus" editions of up to a thousand pages. Readers who know they'll enjoy a particular series but don't buy individual issues are said to be "trade-waiting." A serial comic has to be a catastrophic flop to *not* end up in a trade.

. . .

BUT WHAT ABOUT THE OTHER KIND of graphic novels that you see in bookstores—the kind that aren't serial comics first, usually aren't genre based, almost always have a single writer/artist, and tend to get reviewed in fancier places? That's a second (but, again, overlapping) economy. There are a handful of publishers that have done very well with original graphic novels. Some of them are long-haul operations dedicated specifically to comics, like Fantagraphics, Drawn & Quarterly, and First Second Books. Some have found a particular niche, like VIZ Media, which publishes Japanese comics in translation (*manga* isn't quite the generic word in Japanese, but it's caught on in English). A few conventional publishers that have pulled it off well have long associations with particular creators—Pantheon and Scholastic, in particular.

And a lot of those publishers' operations are linked to another comics economy: conventions. There are the huge annual shows in San Diego and New York, for which the entire entertainment industry turns up; there are local comic-cons that are mostly about cosplay and minor actors' autographs; there are also comics festivals and conventions that are where comics creators of every tier interact directly with their audiences. What they have in common is that they're all where people go specifically to spend money on the stuff they love. And thanks in part to comics' self-publishing tradition, they're where little-known cartoonists go to build their reputations. Jeffrey Brown and Raina Telgemeier, for instance, were very familiar faces at small-press conventions for many years before their *Jedi Academy* and *Smile*, respectively, started selling hundreds of thousands of copies.

On top of all of that, there's another set of comics economies that are growing very quickly: digital comics. Not many people have yet cracked the code of how to make money by selling comics without printing them, but there are a few paradigms in play:

WEBCOMICS. If you can publish something online for free on a regular basis—and it's good enough to attract a substantial audience—then you can make money on related merchandise. This is the "give away the thing itself but sell the T-shirt" strategy, and it works for a certain cohort of artists who are good at keeping to a schedule and funny enough for their work to go viral online. (Not unrelatedly, Brian K. Vaughan and Marcos Martin's *The Private Eye* is a recent experiment in selling digital comics on a pay-what-you-wish basis; it's apparently worked out well for them, although it can't hurt that Vaughan already has a substantial fan base from the likes of *Saga* and *Y: The Last Man*.)

A LA CARTE. This is just like mainstream-comics sales, and in fact what it's selling is digitized versions of exactly the same material, sold an issue at a time and set up for customers to read a page or a panel at a time on mobile devices. The company that's done especially well with this is comiXology, which is now owned by Amazon. (A one-panel-at-a-time view ruins the effect of carefully constructed page compositions and so forth, but it's mighty convenient if you're reading on a smartphone on a bus.)

ALL-YOU-CAN-EAT. Or charging a regular fee for digital access to a big back catalog. The only publisher that's really done this so far is Marvel, with its Unlimited service.

PIRACY. Nearly every comic book published in America is scanned and available for unauthorized downloading within instants of going on sale. This is yet another reason why comics publishers like to emphasize the scarcity of the physical object: at worst it plays into the myth of collectibility, but at best it leads to books that are lovely to hold in one's hands. (It helps that comics readers have decades of experience in fetishizing physical objects.)

There is one other comics-publishing economy that's an elephant in the room, and a fairly dangerous elephant at that: comics, as a field of publishing, has become movie-crazy. Hollywood can't get enough of comics (because a successful comic book has already demonstrated that it works as idiomatic visual storytelling with brand-name recognition); comics can't get enough of Hollywood (because Hollywood means money). *The Walking Dead* owes a lot of its book-market success to the TV show; the *Batman* and *Avengers* and *Kick-Ass* movies have moved truckloads of books and toys and Halloween costumes. This has led to a plague of terrible comics that are transparently movie pitches (or *failed* movie pitches), and a nastier plague of would-be screenwriters wanting to find somebody to turn their hackwork into a comic book so they can cash in on it.

What that sort of grab for the brass ring becomes, at

best, is something that's nominally comics—it has draw-
ings and word balloons and stuff—but is awkwardly stuffed
into a medium to which it doesn't belong, and everyone can
tell. That's not a sniffy aesthetic critique, it's an assessment
of why they invariably tank in the marketplace. The biggest successes in comics publishing come from odd places
(very few people would have guessed that Marjane Satrapi's
Persepolis or Raina Telgemeier's *Smile* or, for that matter, *The
Walking Dead* would become huge enduring hits), but they
almost never come from the creation of extruded comics
product. The most gruesome failures in comics publishing
are almost always extruded comics product. Please don't add
to the pile.

Chris Parris-Lamb & Jonathan Lee

*Chris Parris-Lamb began his career as an assistant at Burnes
& Clegg, Inc., and has been a literary agent at The Gernert
Company since 2007. He is a graduate of the University of
North Carolina-Chapel Hill, and serves on the board of
directors of* n+1.

*Jonathan Lee is an editor at the Brooklyn-based literary
journal* A Public Space *and a contributing editor to*
Guernica. *He is the author of the novel* High Dive
*(Knopf, 2016). His interview with Chris Parris-Lamb first
appeared in* Guernica *in the spring of 2015.*

I n Chris Parris-Lamb's office at The Gernert Company,
a literary agency where staff with shrewd cheekbones
sip herbal teas while managing the affairs of some of
America's top authors, there is a small en suite bathroom in
which I discovered a minor landslide of running shoes. A
couple of pairs looked completely destroyed. A couple of others had the beleaguered appearance of the soon to be dead.
There was one pair in the pile that seemed to be brand new—
stiff tongue, clean toe box, untainted laces—but behind its
game face I thought I discerned an air of resignation. It turns
out Parris-Lamb is a compulsive runner, and at well over six
feet in height he must hit the ground hard. "Sixty to eighty
miles each week," he explained. "Which means I go through
a pair of shoes every six to eight weeks." His most recent mar-
athon time is two hours and forty-eight minutes, which in
1908 would have won him the world record.

Parris-Lamb, who recently turned thirty-three, shot to prominence within the publishing industry in February 2010. That was the month in which he sold Chad Harbach's debut novel, *The Art of Fielding*, to Michael Pietsch at Little, Brown for a reported $665,000. It was his first big head-line success after several years of assisting other agents while slowly building up his own list of authors. The book went on to become a high-profile best seller, and since then, Parris-Lamb has proven himself to be an unusually reliable judge of what the market wants, or soon discovers it wants. This past fall, three books by his authors—Christian Rudder's *Dataclysm*, Peter Thiel's *Zero To One*, and John Darnielle's *Wolf in White Van*—all appeared on best seller lists at exactly the same time, while Darnielle's was also a National Book Award nominee.

One of Parris-Lamb's most recent literary discoveries is Garth Risk Hallberg, whose forthcoming nine-hundred-page novel, *City on Fire*, has already been the subject of much attention, having drawn a nearly $2 million advance. Parris-Lamb has a fondness for wincingly high word counts ("it says something about somebody, in terms of ambition") and he also enjoys getting deeply involved in the process of revision. He's been known to work with an author through six entire drafts before deeming their manuscript ready for submission to editors.

A looming presence even when seated, Parris-Lamb man-ages to be unassuming and prone to thoughtful pauses. On the occasions during our interview when he broke off from quiet logic to offer flashes of frustration ("I frankly think that initiatives like National Novel Writing Month are insulting to real writers"), he usually followed his statement with a wry smile, or a quick glance toward his bookshelves.

JONATHAN LEE: When you look at your unsolicited submis-sions pile, what are some of the common problems you see?

CHRIS PARRIS-LAMB: I just see an awful lot of people who believe that what makes a novel is eighty thousand consecutive words. I just wish I read more submissions where it felt like the author had taken great care with it, had spent a lot of time on it, and had a better idea—or any idea at all—of the books they saw their own as being in conversation with, as well as of how theirs was unique. Most submissions I see feel like someone checking "write a novel" off their bucket list. Readers don't want to spend their $9.99, or even their $1.99—though that touches on a whole other problem—on a book that doesn't give them something. And most of these submissions just don't really justify their existence, or the time spent reading them. They might do something for the author—and that's a perfectly good reason to have written it—but they don't do anything for the reader, which is a perfectly good reason why they shouldn't be published. Time spent writing a novel is valuable, but readers' time is valuable too.

LEE: When you joined Sarah [Burnes] at The Gernert Company, was it hard to find editors and authors who'd take a chance on you?

PARRIS-LAMB: Well, it was difficult and it wasn't. For the first couple of years I was just helping Sarah with her clients, rather than finding my own. But I guess I knew I wasn't going to be happy just assisting other agents forever. A key moment came when a manuscript entitled *Mudbound* was submitted to Sarah. It was by a new writer named Hillary Jordan. I read it for Sarah and sent her an email saying it was great. She wrote back after taking a look at it and said, "You're right, but I'm going to be really busy when I come back from maternity leave." She suggested, generously, that I write to the author, and promised to help sell her on the idea of being represented by a twenty-three-year-old—which, to her credit and to Hillary's, ended up working.

When I sold *Mudbound* a year later, I got the bug. I knew I wanted to be an agent. And I started to realize that it's genuinely true that hope springs eternal in the publishing business. If there's a young, enthusiastic agent or editor around, people will give them a chance. Maybe only one chance, but a chance nonetheless. If you pick up the phone and call a really big shot editor, and they can hear in your voice that you're really excited about something, that's probably going to be the first thing they read that night. They might not have a clue who you are, but they know real enthusiasm when they hear it.

LEE: When was the first time you rang up a big shot editor in that way?

PARRIS-LAMB: I guess *The Art of Fielding*. I sent that book to Jonathan Galassi, whom I'd never met before. I sent it to Michael Pietsch, who—because of [David Foster] Wallace—was the only editor I knew by name when I entered the business. I had met Michael but had never sent him anything. That was obviously a huge deal for me.

LEE: How quickly did they put you out of your misery?

PARRIS-LAMB: I emailed Jonathan Galassi the manuscript at 1 p.m. on a Friday, I think. He emailed me back the next day, on Saturday afternoon, and said it was an extraordinary manuscript. Not so with Michael Pietsch. Michael was completely silent for two weeks after I sent him the manuscript. I had all these editors telling me how great it was, but when we got to the day of the auction, Chad [Harbach] was still saying to me, "What about Michael Pietsch?" It still wasn't clear to me, on the morning of the auction, whether Michael was at all interested in the book. I didn't even know if he'd read the book—not until he called me just before the auction started.

LEE: What did he say?

PARRIS-LAMB: He said, "Hi, it's Michael Pietsch. I'm going to buy this novel from you." Something like that. And, of course, he did.

LEE: It's been a few years since you sold *The Art of Fielding*, and of course you've had several other significant successes since. Do you have a particular group of acquiring editors to whom you now send the manuscripts you're most excited about? What goes into deciding who comprises that group?

PARRIS-LAMB: It happens fairly organically—insofar as drinks and lunches are an organic part of the publishing ecosystem—and you get to know people's tastes. I guess the first thing is the natural winnowing process that happens at each agency and publisher. Not every twenty-two-year-old sticks around to become a twenty-seven-year-old with an expense account. This is a business a lot of smart people enter and which a lot of smart people leave, because it's hard to make your way. But the people who were junior at the same time I was junior have become, largely, the group of editors I send stuff to. So most of the people on any given submission list of mine are people I've known for several years. We've grown up in the industry together and I know what they like. These were friendships forged in the early years of our careers— working very long hours, spending our evenings reading submissions, earning very small amounts of money, and wondering if we'd ever progress.

LEE: Who are the editors you like to submit to?

PARRIS-LAMB: You want names?

LEE: If you feel you can.

PARRIS-LAMB: Noah Eaker at Random House. Diana Miller at Knopf. Allison Lorentzen at Viking. Tom Mayer at Norton. Ginny Smith Younce at Penguin Press. I've gotten to know people outside my microgeneration, as it were, as well, of course, but those are all people I first met when they were editorial assistants and I was an agency assistant, and I think they are all editors with excellent taste. I met Noah in, I think, October of 2004, right after he'd started as Susan Kamil's assistant. I met Diana in 2006, when she was Sonny Mehta's assistant. Tom was working as Bob Weil's assistant when I met him. I remember being so nervous meeting Allison for the first time, because I knew her by reputation as this superstar who somehow managed to be both Tim Duggan's assistant and a cofounder of *n+1*. Now all these people are powerful acquiring editors at publishing houses, but the friendships and mutual respect came long before that.

LEE: The mingling of friendship and business—it must present some problems at times.

PARRIS-LAMB: Yeah, sometimes.

LEE: What happens when you submit to a group of editors that includes several friends, and they all want to buy the book?

PARRIS-LAMB: It's hard. I can't pretend it isn't. Sometimes in the final round of an auction, at the very end, there are very close friends of mine all offering on the manuscript I've sent to them. I don't want to get too specific about it, but with one debut author whose book I sold recently, the last day of the auction was the greatest day of that author's professional life, and in my mind I knew that it was one of the best professional days of my life, too. And yet, calling close friends to tell them that I'd sold the book to another editor? That was one of the hardest things I've ever had to do. It was truly horrible. I guess people on the outside of the industry might hear that and think, "Come on, it's just business, it's not that hard." But it's really, really hard. You have to match your author with the editor who you think will be best for them, and you have to put a lot of weight on who the author has the best feeling about. It's not all about what I think is best—it's about what the author wants. Though it's my job to give them the information they need to make a decision.

LEE: There's been a lot of publicity of late about a new author you took on—Garth Risk Hallberg. You sold his nine-hundred-page novel, *City on Fire*, for a seven-figure sum. It comes out with Knopf later this year. I'm curious—how did Hallberg's work come to you?

PARRIS-LAMB: I met Garth at the wedding of mutual friends. We were seated next to each other, which I think was a deliberate move. The bride and groom knew Garth was looking for an agent. As soon as Garth told me he'd written such a long novel—I think it was 380,000 words, at that stage—I told him I was interested in reading it.

LEE: Seriously? My heart would sink.

PARRIS-LAMB: *Infinite Jest, Ulysses, Middlemarch.* These are my favorite books. I just like long books, I guess. There aren't many of them out there, and it says something about somebody, in terms of ambition, that they're prepared to try and write that kind of novel. Anyway—I read the manuscript, thought it was terrific, and told Garth I'd like to represent him. Garth then took a while to pick an agent. Luckily, he picked me. We worked through a new draft of the manuscript together, and a year after we met, we sent out the book to editors. I first read the manuscript during Hurricane Sandy. I'll never forget that. I knew I had something special in my hands. Four pounds worth of specialness.

LEE: Doing editorial work with an author on a manuscript before you try to sell it—is that common practice for you?

PARRIS-LAMB: Obviously, every agent is different, and every book is different. Every author is different too in terms of what they need and want—macro advice, micro advice, et cetera. I do a lot of editorial work with most of my authors. I want, before the book goes to editors, for there to be as little as possible to detract from my advocacy of the book. If there's something in the novel that I have serious misgivings about, that will detract from my advocacy. So I ask that my authors at least give me a chance to make suggestions for revisions. With *Mudbound*, the first book I sold, I think Hillary and I went through six different drafts before we decided it was ready to send out to editors. It's not my job to tell the author what they want to hear. I have to be honest. That's the main thing. The only thing I can give an author that no one else can is my opinion, and that's valuable. Take away my honest feedback and I add no value at all.

LEE: We talked about your disappointment with the majority of the unsolicited manuscripts you receive. Are there too many people writing, and not enough people reading?

PARRIS-LAMB: There's almost nothing I can say about this that won't bring a lot of rage pouring down on me from the Internet. But, to give a short answer, yes. I try to take a philosophical, and I hope empathetic, view of it all. I mean, we're all going to die, and we have a short time here on earth, and we all want to achieve distinction of some sort while we're here. Meanwhile, we all have Microsoft Word installed on our desktops. We all already spend a lot of time typing. One way to leave one's mark would be to, say, write a great symphony, but most people don't know how to read music. Whereas more or less everyone does have the means to put down words on a page and save them and share them. That's a great thing—I'm all for technology eliminating barriers to communication and expression—but it can lead to delusions. Just because you've written it doesn't make it worth reading. And it's depressing when people forget that you can't be a good writer without first being a good reader.

I frankly think that initiatives like National Novel Writing Month are insulting to real writers. We don't have a National Heart Surgery Month, do we? I'm being intentionally provocative there, obviously—being a good or bad writer isn't a matter of life or death—but I'm also serious. Great writers are as rare as great heart surgeons—maybe even rarer; I don't actually know anything about heart surgeons. But I would argue that it takes as much time and work to perfect their craft, in addition to having talent to begin with that most people just don't. What I really object to is this notion behind these initiatives that anyone can write a novel, and that it's just a matter of making the time to do it. That's just not true.

To be fair, true talent—the Gift, as Lewis Hyde would call it—can come from anywhere, and if National Novel Writing Month causes one of those talented people to finally make time in their life to cultivate their gift, and something great comes of it, then maybe it's all worth it. But I am really skeptical of the idea that, but for National Novel Writing Month, those gifts would go undiscovered. I think part of the nature of the gift is that you can't not give voice to it—having received the gift, you must give it in turn. Which is to say, the people who really do have a great novel in them are going to find a way to write it anyway. If it's not clear by now, I think every writer should read Lewis Hyde.

LEE: Many people in the industry say it's harder to sell a book than ever. Do you concur?

PARRIS-LAMB: It's true. It's harder to sell a book to a big publisher now than it was ten years ago, I think. The block-busterization of the book industry has had the same effect as the blockbusterization of Hollywood—among many other industries. It's the rule of the Power Law distribution—a decreasing number of producers get an increasing share of the rewards. Obviously this is what's happening with income inequality, too. Publishers are buying fewer books and publishing fewer books. If you're an agent, you have to take more time than you might have done in the past to make the manuscript as strong as it can be—because an entire imprint may be only acquiring half a dozen debut authors a year. It's really, really hard to get a book published by, say, Random House now. They're acquiring less. That's the Hachette model, too. That's the Crown model. Of course, when you do have a book that lots of editors love, it's still possible to sell it for a lot of money and get lots of momentum behind the book—if anything, when publishers do really want a book now, they're willing to pay more than ever, for the very reason that they're otherwise not buying much. It's the other side of the coin—it's feast or famine. But big books don't come along every month.

LEE: Is there ever a situation where you'd advise an author not to take a big advance that's being offered?

PARRIS-LAMB: No, not really. Which is not the same as saying they should always take the biggest advance that's being offered. But I'd never advise an author to turn down an advance because it's big. Statistically, your book is more likely to do well if you receive a big advance. There is more pressure on the publishers to make it work and get their money back if they've paid out a large advance. The downside of any advance is always the same—your book might not sell. That's a risk if you get a small advance, and a risk if you get a big advance, so if there's a big advance on the table, take it, and use the money to write your next one.

I think there's this idea that if you receive a big advance and then the book doesn't work, it's a disaster, and your career is ruined. That's just not true. If your first book doesn't work, it's always going to be harder to sell the second book, and that's the case regardless of whether you were paid a big or small advance. If someone wants to make a bet on you, why not take it? If your first one doesn't work, you might have to take a haircut on the advance for the second, but so what?

LEE: I guess one downside specific to really large advances is that all the publicity about the book tends, at least in the beginning, to focus on the size of the advance. That can put an author under a lot of pressure, and I suspect it brings out a certain bitterness in some members of the literary

community, too—people who you'd ideally want as supporters of the book. People love a good underdog story. "Author
gets big advance and goes on to become best seller" isn't one
of those stories.

PARRIS-LAMB: There's some truth in that, and I wish it
wasn't the case. I hate that advances—for my authors or anyone else's—can become public knowledge. But it also drives
me crazy that readers of books get upset about this stuff—
people who presumably love literature and want writers to
do well. Chad Harbach spent ten years writing his novel. It
was his avocation, for which he was paid nothing, with no
guarantee he'd ever be paid anything, while he supported
himself doing freelance work, for which I don't think he ever
made $30,000 a year. I sold his book for an advance that
equated to $65,000 a year—before taxes and commission—
for each of the years of work he'd put in. The law schools
in this country churn out first-year associates at white-shoe
firms that pay them $250,000 a year, when they're twen-
ty-five years of age, to sit at a desk doing meaningless bull-
shit to grease the wheels of the corporatocracy, and people
get upset about an excellent author getting $65,000 a year?
Give me a fucking break.

LEE: How do you feel about Amazon?

PARRIS-LAMB: I feel that the whole dispute with Hachette
said more about the state of Amazon's business than it
did about the state of the publishing industry. Books are,
what, less than 4 percent of Amazon's overall business? So
Hachette—a single supplier—must account for less than 1
percent of Amazon's bottom line. And yet Amazon cared
so much about their profit margin—or cared about being
seen as caring about it—in relation to this little 1 percent

of business that they were willing to take a pummeling day after day in the press—a huge wave of negative media—to preserve their margin. My guess is that Amazon was starting to feel pressure on Wall Street to show a profit—to bring a stop to their pattern of making an operating loss quarter after quarter.

LEE: Putting the retail element to one side, it's interesting to see what's happened with Amazon's literary-publishing arm.

PARRIS-LAMB: Yeah, that has been a big failure. There are good people in that office, I know some of them, but Amazon's attitude toward books is data driven—at the top, they see books as products, just like everything else. That's true at the transaction level, but it's not true beyond that. When you're dealing with art, or even entertainment, all these questions of taste and subjectivity—which can't be quantified—come into play. Almost no one writes books for economically rational reasons, and yet Amazon insists on trying to squeeze books within a rational economic framework. In a traditional economic model consisting of entirely rational actors, an author should not care more about the epigraph on their book than they do about the list price of their book. But let me tell you, they care more about their epigraphs. All of them do. I saw Amazon delete an epigraph from an author's book the day before it went to print, because the author was never told he needed permission to use it. He got permission that very day, and yet they wouldn't restore it in the printed book. To them, it's just an epigraph, they can get rid of it, who cares? To the author, it's a different thing. A book is basically irrational—or fiction is, anyway. That's why we read it. Amazon doesn't seem to be able to get their heads around that. There is a humanity to good books that data can't account for.

LEE: You mentioned earlier that mainstream publishers are publishing fewer books than ever before. I'm getting the impression you think that's a good thing, on balance. But is there a risk that the reduction will lead or has led to a certain conservatism—a narrowness of range—in what's reaching our shelves from the big publishers?

PARRIS-LAMB: I do think it's a good thing that publishers are publishing fewer books. It makes my job and the job of other agents harder in the short term, but there's a net benefit for authors. If you're an author, a good one, do you want to be on a publisher's list with twenty-four books for the season, or do you want to be on the list with thirty-six? It's a fairly simple equation. If you publish less, there's a chance to do more for each book.

That said, I don't mean to presume that we, the much-reviled gatekeepers of the publishing industry, know for certain what books deserve to be read by the public. Of course we don't, which is why it's important that a wide range of books get a chance to break out. Nobody could have anticipated the success of books like *Gone Girl*, or *All the Light We Cannot See*. They were both books by previously midlist authors whose publishers had faith in them over a long period of time—whether you like them or not, you should be happy for their success. They caught something in the public mood, and that kind of serendipity is what makes the business fun. There are self-published books that catch the public mood, too, obviously.

LEE: You don't have a problem with self-publishing, then?

PARRIS-LAMB: There's a role for self-publishing, definitely. But just playing the odds, if you're a new author, it's almost always going to make sense to publish with a big or small professional publisher, if you can—a proper editor, some degree of marketing, some degree of professionalism and advice. Want to upload your book onto a self-publishing platform along with hundreds of thousands of others that month, and hope for the best? That's fine, but you're basically counting on a miracle.

LEE: One of the comforting things about the list you've built and the books you've sold is that they suggest there are still editors out there, at the big publishers and at the independents, who want to take a chance on big, messy, ambitious works of fiction or nonfiction—high-quality literary books that don't conform to the standard idea of a best seller. I assume you feel there's still going to be an appetite for those books ten years from now?

PARRIS-LAMB: I think it's a myth that editors don't want these kinds of books on their lists—that all they want are surefire genre successes. I haven't been in this business that long, but I've found that there are always editors out there who want to take a chance on great writing. I don't think that will change anytime soon. When I send out a big, ambitious literary novel, part of the excitement I hear from editors is precisely because they receive these kinds of books so rarely. If there are big, original, ambitious novels full of bold ideas and great writing that are being turned away *en masse* by literary agents and publishers, by the gatekeepers, then I'm not aware of them.

There simply aren't that many great manuscripts out there, and readers want to be shown what they are. So I don't think gatekeeping is going away anytime soon. Writers might not like it, but readers definitely do, whether they realize it or not. It takes a lot of time to read a book—much more than it does to listen to a song, for instance. People have this misconception that the publishing industry only ever really existed to print and distribute physical books, something that is increasingly unnecessary in the digital age—although I hasten to note that print sales were up in 2014. That's not why the publishing industry exists. It also doesn't exist to give writers a way to publish their books, as much as writers might not want to hear that. It exists to bring readers books that are worthy of their time and attention, which is increasingly scarce and valuable. We sift through the bad stuff so you don't have to. It's not perfect, but it's better than the alternative.

Gerald Howard

Gerald Howard is vice president and executive editor of Doubleday. In 2009, he received the Maxwell Perkins Award honoring his career discovering, nurturing, and championing American fiction. His essays and reviews have appeared in the New York Times Book Review, Bookforum, n+1, Tin House, Slate, *and other publications.*

A few decades ago I was sitting in a college seminar room listening to the professor discourse quite penetratingly on Thomas Mann's monumental and once ubiquitous novel *The Magic Mountain* when my mind wandered to the question of just how this novel came to be published. Presumably, that callow and ignorant undergraduate in the basement of Goldwin Smith Hall thought someone—some *editor*—must have read the thing and recognized it for the great book that it was. And how hard could *that* have been anyway? Hell, even I knew it was a great book, if a bit long and occasionally opaque in meaning. I was a senior and the unpleasant prospect of graduation and the necessity to find some paying work was weighing on my mind. Why couldn't *I* become that guy? I loved books, loved them even more than my other obsession, basketball. That might be a satisfying line of work.

And so it has turned out to be—albeit orders of magnitude more complex and riven with stress and uncertainty than my younger self could have imagined. Oddly enough, I now work in something called the Knopf Doubleday Group as a Doubleday editor, and our sibling imprint Knopf published *The Magic Mountain* in 1927. Its paperback line, Vintage, still has it and most of Mann's other works in print. In truth it really wasn't all that hard for Alfred Knopf to decide to publish *The Magic Mountain*. His relatively young and thrifty firm—started in 1915 on, no kidding, $5,000 worth of capital after a couple of years of apprenticeship at, yes, Doubleday and Mitchell Kennerley—had made its reputation as a publisher of literary books of high quality in translation, and in 1921 it had signed a contract with the German publisher Samuel Fischer for the exclusive rights to Mann's works in English. The first fruit of that agreement was the 1924 American publication of Mann's epic family saga *Buddenbrooks*. (Rather shockingly to me, the book had been published in Germany in 1901 and remained un-Englished for more than two decades. It was a larger and slower world.) *The Magic Mountain* was published in Germany in late 1924 and was immediately hailed as a masterpiece of modern European literature, so it was, as we say, a no-brainer for Knopf to continue with Mann. (Since Knopf did not read German he would not have read *The Magic Mountain* until H. T. Lowe-Porter translated it, but we can assume that he was guided by a reader's report from someone who did—maybe his friend and informal adviser H. L. Mencken—as well as by the European reviews.) Their author-publisher relationship would ripen into a lifelong friendship and became one of the most storied such associations in American publishing history.

Sadly, *The Magic Mountain*, once a fixture of every middle-brow household's bookshelf, has fallen off sharply in its sales and cultural currency, as has the rest of Mann's oeuvre. He and it are too forbidding, demanding, and German for contemporary tastes. I just checked the sales pace of his Vintage paperbacks, as telling a data point on the matter as you can imagine.

I love being able to do that, as I love just about every other aspect of my job here in the heart of New York's literary-industrial complex, for which, it seems, I have been selected to speak. As much as I'd like to conceive of myself as a sort of free-floating and entirely independent literary sensibility and quality inspector, the fact of the matter is that I am utterly a creature of corporate publishing. My first job in publishing was as a copywriter in the college textbook department of Harcourt Brace Jovanovich, which had been transformed by the buccaneering William Jovanovich into a huge communications conglomerate that included, no kidding, Sea World as one of its holdings. (Insert Flipper joke here.) Then I became an assistant editor in the education department of New American Library, the large and once pioneering mass-market publisher owned at the time by the Times Mirror corporation. Two years later, I became an editor at Viking Penguin, the American wing of the truly global Penguin Books, owned by the Pearson Corporation. Eight years on, Penguin bought New American Library from Times Mirror, and not coincidentally I moved to the independent and, uniquely, employee-owned W. W. Norton for ten years. A major player in the textbook market, no one could plausibly call Norton a small press—it had the resources to play with the big boys and occasionally it did. In 1998 I came to Doubleday, which was at the time part of Bantam Doubleday Dell, owned by the German communications conglomerate Bertelsmann. Within a year the Newhouse family-owned Advance Publications had sold Random House, which comprised the imprints Random House, Knopf, Ballantine, Vintage, Crown, Pantheon, and several smaller entities, to Bertelsmann and so we became Random House, the world's largest trade publisher at the time, with publishing companies in more than a dozen countries. And just two years ago a joint-venture merger between Penguin and Random House was completed to create Penguin Random House, a staggeringly large (in publishing terms, at least) international behemoth with gross revenues of almost $4 billion dollars annually. Whoa.

And what do I think about this, and how does all this stunning and obviously inexorable consolidation in my part of the publishing world affect my work as a book editor? In answer to the first question, I am enough of a nostalgist and publishing geek to look back with longing to the so-called golden age, when the great houses—Knopf; Scribner's; Random House; Viking; Doubleday; Farrar, Straus and Giroux; Henry Holt; Simon and Schuster; Pantheon; Harper Brothers; *und so weiter*; and the mass-market giants Bantam, New American Library, Fawcett, Pocket, and Avon—stood firmly on their own financial feet and had distinct editorial identities and idiosyncrasies. I came on the scene in the seventies just as the wave of mergers and buyouts was gathering force, and I witnessed enough traces of the old order to have taken its measure. But I'm enough of a realist to understand that things happen for a reason. Clearly the forces that have shaped trade publishing for the past four decades dictate that houses must go big or go away. These forces may be deplored, but they will not be argued away or resisted.

As for the second question, my work as an editor is both entirely unaffected by these huge changes in corporate alignments and profoundly in sync with them. What do I mean by these seemingly contradictory assertions?

At the simplest, most basic level, I've been reading for a living for thirty-seven years. I arrived at New American Library with a literary and intellectual sensibility formed by the unruly rebellions of the sixties and the spiritual defla-tions of the seventies, with a taste for the novelists and thinkers who had either helped to cause or best reflected and interpreted those rebellions and deflations. I've read thousands of books and proposals since then, and I believe

I am a better reader than I was at age twenty-seven—I know more because I've read more and my judgments are (I sure hope) better informed and more mature. But at the primal level where reader meets text and experiences emotions ranging from boredom and impatience to I-love-this-and-have-to-*have-to*-publish-it excitement, I think I am still that young man in the hunt and on the make, always searching for the big wow. This process takes place in the private arena of the mind and is entirely unrelated to the corporate arrangements of my employer. It is, quite literally, where I live, where I feel I am most myself.

As for the editing of those books that wow me when happy circumstances dictate that I get to acquire them, that process too takes place in a private arena. When I encounter a sentence that is inelegant or ungrammatical or inefficient or ambiguous in meaning, or a scene in a novel that is implausible or overdone or superfluous, or a plot that drags or goes off course or beggars credulity, or a line of exposition that falls short of the necessary clarity, or feel that some subject is missing and requires coverage, I point those things out to the author and with a carefully calculated mixture of firmness and solicitude suggest ways they might be remedied. I do this usually at nights and on weekends, sometimes on my bus ride to and from work, very occasionally in my office on slow days with my door closed (yes, I have an office with a door that closes), with a complete absence of business calculation beyond the largest context—that a book that is bad or just not good enough is a book that will embarrass me and my employer and be poorly received and will not sell.

But as I read those submissions and edit those manuscripts, on another cognitive plane I am reality testing what I am reading. What other books—the fabled and often tiresome "comp titles"—are like this one, and how did those books sell? (We are always fighting the last war.) Is it too

similar to something we published recently or are publishing in the near future, or to a book some other house has or
shortly will publish? Are there visual images in the book that
might be utilized on the cover? What writers of note can
I bug for prepublication blurbs? Is there something about
the author, some intriguing or unusual backstory, some cha-
risma radiating off the page (and maybe the author photo?
Don't act so shocked) that suggests that he or she will be a
publicity asset? What might a reasonable advance be, given
the amounts that have been paid recently for similar books,
or might reason for some reason be thrown out the window? (A friend and colleague of mine refers to this feeling
as "Let's get stupid." More on this matter shortly.) What
colleagues in the company, in the editorial department, in
marketing, publicity, and sales, could I ask to read the book
to drum up support for it? What is my "handle" going to
be—the phrases or brief sentences that briskly encapsulate
a book's subject matter and commercial appeal? These and
all sorts of other questions will be popping up in my brain,
and inevitably there is some crosstalk and bleed-through
between the two cognitive spheres. If you want total purity
in these matters, go join an Irish monastery and work on
illuminated manuscripts, not a New York publishing house.
Or at the very least a quiet and scholarly and well-endowed
university press.

Nobody really knows how an editor works besides his or her
authors and possibly his or her assistant. Yet I am quite certain
that, allowing for differences in personal style—some editors go
for close-in textual work, some prefer to hover somewhere above
the text and make broader observations and suggestions—the
process described above is close to the way that my fellow New
York editors operate. And there really are not too many of us. I
would say that, taking in the six major corporate houses and the
handful of sizable independents, that there might be something

like 250 editors at a rough count working in adult trade publishing. It's a fairly clubby group. Most of us know each other either
personally or by reputation, and we watch each other's activities,
especially acquisitions, obsessively, aided by our very own digital
town crier, the website Publishers Lunch. The society of editors
has, of course, its doppelgänger or shadow world in that of the
literary agents with whom we deal and whose functions—chiefly
the discovery and care and feeding of writers and creating the
market for their wares— overlap considerably with ours. Let's put
the number of agents who count (sorry, but we think that way in
this town) at 150, and you can grasp how really small-town and
incestuous and ingrown the literary ecosystem of New York publishing is. In such a small and hyperconnected world, fueled by the
twin forces of ego (our sense that we are at the top of the heap)
and insecurity (our sense that we might vanish any year now
under some technological *Anschluss*, that we are in economic terms
pissants compared, to, say, the computer-game industry, and
how many people in this country care about books anyway?), the
arrival of a literary property that holds the promise of both review
and publicity glory *and* substantial sales, can instantly engage the
forces of irrational exuberance. And that brings me to the subject without which no consideration of the work of the New York
trade editor can be complete: money.

Lord, we have a lot of it. And lord, we need a lot of it.
I work in a fifty-story mixed-use office and condominium
complex in Midtown North, bordering on Hell's Kitchen.
When I approach this building arriving at work in the
morning or returning from one of those storied publishing
lunches, I look up at it and start doing calculations in my
head as to what our offices must cost to rent, and to heat
and light and air-condition, let alone the expense of paying
the salaries and the benefits and the T&Es of all the people
working here. Then I add on the cost of our *humongous* and
totally up-to-the-minute warehouse and fulfillment center

in semirural Maryland and all the folks who work there, and I ask myself what have I done to help my company cover the truly enormous nut that *one day's* operation must entail and try to avoid the obvious answer that, whatever it is, it is not enough. So I head through the revolving door and up the elevator and tank up on the not-at-all-bad Flavia coffee in the common area that looks like it was decorated with fixtures from the set of some late sixties Polish science fiction film and start answering the e-mails that have piled up since the day before. Welcome to my world.

What is both odd yet understandable is that the response to the inexorable financial thirst of corporate publishing houses on the part of its editors is less the exercise of thrift and discipline in the matter of acquisitions than a profligacy that is sometimes truly jaw-dropping. I am the son of Depression-era parents, part of the last generation of Americans to be told to close the refrigerator door because it wastes electricity, and I have to say, this really bothers me. Especially when I do it myself. Because, you see, we are all English majors, and while few of us are truly innumerate, finance and accounting are not where we live, and agents have become immensely skilled at orchestrating competitive bidding situations, even for first novels by complete unknowns, the results of which sometimes reach so many hundreds of thousands or even millions of dollars that the amount begins to feel abstract, even as what Lord Keynes called our animal spirits become aroused and engaged and the amount goes even higher. Plus, by the way, we are not crazy, or at least not always. We publish into a winner-take-all marketplace where one or two high-risk/high-reward properties can make a publisher's fiscal year, so there is a definite financial logic to this sort of behavior, even if, as often happens, we are disastrously wrong. And this inflationary dynamic extends backward from the megasellers, actual and merely hoped for, to the books we term midlist, to the point where only a small percentage of the books we publish end up earning out their advances. We're leaving the refrigerator door open most of the time, and a hell of a lot of electricity is being wasted.

That's New York publishing for you, the literary home of the wider Gotham disease that Tom Wolfe dubbed the Big League Complex. This suggests a sports analogy to me. There has been an American publishing industry for a little under two centuries, once widely dispersed across a number of urban centers, but now almost entirely concentrated in New York; let's call it the major leagues. Over the past seventy years there has arisen, for reasons too complex to unpack here, an increasingly widespread and professionalized creative-writing industry, and just as the major college athletic programs groom and showcase top-tier talent for drafting by the National Football League and the National Basketball Association, so do the MFA programs groom and showcase top-tier literary talent for the New York publishing houses. There are these days about as many uncredentialed walk-ons in our literary fiction as there are walk-ons in major league baseball.

In 2013 Chad Harbach, author of the widely acclaimed novel *The Art of Fielding*, holder of an MFA from the University of Virginia, and a founding editor of *n+1*, published in that magazine an acute anatomy of what he characterized as the two dominant cultures of American fiction, "MFA vs. NYC." By "MFA" he means the university-based degree-granting system, which now numbers an amazing and, to a book editor, unnerving 1,269 such programs. By "NYC" he meant not only the New York-based publishing houses and the prestige-conferring magazines such as the *New Yorker* and the *Paris Review,* but the whole society of writers and editors and agents and publicists and booksellers and, yes, even

MFA teachers who make their home and their living here. Broadly and reductively described, the MFA world runs on credentials and degrees and connections, a highly networked "system of circulating patronage," as Harbach puts it, largely detached from commercial imperatives. Broadly and reductively described, the NYC world runs on money and prestige. NYC is, of course, also highly networked, and one can cite many NYC-ish writers whose prestige is decoupled from their sales, but by and large and in the end we are all highly aware of and finally judged by the metrics of the market.

Yet, as Harbach admits, NYC is where a good part of the MFA sets its cap, for here is where the big payoffs and the lasting glory are to be earned. So to complete the sports analogy, one might propose that the AWP (Association of Writers & Writing Programs) = NCAA (no explanation needed). Both have a limited number of top drawer competitive programs where the truly talented gravitate, and those programs are devoted to preparing the truly talented for their sometimes highly compensated entry into the big leagues. NYC does not formalize this process with anything like a draft (though that would be quite an amusing thing to contemplate); in its place is a system of recommendations whereby the marquee writing instructors pass along their most promising students to their agents, who bring those young writers and their work to editors with all the smarts and salesmanship and market knowledge at their command. When the stars are in alignment—when the right book hits the market at just the right time with just the right spin and buzz—the payoff can be immensely lucrative, approaching and in some cases exceeding a million dollars for a first novel by a hitherto unknown writer. (Such news is usually greeted by a soundtrack of bitching and moaning and gnashing of teeth by hitherto known writers.)

On occasion the books so singled out will earn back their advances, and their authors will go on to notable careers. But just as many a number-one draft pick will, despite their heroic compensation, struggle as a professional athlete and slowly fade into obscurity, the good fortune of such a young writer can prove temporary and illusory. The excitement that accompanied the first novel's acquisition somehow does not carry over into the reception by the reviewers and the reading public; the sales disappoint; and in a New York minute, yesterday's hot property becomes today's expensive liability.

We've traveled a long, long way from the storied four-decade publishing association of Alfred Knopf with Thomas Mann, nostalgia for which is a fairly useless emotion in our Godzilla vs. King Kong world of death-match throwdowns against Amazon and Apple and Google and the Justice Department and adversaries yet undreamt of. So whither "the art of literary editing" in such a world? (It's really a craft and a profession, but let it pass.)

My crystal ball is cloudy, but it seems to me that unless the creation and dissemination of written artifacts of literary intent becomes a fully digitized and DIY enterprise— and it might, every typing man and woman his or her own imprint—the exercise of informed taste and judgment, the expert guidance, and the infectious enthusiasm that are the editor's stock in trade and unique contributions to the publishing enterprise will remain indispensable. For all the wrenching changes in trade publishing in the past decades, I know that my colleagues and I pretty much go about the thing in a fashion very similar to the way the editors I watched and learned from were doing it in the seventies, and they were doing in a fashion very similar to the editors they learned from. Sometimes I think we're like blacksmiths or bespoke cobblers—how many ways are there, really, to shoe a horse or a human?

But here's an ironic and unexpected note to finish on: it seems that Alfred Knopf took a somewhat dim view of editors and did not regard them as so central to the publishing process as many (including editors) would have it. In his generous review in 1950 for the *New York Times Book Review* of the marvelous collection *Editor to Author: The Letters of Maxwell Perkins,* Knopf gives full credit to Perkins for his almost superhuman tact and patience and graciousness and his central place in the creation of the American literary canon of the first part of the twentieth century. This was something, of course, that he would have witnessed in real time as a competitor to Scribner's, which employed Perkins. But towards the end of his review Knopf registers this demurral: "Perkins's influence on his own authors was clearly all to the good, but his influence on other publishers' editors and consequently on American publishing, as a whole, has been something else again." He goes on to argue that, for one thing, novelists in an ideal world would deliver their novels to their publishers without needing or expecting Perkinsesque editorial aid and comfort, and for another that publishers themselves have become so focused on the business aspects of their enterprise that they have become too dependent on editors to tell them what they should publish rather than reading the books themselves. He concludes, "I can only hope that this trend may be reversed, that the harassed publisher will consider hiring instead of an editor, say, a very competent business manager and thus become freer himself to spend more time with the people who write books for him and for others. For we have seen only one Perkins in a generation." That must have been a fun review for the editorial staff of Knopf to have read on a Sunday morning in March 1950.

And with that mixed and chastening message, farewell for now from the Knopf Doubleday Group.

A CULTURE OF COMPETITION: SOME NOTES ON WRITING CONTESTS & LITERARY PUBLISHING

Kevin Larimer

Kevin Larimer is the editor-in-chief of Poets & Writers, where he edits Poets & Writers *magazine; oversees the organization's website, pw.org; directs Poets & Writers Live; and cohosts* Ampersand: The Poets & Writers Podcast. *He holds a degree in journalism from the University of Wisconsin in Milwaukee and received his MFA in poetry from the Iowa Writers' Workshop, where he was the poetry editor of the* Iowa Review. *He has presented lectures on publishing at the Academy of American Poets' annual Poets Forum, the Writer's Hotel Master Class, and the International Poetry Conference in Koprivshtitsa, Bulgaria, and has served on a number of panels on publishing at events such as the Library of Congress National Book Festival, the Sozopol Fiction Seminars, the Slice Literary Writer's Conference, and Poets Forum. His poems have appeared in* Poetry International, Fence, Pleiades, Verse, *and a dozen other literary magazines. He has written book reviews for* American Letters & Commentary, American Book Review, Chelsea, *and the* Pittsburgh Post-Gazette.

Howard Buck graduated from Yale University in 1916, went on to serve in the American Expeditionary Forces during World War I, then returned home and wrote a collection of poems, which he submitted to a new writing contest open to poets under the age of forty who had not yet published a poetry collection. He won and, as a result, received an award uncommon at the time: the publication of his book. *The Tempering: Leaves From a Notebook* included the following publisher's note upon its release in 1919:

> The Yale Series of Younger Poets is designed to afford a publishing medium for the work of young men and women who have not yet secured a wide public recognition. It will include only such verse as seems to give the fairest promise for the future of American poetry—to the development of which it is hoped that the Series may prove a stimulus . . .

The unremarkable poems of Howard Buck have become a footnote in the rich history of the Yale Series of Younger Poets, which claims to be the oldest annual literary award in the United States. As George Bradley writes in his excellent introduction to *The Yale Younger Poets Anthology* (1998), "His was schoolboy verse, and it is not his fault if the series his volume initiated has gone on to greater things." The contest's list of winning poets started to get interesting in the early 1930s, with the addition of names such as James Agee and Muriel Rukeyser, then hit its stride in the 1950s, with Adrienne Rich, W. S. Merwin, John Ashbery, James Wright, and on and on, up to the present day. The award is significant not only for having showcased a good portion of the important modernist poetry written in the United States following World War I, but also for introducing a new model for literary publishing in this country. Indeed, it provided a stimulus for the future of American poetry, but not only in the way Yale University Press intended. As Bradley writes, "Through it all, the Yale Series has set an example. It has shown others what professionalism in a literary competition might be, and its long-term success has inspired other presses to initiate similar programs. Thus, the Yale Series of Younger Poets has occasioned young poetry series even as it has fostered young poets."

As the editor-in-chief of Poets & Writers, I edit *Poets & Writers* magazine, oversee the organization's website, and direct a series of national events, Poets & Writers Live. I am charged with ensuring that all three programs deliver a balance of practical information for writers and of creative engagement and inspiration, in keeping with the nonprofit's mission: to foster the professional development of poets and writers, to promote communication throughout the literary community, and to help create an environment in which literature can be appreciated by the widest possible public. Much of my time on the magazine is spent assigning and editing craft essays, author profiles, interviews with agents and editors, and articles about nearly every aspect of the lives of writers and the business of publishing for the magazine's approximately one hundred thousand readers. A good deal of my attention is also directed to the many thousands of listings in our databases—small presses, literary magazines, MFA programs, writers retreats, reading venues, and so on—as well as the events calendar and directory of authors at pw.org, which attracts approximately 1.6 million visitors each year.

Every day I'm reminded that writers are hungry to know how to get an agent, they are eager to know about new markets for their work, and they want to learn about the work of their peers. They want to know how authors—some well-known, others less so—are able to juggle the pursuits of writing, publishing, and promoting their work with the real-life pressures of making a living, maybe raising a family, and simply being a responsible human being in this early twenty-first-century writing community. But there is one topic that rises to the top of nearly every survey we conduct and every dizzying examination of page views, as ranked by Google Analytics: writing contests. Writers consistently search our database of contest deadlines more than any other resource on our website. Readers flip first to the Grants & Awards section of *Poets & Writers* magazine before making their way to the author profiles and advice columns. Years of research and anecdotal evidence point to one common truth: when most beginning and emerging writers think about publishing their work, their thoughts nearly always turn first to writing contests. The competitive culture of literary publishing (in which a limited number of editors, with or without the help of a limited number of literary agents, acquire and publish a limited number of books from a vast pool of available talent) has been enhanced by an equally competitive culture of literary contests.

The Grants & Awards section of *Poets & Writers* magazine features deadlines of forthcoming writing contests as well as information about recent winners. We list state, national, and international prizes in poetry, fiction, and creative nonfiction that offer prizes of $1,000 or more, prizes of less than $1,000 that charge no entry fee, and some prestigious nonmonetary awards. While the section doesn't represent the entire field of writing contests in this country, it encompasses a broad spectrum of contests that matter—those that are established, have proven to be trustworthy, and can have a significant impact on a winner's career. It also covers nearly every book-publication prize (that is, those prizes that result in the publication of a book, like the Yale prize) available in this country. As long as I've been working on the magazine (going on seventeen years now) I've kept track of the numbers behind Grants & Awards because, as the numbers continue to climb, they offer an intriguing snapshot of contemporary literary publishing as a whole—and poetry publishing in particular.

In 1973, the first issues of *Coda*, the magazine's news-print predecessor, featured 45 winners of listed contests. By 2001, that number had risen to 975. Over a decade later, the number of contest winners consistently climbs over 1,100 annually. Some of the winners are acknowledged for single poems, stories, or essays, and others for chapbooks, or previously published books. Most receive some money, perhaps a publication in a literary journal, maybe some time at a writer's residency. Most important, they receive a sense of support and a feeling of acknowledgment and validation—the next stepping-stone in an often twisting and uncertain career path. But then there are those prizes that offer something more—the publication of a book—and these have had an impact on more than just the lives of the writers who win them. Back in 1918, when Howard Buck won the Yale Series of Younger Poets and was awarded the publication of his book, he and Yale University Press started a trend that has grown over the past century, as book-publication prizes have multiplied and evolved into a viable model for a rising number of poetry publishers.

In 2004, the Recent Winners section of *Poets & Writers* magazine listed 135 winners of contests that directly resulted in the publication of books. Ten years later, the number had risen slightly, to 138 winners. Of these, the vast majority are poets. (Of the 135 books published through listed contests in 2004, 104, or 77 percent, were books of poetry; of the 138 prizewinning books published in 2014, 107, or 77.5 percent, were poetry.) This is not surprising, of course. For the most part, poets have become accustomed to standing on the outside looking in at the world of literary agents, commercial publishing, and multibook deals. But thanks in part to the rise of book-publication prizes (as well as tremendous growth in the number of independent presses in general) there are more publishing opportunities than ever for poets. All that's

required is a manuscript and usually an entry fee, which typically falls anywhere between ten and twenty-five dollars.

In both 2004 and 2014, the majority of the magazine's
listed winners were awarded and published by independent
presses, with the number of independent presses that publish award winners rising by nearly 8 percent in that ten-year
span: 70 (or 52 percent) of the 135 winners in 2004; 82 (or
59.5 percent) in 2014. In the same time period, the number of
university presses sponsoring publication prizes dropped by 6
percent: 58 (or 43 percent) in 2004 to 50 (or 37 percent) ten
years later. The small handful left over were sponsored and
published by nonprofit organizations (2 in 2004; 3 in 2014)
and commercial publishers (with the radical transformations
that have marked the Big Six, now the Big Five, in the past
decade or so, it is not surprising to see their number of contest
affiliations decline from 5 in 2004 to two in 2014).

In 2004, the commercial presses publishing writers via writing contests included Houghton Mifflin,
HarperCollins, and Penguin. Houghton Mifflin published
two of the books that won Bread Loaf's Bakeless Prize,
and HarperCollins published the winners of the National
Poetry Series and the National Writers United Service
Organization's Bellwether Prize. Today, only one listed
contest, the National Poetry Series, includes publication by
commercial presses, Penguin and HarperCollins.

·   ·   ·

BOOK-PUBLICATION CONTESTS EMERGED IN THE
last century, and flourished in the last quarter century, as a
way for independent and university presses to not only cast
a wider net to find new poetic talent, but also to offset costs
in the publication of books that do not often otherwise fit in
a publisher's profit-and-loss reports. The appeal for writers

is clear. It's an open system: anyone can enter as long as basic guidelines are followed, so there is no need for an agent. For the most part, it is also, finally—after years of suspicion then flat-out accusations of unfairness and charges of nepotism at a number of contests—a transparent system. Since there is usually an entry fee, and therefore higher scrutiny of the mechanics of the process, sponsoring organizations often employ a multitiered system for the review of manuscripts that involves more than one pair of eyes on each submission. Writers who are skeptical of editorial objectivity can also take some solace in the common contest guideline stipulating that submissions be scrubbed clean of identifying details before they are read. Book-publication prizes also offer writers the dream of having one's manuscript published not only under the imprimatur of a trusted press but also with the stamp of a judge's approval—often a high-profile author whose popularity draws the highest number of submissions.

A few years ago I conducted a roundtable interview with representatives of four book-publication contests—the Bakeless Literary Publication Prizes, which until 2012 were sponsored by the Bread Loaf Writers' Conference and offered publication by a participating press, first Houghton Mifflin, then Graywolf Press; the Cave Canem Poetry Prize, sponsored by the Cave Canem Foundation and offering book publication by one of three participating presses to an African American poet; the Walt Whitman Award, sponsored by the Academy of American Poets and also offering publication by Graywolf Press as well as a six-week residency at Italy's Civitella Ranieri Center and distribution to thousands of the Academy's members; and the Colorado Prize for Poetry, sponsored by the Center for Literary Publishing at Colorado State University in Fort Collins and offering publication by the Center. When I asked each of the coordinators how they saw contests changing the landscape of literary publishing, they all pointed to contests as alternatives to a traditional system of publishing hobbled by the bottom line.

Stephanie G'Schwind, the director of the Center for Literary Publishing, went so far as to say, "We love publishing poetry books—it's very rewarding—but we couldn't do it without the contest model."

Camille Rankine, who at the time was the program and communications coordinator at the Cave Canem Foundation, said contests have led to a greater sense of diversity in poetry book publishing. "There's more diversity in the field now, because there are so many more people choosing who's being published," she said. "It's not just the people working at the presses, the poetry editors, anymore. It's poets. And I think all these different ideas of what a book should look like and what poetry should be are being expressed now more than they would be without these prizes."

Michael Collier, director of the Bread Loaf Writers' Conference, pointed out the benefits of the open system of contests while acknowledging a long-standing criticism of the writing contest as a force in the democratization of the art. "To be able to just send a manuscript out somewhere and know that, okay, you have to pay a fee, but you know it's going to be read, it's going to be considered. You don't have to have an agent; you don't have to know anybody," Collier said. "On the other hand, it does give the impression that there is an institutionalization of this, and that can have its drawbacks as well. Whenever you institutionalize something, there are certain perceptions that go along with it that are generalizations of a process. But by and large, the fact that anybody can send a manuscript out and have it looked at. . . . And because those judges are always changing, you know your chances are always changing."

In an article written at least partially in response to that interview and published by the *Huffington Post*, poet and critic

Anis Shivani questioned—and ultimately condemned—the contest model as a system of publishing new poetry books. "Is this the best way to discover new poetry talent in the country?" he asked. "What happens to editorial judgment, consistent aesthetic vision, commitment to particular values, building a movement, advocating for a particular style, and creating a critical mass of new writing if the contest model is allegedly based in 'impartiality' and 'blindness'— in other words, pretends to be the exemplar of democracy, egalitarianism, and disavowal of values? Has institutionalization gone too far? Would we all be better off—far-fetched as it sounds—if the contest model were eliminated and consistent editorial judgment were allowed to enter into the process of first book publication again?"

One element that is surely missing from the writing-contest model is a framework that aids in the development of lasting relationships between poets and publishers: the book-publication prize is essentially a one-and-done agreement. And when it comes time for prizewinners to place their second books, they often find themselves back at square one, without the support of an editor and a publisher that specifically chose their books for publication. Once the original press has fulfilled the obligation to publish the winning book, the editors may consider a subsequent book, but more often than not the poet must look elsewhere. By and large, the poets who stick with one publisher through the release of multiple books are those who go the traditional route and are able to develop relationships with the editors, who in turn commit to their authors and their future books. Wave Books, an independent press in Seattle that, under the editorship of Joshua Beckman and Matthew Zapruder, has published multiple books by Matthew Rohrer (whose first book was published by W. W. Norton, through the National Poetry Series, but who has been with Wave ever since), Noelle Kocot, Mary Ruefle, Dara Wier, and many others, is an excellent example—as is Graywolf Press, Four Way Books, Copper Canyon Press, and on and on.

While it's true that the contest model subverts the traditional notion of the editor (a staff member of the press) as arbiter, contests are hardly the only elements of publishing that employ a changing roster of name authors as tastemakers. Consider popular anthologies such as Houghton Mifflin Harcourt's annual Best American anthologies, which collect everything from poetry and short stories to comics and travel writing, and employ a different guest editor for each new volume. The argument against writing contests also ignores the simple truth that even in traditional publishing, not every submission makes its way to the eyes of the editor, but rather gets filtered out of the stacks by interns, entry-level assistants, and others.

Of course, the community of writers and literary publishers in America is big enough to allow for both models. There is a dizzying array of small presses that publish amazing books with or without the aid of contests. For every independent press that runs a book-publication contest, there are at least two more that don't. And there are some that denounce this kind of competition all together.

The editors of *Barrelhouse*, a literary magazine based in Washington, D.C., that also publishes books, recently told Travis Kurowski, a columnist for *Poets & Writers* magazine (and a coeditor of this volume), that they consciously abstain from sponsoring contests. "We did one contest and took an entry fee for it and then felt pretty icky about that," said cofounder Dave Housley. Icky or not, writing contests have provided a stimulus for poetry in this country, just as the editors of the Yale Series of Younger Poets predicted. At the end of the day, publishing is a competition. The real question is whether you want to pay an entry fee to be in it.

Of course, fees are not solely the domain of writing contests. There are plenty of reputable presses, such as Copper Canyon Press and Four Way Books, that charge reading fees. In the case of Copper Canyon, a poet is asked to pay thirty-five dollars during an open reading period; in exchange, she receives two Copper Canyon books and the knowledge that at least one staff member of the press has read her manuscript. Four Way Books, publisher of the 2014 Pulitzer Prize winner Gregory Pardlo, accepts submissions during the month of June with a twenty-eight-dollar reading fee (the same amount, it is worth noting, as the entry fee to its Levis Prize in Poetry).

An open submission period that requires a reading fee is really not all that different from a writing contest, except that there is no famous judge, the press is under no obligation to name a "winner," and the chosen poet doesn't receive a cash prize but rather a publishing contract.

. . .

SO WHAT DOES ALL THIS TELL US about the state of literary publishing? For one thing, there are a lot of poets who are willing go to great lengths for the chance to publish a book. With the preponderance of fee-based publishing structures, it's easy to see why so many of them assume that publication by a top-tier press requires a not-insignificant amount of either money (spent in the form of reading fees or entry fees) or luck (to be chosen by either a judge or an editor who somehow takes an interest)—or, more often the case, both money *and* luck. This is quite different from the traditional model, wherein a talented writer approaches a publisher, or a publisher goes out and identifies a writer whose talent and literary promise justify a financial investment—in the form of an advance and the costs of publication—with the hope that there will be a return on that investment, in the form of sales of that particular book as well as subsequent books.

Considering sales of poetry in this country, it's clear why so many publishers are keen on contests and why so many poets are willing to take the short-term deal. How many publishers have the resources to invest in a debut poet who isn't plucked from relative obscurity by a famous poet-judge and who doesn't come with the extra padding provided by entry fees?

The increase in writing contests, specifically book-publication contests, has slowly altered the ecosystem of literary publishing—poetry publishing, in particular—but has it influenced the quality of the writing published as a result of those contests? Only insofar as the relationships between publishers and new prizewinning authors are necessarily uncertain—not forged in the fires of the traditional acquisition process but rather loosely tied by an obligation to publish a winner as chosen by an outside judge. When looked at from this perspective, prizewinning authors are often cast out into the wilderness and forced to hunt for the next publishing opportunity, rather than being nurtured by a press and given the luxury of being able to concentrate on the next book with the input of a committed editor.

Still, it is comforting to know that the number of presses where those wandering prizewinning authors can land is growing at a rate that seems to be outpacing the growth of contests. (As of this writing, the curated database at pw.org includes more than 425 of them.) And that's the real beauty of literary publishing in the twenty-first century: the scrappy, entrepreneurial spirit and passion for new literature that is at the beating heart of so many small but successful indie presses is contagious, and ensures that for every talented writer who doesn't want to spend money to be published, there is always another option.

Daniel Slager

Daniel Slager is the publisher and CEO *of Milkweed Editions. Previously he was an editor at Harcourt Trade Publishers and associate editor of* Grand Street. *He is a widely published translator from the German; his book-length translation of Rainer Maria Rilke's* Auguste Rodin *(Archipelago Books, 2011) received the American Translator Association's Ungar Prize.*

At a dinner party recently, I was asked what I do. "I'm a book publisher," I replied, only to receive what has become, with modest variation, a common response: "So, what does it feel like to be part of a dying industry?"

I am no longer surprised by the question. In fact, it is not unusual these days to hear gleeful pronouncements about the imminent end of books, often accompanied by an unquestioning embrace of the digital age. The Internet, this line of thinking goes, offers a more vibrant and democratic forum, where all voices can be heard without the mediation of traditional gatekeepers such as publishers. The implication is obvious if generally unstated: this "disintermediation" will inevitably render irrelevant those fusty elites who have somehow inserted themselves between writers and readers for generations.

I almost always feel inclined to respond in a subtly argumentative way to this manner of thinking about books and the paradigm change that clearly is underway for all of us who work with them in some capacity. But before elucidating my response in a bit more depth, perhaps I should explain where I am coming from, and how my perspective on the current situation has been informed by my own experience in the book business.

I have been interested in books for as long as I can remember. Apart from a three-year interval in Amman, Jordan, I grew up mostly in Michigan. And as a student at the University of Michigan, my adolescent interest in books blossomed into an obsession. Apart from the hours in the library, I spent a great deal of time during these years in the original Borders store in Ann Arbor as well, and it was there that I began to discover the world of literary magazines and journals.

On graduating from Michigan in 1988, it was clear to me that literature was my passion, and I was determined to pursue it. And so I decided to move to New York, as I knew that most of the publishing industry—along with many of the writers and magazines I found most interesting—was centered there. With just a few hundred dollars and almost no contacts, I enacted the classic American trope, migrating from the Midwest to our cultural capital.

After looking for a couple months, and enduring dozens of interviews that invariably entailed typing tests, I was offered my first job in publishing. At William Morrow, I was the editorial assistant to senior editor Maria Guarnaschelli, who was publishing some of the best cookbook authors in America at the time—Rose Levy Beranbaum, Jeffrey Smith, Julie Sahni, and others—along with a tasteful if smallish list of literary authors, from Sven Birkerts to John Irving. When I was walked to my desk that first day at William Morrow, I found a typewriter and a telephone, the tools of the trade at the time. All correspondence was posted and delivered by workers from an actual mailroom, and submissions arrived from agents in manuscript boxes, often via bicycle messengers.

I learned a great deal from Maria Guarnaschelli, but that first position was to be a short stop for me. William Morrow simply wasn't the right fit for the kind of books I was interested in. And on a more pedestrian level, in retrospect I wasn't mature enough to hold a full-time office job. So I left this one after just six months, not knowing what was next.

I spent the next few years working in restaurants in New York and traveling. I continued reading voraciously, and increasingly my interests led me to literature from all over the world. I had learned German in high school and college, and it was in these years that I began reading broadly in German-language literature and philosophy, eventually deciding that I wanted to go back to school. And as I considered my interests and explored programs, comparative literature—multiple languages, interdisciplinary approaches—seemed right. I applied to a number of programs and headed off to Europe for a year, with an eye to moving my competence in German and French to a more advanced stage.

In the fall of 1992, I began three years of coursework leading to a PhD in Comparative Literature at New York University. I remember this time as a kind of penurious golden age. One was actually expected to read all the time; the students and faculty were knowledgeable, interesting, and refreshingly diverse; and the immersion in thinkers such as Theodor Adorno, Walter Benjamin, and Michel Foucault was electrifying.

In my second year, a colleague who knew of my growing interest in contemporary literature told me that a prominent quarterly magazine, *Grand Street*, was looking for someone to read and report on texts in German. After an exploratory call, I walked across the Village to their offices, met associate editor Deborah Treisman, and left with a handful of books and catalogs under my arm. I was to read work that had been submitted by trusted sources, and find forthcoming work that would suit the editors' tastes.

As coursework gave way to preparation for comprehensive exams at NYU, I continued reading for *Grand Street*, and began translating some of the work I found most interesting for publication in the magazine. My interest in translation had been encouraged by Richard Sieburth, a scholar and acclaimed translator from both French and German whom I had been fortunate to claim as my advisor at NYU. And now I was in a position to select contemporary texts and render them. Astonishingly, I was paid for this work.

Soon I was translating previously undiscovered work by Franz Kafka and Bertolt Brecht, and the first texts to appear in English by writers such as Durs Grünbein, Marcel Beyer, and Terézia Mora, all of whom went on to have book-length work published by major houses in the United States. Then when Deborah Treisman moved on to the *New Yorker*, I was invited to join the staff at *Grand Street* as associate editor, a decision that surely had to do with the fact that the next themed issue was to be on Berlin. In any case, while I first thought of the position as dissertation support that promised to be more fun and lucrative than graduate-assistant teaching, it proved to be far richer than that.

Resources were never an issue at *Grand Street*, though it was only later that I would learn how atypical this is throughout the literary-publishing ecosystem. Rather, our charge—supported in every way by the inimitable Jean Stein, who funded and ran the magazine from her place uptown—was to find and publish the most interesting and original writers from around the world. On one hand this meant soliciting work from English-language writers who were like gods to me at the time—Mike Davis, Alexander Cockburn, William T. Vollmann, and many more—and on the other hand it meant discovering and publishing writers who were new to me. Roberto Bolaño, Victor Pelevin, Yehuda Amichai, José Saramago—we had the resources to find and translate the best short-length work from the world's best writers. Published alongside art portfolios curated by the legendary Walter Hopps, these texts introduced a good number of major international writers to American readers. And for an editor just beginning to learn the craft, it also presented an opportunity to work with a wide range of dispositions and tendencies.

I had been at *Grand Street* eight months or so when Jean Stein made clear that the future of the magazine would be online. This wouldn't happen exactly as intended, but the change in vision provided an impetus for my departure from the magazine. A dissertation on Robert Musil and *The Man Without Qualities* beckoned, along with a growing number of opportunities to translate work I cared about. So I left *Grand Street* and returned to writing and translating, piecing together a precarious living.

I was only back at this relatively solitary life for a few months, however, when I received a fateful call. Drenka Willen, who had been a contributing editor for *Grand Street* for years, was looking for an associate editor at Harcourt, someone who could work closely with her to publish what was arguably the best list of world literature in New York at the time, a list featuring Octavio Paz, Italo Calvino, Günter Grass, José Saramago, Wisława Szymborska, and many others. I hemmed and hawed foolishly, not understanding what a break this was, but eventually I did accept the position and began work at Harcourt in the summer of 1999.

General Cinema owned Harcourt when I began there, just as most of the household-name New York houses were owned at the time by entertainment conglomerates, a phenomenon that had begun in the seventies and accelerated in the eighties. Drenka presided over what had been the Helen and Kurt Wolff Books imprint, a connection to central European modernism that had considerable resonance for

me. This role meant not just working with many outstanding writers and translators, but also entrée to a rich network
of international publishers, annual trips to the Frankfurt
Book Fair, and, perhaps above all, protection from the
increasingly corporate pressure that was evident across the
commercial book-publishing scene in New York.

I worked with Drenka for nearly six years, a mentorship
that provided me with an absolutely invaluable education in
editing and publishing literature. We spent countless hours
talking over submissions, and then developing those we had
acquired into publishable books. I learned from Drenka
how to see and address substantive challenges in manuscripts, how to fix sentences, and how to work fruitfully with
writers. And as she always liked to say, when a manuscript
was ready for publication, our work was just beginning. For
then we had to see it through design and typesetting, and to
describe the book in ways that would appeal to intelligent
readers, providing our sales force and publicists with the
tools they would need to interest booksellers and librarians
along the way.

In the summer of 2005, I received another fortuitous call
out of the blue, this time from Minneapolis. A search firm
was looking for an editor-in-chief for Milkweed Editions,
an independent literary press. I didn't know much about
Milkweed or the independent book-publishing scene at the
time, but someone had provided my name to this firm, and
a nice woman sounding very much like Minnesota asked if I
would ever consider such a move. I responded affirmatively,
and was in Minneapolis to interview a week later.

When I was offered the position the following week,
I had an interesting decision to make. Drenka had always
talked as if I were being trained to inherit the list she had
built and presided over for several decades at Harcourt, a
prospect that was obviously very appealing. And yet I had no

idea how realistic this was in light of the fact that Harcourt
seemed to change corporate hands every few years, an experience that was always accompanied by a sense of forebod-
ing. And then it was also true that many of the friends and
colleagues I had in New York who were interested in literature in the way I was were drifting away from the commercial publishing scene.

On the other hand, Milkweed had a respectable history of publishing excellent literary books and an impressive board of directors, and it was a stable nonprofit organization with a compelling mission. Leaving New York for
Minneapolis would represent a reversal of the direction I
had taken on graduating from college, I thought, but New
York—the city and the book business—had changed dramatically over the fifteen years I had lived there, and in
ways that had me wondering if the future for publishing
the kind of books and writers I was interested in might be
elsewhere—not necessarily centralized in New York, that is,
and not necessarily for-profit.

I had a lot to learn on arrival in Minneapolis, of course.
Grant proposals, fund-raising, managing a nonprofit organization that operates with an eye to the public trust and a
mission rather than to profit growth: these and other elements of work at Milkweed Editions offered a steep curve.
But over the decade since making the move, I have grown to
embrace the fact that our business model makes it possible
to spend the time it takes to develop manuscripts editorially, to market and sell the books we publish effectively, and
to keep books in print in perpetuity following their initial
publication. Also, as an independent publisher, I am in far
more frequent and meaningful contact than I had been at
Harcourt with the various individuals involved across the
book business, from our preferred printers to reviewers to
the independent booksellers who are absolutely essential if

we are to see the books we publish find their way into readers' hands. In this sense being a relatively small independent
publisher today is arguably akin to what it meant to be one
in the first years after moveable type was invented in the
mid-fifteenth century, when the ties between and among
authors, publishers, printers, booksellers, and readers were
intricate and close, financially and otherwise.

Much has changed in the book business over the twenty-five or so years since I took my first editorial position.
Most obviously, the telephone and typewriter that greeted
me at William Morrow have given way to e-mail and the
Internet, technological changes with ramifications extending far beyond the ways we communicate in the book world.
With the Internet and e-books, the reach of publishers is no
longer limited to the physical range of our distribution—to
the shelves in bookstores and libraries, where readers have
traditionally found our offerings. Awards lists almost always
include books published by relatively small independent
presses from around the country these days, and when I
reflect on the books I care most about, the number of them
published by independent houses based outside New York
seems to grow with each passing year.

And yet while it does seem clear that the book world
is undergoing a change greater than any since Gutenberg
invented the modern printing press some five hundred years
ago, it is also true that much remains the same. Literature of
lasting value does not grow on trees. Apart from the curatorial role played by publishers in developing a list, literary
books often need nurturing and editorial development,
which requires investment that can exceed potential financial returns. Once the books we publish are ready for market, we seek to generate the kind of attention for them that
will interest potential buyers, and we still need commercial
networks that enable us to distribute and sell them. And

then finally, just as the rise of the book in the century following Gutenberg's invention of moveable type would have been inconceivable without the rise of a literate public whose demand drove the innovations that made mass-produced books possible, so do we need new generations of readers who care enough about books and the kind of thinking and feeling they enable to engage with them.

At Milkweed, we seek to retain what has long been essential in traditional publishing, and to embrace the opportunities offered by new technologies. We publish our books simultaneously as printed and electronic books, and sales of the latter have become an important source of revenue. We invest a growing portion of our revenue in the generation of digital content, aimed not only at increasing interest in our books and authors across North America, but also at generating the kind of conversation that is animated uniquely by literature around the world. And yet with each passing year, we place growing emphasis on crafting beautifully made books, investing in world-class design, artisanal printing, and original book art.

Perhaps the biggest contrast between my previous experience and where I am now, however, lies in the nature of our relationship with the writers we publish. This begins with the curatorial function that has been elemental to publishing since Gutenberg. Because contributed income supplements revenue generated by sales, the composition of our list is directed not by a desire for commercial success, but rather by a determination to find and nurture writers whose work is transformative. Similarly, when I acquire books and negotiate contracts, I am motivated ultimately not by the enrichment of shareholders, but rather by a desire to find the place where the writers we are publishing are paid reasonably well while we too retain enough income to continue publishing those who will follow. Once we have acquired a project, we are committed to developing it editorially, a costly process that can extend over years and several rounds of revision. And then, finally, because selling books is generally how we connect the writers we publish with readers, and because the revenue generated by these sales is essential both to our business model and to the livelihood of many writers we publish (in the form of royalties), we promote the books we publish energetically, often generating results that would be pleasing in any publishing house in America today.

While it is not always perfect, I seek to build relationships with writers based on an ethos of stewardship. My experience has left me with an understanding of the literary world as akin to a cultural ecology. A vibrant ecosystem requires healthy populations of individuals and species whose activities are complementary. Writers need readers, readers appreciate guidance with regard to what they might read, and we all need libraries and bookstores. It may be the case that the new connective technologies facilitate greater intimacy between readers and writers, but it is also true that those who finance and develop books, and then work to bring together writers and readers, remain essential. The dawn of the digital age has changed none of this.

Indeed, there is to my mind a somewhat troubling side to the unquestioning embrace of new technologies and media at the expense of book publishers. For while the Internet is often hailed as an unprecedented democratizing force, it is also undeniable that insofar as the power and authority of the traditional gatekeepers wane, they are being replaced by that of the giant media companies—Amazon, Google, Apple, and Facebook, most prominently—and while access to information has undoubtedly increased in this new regime, creative work such as writing literary texts has diminishing monetary value, rendering many writers digital sharecroppers of sorts, free to compose and spread texts and images through networks controlled by a handful of companies that profit from the traffic.

We have undoubtedly reached a critical moment of cultural and economic restructuring, with implications for those of us who care deeply about literature. As consolidation accelerates across the commercial book-publishing industry while commercialism and the logic of advertising increasingly dominate the media spectrum, what I am interested in—writing that moves me, writing that illuminates new perspectives, writing in which language is used to convey more than information, to borrow Walter Benjamin's definition of literature—really has not changed very much at all.

As is the case with most publishers and editors I respect, I am devoted to a craft whose reward lies in the activity itself, rather than its financial outcome. Publishing literature has never been easy, nor particularly lucrative. Like generations of publishers, editors, and translators before me, I found my way into this line of work because I gave myself over to a passion for literature. And much to my surprise, I have found myself in the midst of an enormous cultural transformation, with ramifications that promise a lifetime of creative adventure.

Emily Louise Smith

Emily Louise Smith is director of the Publishing Laboratory at the University of North Carolina Wilmington, cofounder and publisher of Lookout Books, and publisher of the literary magazine Ecotone. *Her honors include fellowships from the Truro Center for the Arts and the Hub City Writers Project, as well as a Dorothy Sargent Rosenberg Prize. Her poems appear in* Best New Poets, *the* Southern Review, *and* New South, *among other places.*

I held my breath those mornings in 2003 as I walked past the cases of taxidermied shorebirds, a dried puffer fish, and other specimens floating in formaldehyde on my way to work in the Publishing Laboratory, housed then in a defunct science lab on the campus of the University of North Carolina Wilmington. (We stored our paper trimmer under a fume hood.) The Pub Lab, as we refer to it, was the newly founded teaching press and brainchild of a visiting professor and retired head of HarperCollins Canada, Stanley Colbert, my new supervisor. An eager refugee of advertising and development, I was one of three graduate assistants and his newest recruit. On each of seven portable desks sat one of those hulking, now extinct iMac G3s, its innards exposed behind blue plastic. A particleboard slab covered the sinks and propped up the glue binder. Every once in a while someone would accidentally catch an elbow on the switch and rouse the giant lung of the ventilation system.

I didn't fully understand then that our machines were training-wheels versions of those used at commercial printers, but as someone blissfully embarking on an MFA in poetry after five years bereft of classroom discoveries, I did know this: I wanted desperately to join this grand experiment. I wanted to write and make books.

Housed under the same roof as the creative-writing department since 2008, the Pub Lab is today a state-of-the-art desktop publishing facility with twenty slender iMacs and an adjacent bindery. On any given day, the machines—including the trusty original binder and a new guillotine trimmer—trill and slice, scan and hum. The Lab has become a hive where students congregate, not only to take formal publishing courses and create their own chapbooks, but to intern for our national literary magazine, *Ecotone*, and book imprint, Lookout; among other tasks, they design layouts, research cover art, edit, proofread, fact-check, and write blog posts. In late 2011, when Edith Pearlman's *Binocular Vision: New & Selected Stories*, the debut title from Lookout, was announced over public radio as a finalist for the National Book Award, I felt the students' collective gasp through my office ceiling.

. . .

WHEN FACULTY MEMBER DAVID GESSNER founded *Ecotone* in 2005 as the department's first literary biannual, the Pub Lab was instrumental. On a collapsible dry-erase board beside the fume hood, we brainstormed the subtitle *reimagining place* and listed ways the magazine could move beyond the hushed tones of some nature writing to publish thorny pieces that push readers to engage with our environment. An ecotone is a transition zone between two adjacent ecological communities, containing the characteristic species of each—and in our pages we conceive of it as a testing ground, a place of danger or opportunity. Our first issue featured an exemplary essay by Reg Saner—about children and mountain lions sharing a cul-de-sac in his Colorado neighborhood—and "Homesick," a poem by Gerald Stern later reprinted in *The Best American Poetry*. Before we knew it *Ecotone* had matured from an idea to a nationally recognized magazine with poetry, stories, and essays collected in the Best American series and *The Pushcart Prize*. Although we attracted the work of established writers, we prided ourselves on providing a home for emerging voices.

I remember a colleague asking during my interview for director of the Publishing Laboratory where I envisioned the program in five years. This was midway through my year as interim director of the Lab, and I knew already that the enterprise was on the cusp of something extraordinary. Having shepherded more than half the titles on our backlist (several successful regional books and the department's textbook, *Show & Tell: Writers on Writing*), I longed for a new creative challenge, as well as a chance to discover and publish book-length literary projects more in keeping with the work in *Ecotone*. "What if we combined *Ecotone*'s editorial strengths with the Lab's design and production expertise?" I proposed. A new literary imprint would enable the magazine to highlight its best authors and offer the Lab a chance to grow beyond its regional roots to become a boutique literary press. We'd certainly laid the foundation; by 2011, UNCW had been publishing books under the Pub Lab name for nearly ten years and had distributed them nationally for another five. And *Ecotone*, in its first ten issues, had established itself as one of the country's preeminent venues for original fiction, nonfiction, and poetry. (Which is to say: anyone who later deemed Lookout Books an overnight success hadn't done his homework.)

I'll never forget my first phone call with Ben George, who would join our faculty the following year and become my accomplice in all things *Ecotone* and Lookout. Ben and

I had both cut our teeth in publishing—me as an editor, book designer, and publicist at Hub City Press in South Carolina, and Ben in Portland, where at *Tin House* his reputation for meticulous editing preceded him. In our first few years together, we unveiled a sleeker *Ecotone* logotype and a larger trim size. The redesigned layout featured a new typeface, pull quotes, and a compelling image on each opening spread. New departments, including The Strip, for visual stories and essays; Reclamation, in which a modern master reintroduces a neglected story; and Correspondents, for letters between an editor and a writer, soon followed. But despite these enhancements, we were also custodians of *Ecotone*, carrying out, and often reinterpreting, the vision of its founding editors. Lookout, on the other hand, offered us the rare opportunity to build an imprint that reflected *our* tastes and interests. Years later we'd be able to look back and say *we built this*.

Ben and I jotted pages of potential names and crossed through them, until *Ecotone* contributor and North Carolina native Ben Fountain reminded us of Cape Lookout, just up the coast; a nod to our local landscape, the word also defines our publishing philosophy. Lookout Books provides a home for poetry, story, and essay collections, as well as debut novels—manuscripts that by virtue of their originality or newness or audience might not present themselves as predictable successes. If we love it, we find a way to sell it, not the other way around. Though we welcome agented submissions, our partnership with *Ecotone* allows us to discover and nurture emerging talents, and to cultivate lasting editorial relationships that often lead to book acquisitions.

At the time we founded Lookout, VIDA was also in its first year, and as a young poet poring over journals in search of places to submit my own work, I was becoming increasingly aware of the gender divide, among other disparities, in literary publishing. It was imperative to me that this new imprint champion works by emerging and historically under-represented voices, as well as overlooked gems by established writers.

Also, the surge in e-readers had prompted publishers to respond with beautiful, collectible print editions. Even the paperback was experiencing a renaissance as art object, spruced with deckled edges and French flaps. The vellum jacket for Haruki Murakami's *1Q84*, designed by Chip Kidd, was widely credited with the nine-hundred-page book's impressive print sales—far more popular than its digital counterpart. I've long believed that readers intuitively associate the well-designed and well-written book, and with every Lookout title, I've tried to honor that intimacy between writer and reader by publishing books as beautiful to hold as they are to read.

When it came time to acquire Lookout's first book, Ben suggested Edith Pearlman, who had been quietly writing remarkable stories for decades. The author of three award-winning collections, all with small presses, and stories reprinted in *The O. Henry Prize Stories*, *Best American Short Stories*, and *The Pushcart Prize*, she somehow still wasn't widely known. Authors Ann Patchett and T. C. Boyle, among others, considered her a master of the form. She fit our mission perfectly, and so we approached her about pairing the best stories from her previous books with new, unpublished stories, making her Lookout's debut author. The idea was to create a narrative of discovery around the collection, inciting late-life acknowledgment and a wider readership. As Patchett wrote in her introduction to *Binocular Vision*, "Of course by not having the level of recognition her work so clearly deserves, she gives those of us who love her the smug satisfaction of being in the know. Say the words *Edith Pearlman* to certain enlightened readers and you are instantly acknowledged as an insider, a person who understands and appreciates that which is beautiful."

In retrospect, the plan was remarkably simple, if grandiose. But as Simon Michael Bessie, who founded Atheneum, once wrote, "I suggest that we would not be publishing books—any of us—if we didn't want to play a role in the development of the ideas and insights which aim to make life more intelligible and more beautiful as well as more enjoyable." So it came as both unimaginable and somehow exactly what we'd hoped when *Binocular Vision* made publishing history—initially as the first debut book by an independent press to be reviewed on the cover of the *New York Times Book Review*, and later as the first book to win the National Book Critics Circle Award and also be named a finalist for the National Book Award, the Los Angeles Times Book Prize, and the Story Prize.

Binocular Vision is by now well known as one of independent publishing's success stories, but for me, it was the daily joy of ushering it into the world, championing it alongside Edith and Ben, that made publishing it so sweet. Edith opened doors that everyone at the imprint—future authors, editors, and students—will appreciate for years to come. In trusting us and offering us the gift of publishing her collection, she brought Lookout to life.

. . .

SAMPLE THE MISSION STATEMENTS OF young presses and you will discover the variety of ways we see ourselves filling gaps left by decades of consolidation and homogenization in the industry. "By publishing diverse and innovative literary translations," Archipelago is doing its part to change the lamentable fact that "less than 3% of new literature published in the United States originates outside the Anglosphere"; Black Balloon champions "the weird, the unwieldy, and the unclassifiable"; Tiny Hardcore Press "fosters access to emerging and experimental poetry and prose"; Bellevue Literary Press, publisher of the Pulitzer-winning novel *Tinkers*, devotes itself to literary fiction and nonfiction "at the intersection of the arts and sciences"; and Akashic claims "reverse-gentrification of the literary world."

The shift in landscape—from family-run publishing houses to ownership by multimedia conglomerates—has made way for the burgeoning of hundreds of small presses. In the ten years I've been at this, my students and I have followed along as national bookstore chain Borders collapsed, the formation of Penguin Random House brought the Big Six to Five in the largest merger in book-publishing history, and Google won dismissal of a long-running lawsuit by Authors Guild members who accused it of scanning millions of books without permission. Finalists for the country's preeminent prizes are now as likely to include books from Bellevue, Copper Canyon, or Graywolf, as from heavyweights Farrar, Straus and Giroux; W. W. Norton; and Knopf.

More genuinely interesting, genre-bending manuscripts cross my desk than ever, those that don't fit comfortably in any one bookstore category. Is it an essay collection, or a memoir? Literary or historical fiction, or both? Kathy Pories, senior editor at Algonquin Books, said years after acquiring Daniel Wallace's *Big Fish*, her auspicious debut, that you have to have a feeling that something is risky; those are the books that are the most exciting to publish. Fortunately for us, those risky books are finding their way to smaller houses, and we're increasingly adept at helping them reach their readers. Perhaps we won't rescue the industry from whatever imminent collapse the media outlets keep predicting, but we just might preserve the *culture* of literary publishing—that penchant for the original and new, risk and innovation, bequeathed to us by our editorial predecessors. While large houses are as equipped as ever to acquire best-selling authors, we're at least as well, and perhaps even uniquely, suited to discover and nurture them.

Small presses publish fewer titles a year, and in Lookout's case only one or two, so we're especially mindful of fit. In fact, while building our catalog, I've thought a lot about the days when a publisher's colophon—the sower, borzoi, or three fishes—stamped on the spine told readers what to expect. Established authors still transcend publishers when it comes to reader loyalty, but we small presses are increasingly better at building community. We sell books at a discount on our websites, and we curate accompanying blogs that let readers in on what we and our authors are thinking about and working on behind the scenes. We convey our distinct editorial mission and visual aesthetic across our website, blog, and social network, and extend the conversation around our books.

Under my direction, UNCW students help execute book design and layout, so we eliminate that expense. Though we can't afford large advances, the fifty-fifty model I first tested for Pub Lab titles has worked well for the imprint too. After recovery of any direct costs—essentially printing and licensing of cover artwork—we divide profits evenly with the authors. We ask them to partner with us in selling their books. Especially before Lookout earned national credibility, the only fair compensation for their faith in our fledgling imprint was to share profits. Five years later, our arrangement has proven in some cases more profitable than a traditional royalty structure. Though we print in batches to avoid remaindered books, we're nimble enough to respond promptly to market demand. We publish handsome but affordable paperback originals, and because we're forced to be resourceful, we always personalize promotion and develop shrewd marketing strategies. Which is to say: we evangelize for our books. "Scrappy and shoestring" is how then-president Eric Liebetrau referred to us at the National Book Critics Circle Awards ceremony.

While alchemy plays a role in every publishing success, I can in retrospect identify the ingenuity and sweat equity that helped *Binocular Vision* along the way. For one, we picked an opportune time to found a literary imprint. In 2010, the novel *Tinkers* won the Pulitzer, making it harder for review outlets to overlook small-press books. Every Sunday, I notice more of the longtime arbiters making space for small-press titles, even reviewing paperback originals. An assigning editor at the *New York Times* told me that he plucked *Binocular Vision* from the bin in part because he recognized Edith Pearlman's name but also because of the compelling package, including an advance reading copy that featured endorsements from T. C. Boyle, Brock Clarke, Yiyun Li, and Alice Mattison.

Soliciting a foreword from Ann Patchett was our first coup in a string of them. As guest editor of *The Best American Short Stories* in 2006, she included Edith's "Self-Reliance," but it wasn't until her brilliant introduction arrived that we learned that in fact *two* of her favorite stories in the more than one hundred she was given to choose from were by Edith Pearlman. Later that year, Patchett would open Parnassus Books in Nashville and almost overnight become the unofficial spokesperson and a fierce advocate for independent bookstores nationwide. When she appeared, again and again, on radio and television programs, she was asked—what else?—to recommend books. And so it was that *Binocular Vision* benefited from guest spots everywhere from *The Martha Stewart Show* to a *New York Times* op-ed reproving the Pulitzer committee for not awarding a fiction winner.

As important as any advance reading copy mailed to a reviewer were the dozens I sent to independent booksellers across the country, introducing them to the mission of Lookout Books and the work of Edith Pearlman, and requesting their help spreading the word. Similarly, I've always submitted qualifying titles for national and regional awards. Even if they aren't named finalists, judges and influential readers each year become aware of Lookout authors and the writing we publish. Maybe they mention one of our books in an interview later, or just in dinner conversation. Either way, it's a worthy investment.

As a nonprofit, we're also eligible for federal and state grants, and thanks to generous support from the National Endowment for the Arts and the North Carolina Arts Council, I was able to send Edith Pearlman and, after her, numerous other Lookout authors on tour to extend their audience and book sales. Because platform building is unique to each author, poet John Rybicki's unconventional tour included not only readings from *When All the World Is Old*, his collection about his wife's sixteen-year struggle with cancer, but also workshops for health professionals and patients at oncology centers, and visits to schools. His tour culminated in a video trailer, produced by my students, to promote his work as a *Time Magazine for Kids* outstanding writing *teacher* and, in turn, his book.

Along the way, Lookout also benefited from what John B. Thompson has termed the economy of favors, which is to say that because of our common vocation and shared mission, we independent presses and booksellers help each other. The advice I received, so invaluable at the outset, became indispensable that first head-spinning year when I wasn't sure how many copies to reprint after *Binocular Vision* won the National Book Critics Circle Award and back orders climbed to the thousands overnight. Bless our generous tribe, pioneers at Algonquin, Bellevue, Hub City, Milkweed Editions, and Tin House, among many others, who offered sound advice. I try to return the favor any time an upstart press calls for help.

Perhaps any editor not quite blind as a bat knew of Edith Pearlman's work by the time we acquired her manuscript in 2009, but she was without question the right *fit* for Lookout—perhaps the most important factor. While we weren't the first to court her, I believe that by publishing her as thoughtfully and charismatically as we did, and launching her as our debut author, we made a little publishing magic.

. . .

AMONG MY FAVORITE THINGS ABOUT working for a boutique literary imprint and magazine is the opportunity to be involved in every facet of the publishing process—and my students are in turn exposed to the full spectrum; they grasp how the advance amount is directly related to print run and foreign sales potential, for example, and understand the layering of publicity, audience reach, and grant support. A day hasn't passed in which a Lookout title didn't serve as a reference in my classroom. Over the course of an internship with the press, I hope to reveal the unlikely but beautiful marriage of art and commerce that makes publishing so distinct. Our projects aren't just simulations. Everything we produce on behalf of the magazine and imprint has to be of the highest quality, meticulously edited and designed. Lookout's books and promotional materials have to compete in the marketplace with those produced by professionals at houses with far greater resources.

Having worked exceedingly hard over the years to help the Pub Lab and its imprints achieve success, I expect that same level of commitment from everyone who works for us.

I want to inspire students to carry into the world beyond our hallways their appreciation for intelligent editing and imaginative design, an unflagging belief that books enlarge our sympathies. To that end, I focus on shared discovery and grant them enough autonomy to ignite their sense of leadership and responsibility, even allowing them to make mistakes—though, of course, I'm always guiding their steps. From the earliest days of the Publishing Laboratory, students helped shepherd the beautiful regional books we brought out, but since the establishment of Lookout, I've watched their level of investment and proficiencies increase · exponentially. By acknowledging their talents and passions, I hope that my students learn to recognize in themselves the power they have to shape literature.

Whether they go on to publishing careers or not, their apprenticeship will serve them well. After all, by teaching them to craft stories around our titles, we're empowering them to pitch their own ideas, to compel investors and clients, and thus succeed in any field. Those who eventually publish their own writing will be better informed and more engaged authors, respectful of the resources publishers invest in their books. I counsel the aspiring publishers in my classes to find a niche that isn't being filled and claim it. If they don't like the books available to them, they can employ the skills they've learned to publish the manuscripts and champion the authors they believe in, eventually even to start their own presses. Poets House founder Stanley Kunitz said on many occasions that when he did not find the community he needed, he felt compelled to make it. It's what the best houses do, I think, and what I pledged in cofounding Lookout: to create a haven for books that matter and to build meaningful conversation around them.

The initiatives my students have breathed life into, and the ones still to come, are the Pub Lab's legacy as much as Lookout, *Ecotone*, and the authors we've launched. They serve as proof that our teaching-press model fosters the innovation that will sustain independent publishing. One Pub Lab alumnus, the intrepid Sumanth Prabhaker, established Madras, through which he publishes novellas in a beautiful square format and distributes the proceeds to nonprofit organizations chosen by Madras's authors. Alumna Corinne Manning founded the *James Franco Review*, an online magazine that garnered national notice with its first issue for encouraging editors to read submissions blindly and to "allow room for what isn't supposed to happen, characters you don't always get to see" in an effort to increase the visibility of underrepresented artists and narratives. Meg Reid, now the deputy director of Hub City Press in South Carolina, led an anticensorship campaign to bring attention to the state legislature's censure of two university common-read selections with LGBTQ themes—one of which, *Out Loud*, Hub City published. (Hundreds of writers and booksellers took to social media in the spring of 2014 wearing neon, I'M SPEAKING OUT! T-shirts that the press created.) Alumnus John Mortara found his niche publishing poems submitted by voicemail, and Anna Sutton cofounded The Porch, a Nashville-based community organization that connects writers through classes and events.

As proud as I am of the foundational coursework we've implemented at UNCW, I know that my best teaching happens by apprenticeship, when I model passion and creativity in my work as a publisher. Even before my students can fully appreciate the considerations and conversations that lead to acquisitions and rewarding editorial relationships, much less the financial risk and reward, I let them in on my research and decision making—when we're successful and when we lose a manuscript to another house, when a clever publicity campaign results in widespread media attention and when, despite our best efforts, a deserving book doesn't reach the audience we'd anticipated. Through the choices we make at Lookout, they learn to be resourceful and imaginative, to problem-solve.

Every year, our students join us at the Association of Writers & Writing Programs Conference to help promote our authors and staff our book-fair table. They witness the excitement and exhaustion that accompany the digital uploads of grant proposals and issues of *Ecotone*. They arrive eager to wield red pens and leave our program with an appreciation for penciled queries, knowing that the best solution is almost always the one the author arrives at herself. They see us deep in InDesign files, setting one letter next to another so the words will seem to lift off the page, honoring the white space that carries the silence around poems. They hear us go to bat, sometimes vociferously, for writers we love, and I hope they lean in closest when I sing about books from other presses with all the charm and fervor I would one of my own.

Perhaps it's fitting that we came of age in a defunct science lab. Our students will have to solve the industry's next challenges, to translate the power of the book digitally and satisfy the proclivities of readers who increasingly engage through handheld devices. The tumult makes it an extraordinarily exciting time to enter the profession. Like the late Stanley Colbert, who founded the Pub Lab to demystify the publishing process and challenge the old paradigm, our students will further innovate to close the gaps between author, publisher, and reader. Though I wasn't around for that first year when the Lab consisted of two salvaged computers in the custodian's storeroom, I know very well the audacity it takes to see a publishing house in a closet, and the resilience required to carve out a place for it in the larger literary conversation. It's what—more than anything—I hope to pass along to my students.

Jessica Faust & Emily Nemens

Jessica Faust is coeditor and poetry editor of the Southern
Review. *She has been on the staff of the* Southern
Review *since 2004.*

Emily Nemens is coeditor and prose editor of the Southern
Review. *She has been on the staff of the* Southern Review
since 2011.

This year, the *Southern Review* celebrates its eight-
ieth anniversary. Editors Robert Penn Warren
and Cleanth Brooks began publishing the journal
in 1935, at the height of the Great Depression. As we editors think about publishing the journal today, we would be
remiss if we did not acknowledge that our long and storied
past remains ever present. The journal's role in publishing
some of the greatest writers of the twentieth century, such
as Katherine Anne Porter, Wallace Stevens, Peter Taylor,
T. S. Eliot, and many others, has positioned us as a publication known for featuring engaging literature from writers
who are beginning their careers as well as those who have
already achieved various levels of—even tremendous—
success. The aforementioned writers are just a few of the
upwards of three thousand contributors we've published
across fifty volumes. That storied past also includes the
efforts of the ten editors and coeditors who came before us,
assisted by dozens of assistant, associate, and managing editors; business managers; resident scholars; and graduate and
undergraduate students. Our collective effort has created a
library that, chronologically arranged, takes up more than
twelve feet of shelf space.

We do not consider, however, this voluminous past to be a burden. Rather, we see it as an opportunity to build on the journal's reputation and original ambition, as described by Cleanth Brooks in a 1985 documentary celebrating the journal's fiftieth anniversary, to publish good writing, of course, but also to have "some kind of personality and character" that would allow the journal to stand out "nationally and internationally" by having its own "flavor." To honor this mission, we have developed the journal in ways that allow it to thrive and continue to be relevant, engaging, and intelligent. In order to establish continuity in the journal from series to series, editor to editor, various directors have published some of the same contributors, and this, too, reinforces the journal's flavor, even as it has shifted over time to reflect the taste of the current masthead.

As we often find ourselves explaining to people who may not be familiar with the *Southern Review*, the journal was never particularly "Southern," despite its name. As second-series (1965–) editors Lewis P. Simpson and James Olney pointed out, the same writers who appeared in the original series, which ran from 1935 to 1942, also appeared in the *Partisan Review*, a New York-based magazine. Yet for all of its national and international ambitions, the *Southern Review* did also go to great lengths to establish and promote its role in Southern letters, capitalizing on the unique opportunity our geography and history provided. The Writing in the South series appeared in sixteen issues between 1968 and 2002, and offered to readers everything from William Faulkner's unpublished introduction to *The Sound and the Fury* to correspondence between the Vanderbilt Fugitives.

When asked, in a 1972 interview that appeared in the journal, about her relationship with the *Southern Review*, Eudora Welty said, "Why, it just gave me, you know, my life to get my stories into print at that time [the late 1930s], and they printed a number of them. They were marvelous to me." Equally fond memories existed on the other side of the editor's desk. Brooks recounted in his essay "The Life and Death of an Academic Journal" that he and Warren had never heard of Welty, since at that point she had only published one story in a "very little, little magazine," but recognized her as a "young first-rate story-writer," and they would go on to publish seven of her stories between 1937 and 1941.

We recognize that there are many journals available to writers, some of which pay more than our funds allow, so we feel that, in addition to giving the writers space in our pages, we can also offer careful editorial attention as a way to keep good writers coming back. We've received numerous notes and letters from contributors expressing gratitude for our close editorial work, and our authors sometimes say that no other journal provides as much guidance in that area as we do. While reworking an essay for the most recent issue, one author likened Nemens to Maxwell Perkins, and one poet told Faust that, when he is hoping to place new work, she is second on the speed dial only to the *New Yorker*. Working in relative isolation from our authors, this kind of feedback encourages us to continue the hard and satisfying work of advising our authors toward sharpening their already-outstanding work.

Brooks also noted in his essay that when the *Southern Review* began, it "enjoyed a special advantage because of the limited number of places where certain kinds of material could be published . . . particularly . . . with regard to poetry and fiction." For this reason, "the pickings were good, not only in quantity but in quality." While the number of journals in print today far exceeds those in 1935 (despite the closing of well-known journals every year), our long-standing reputation has ensured that we receive an abundance of good work.

It's difficult for us to count the multitude of Pulitzers and Pushcarts, Nobels and National Book Awards that our authors have accrued over the years, but we are always honored when an award-winning writer we admire and have read for years sends us work. One of the thrills of working as an editor at such a well-regarded journal is being able to correspond with writers you've admired from afar and have them happily send work your way because they respect the journal and want to be published in it. In the early days of the *Southern Review,* the editors published both established writers, like Aldous Huxley, as well as brilliant new writers who were virtually unknown at the time, like the twenty-three-year-old John Berryman. The goal was to present great writing and maybe even help launch careers. Of course, no one can predict the future of a writer's path or a trend in literature, but the possibility of discovering and supporting new talent is why we continue to seek out new writers through our general submissions and by soliciting them when we are struck by their work. We consciously ensure that each issue of the quarterly comprises new writers from the general mail as well as familiar literary names, with the aim of promoting great literature from every stage of writers' careers. Similarly, while the content has always reflected the specific and diverse concerns of the day, now more than ever we're also mindful that our authors reflect diversity across gender, cultures, and generations.

Just as the original series published newcomers alongside luminaries, we have, for example, recently included a posthumous W. D. Snodgrass translation and featured former U.S. Poet Laureate Charles Simic alongside nine writers who had never before appeared in the journal. Good writing is good writing and "does not have to be attached to a man or woman of distinction," said Brooks in support of the journal's selections. And while all editors probably aim to have the foresight to spot a future Pulitzer winner, finding an outstanding piece of writing is often satisfying enough. "I have no regrets that we published a good many stories by young and unsung authors who did *not* go on to glory," declared Brooks. Still, as editors we find it rewarding and reassuring when external accolades support the editorial choices we've made.

Resting on the past achievements of the journal or stifling the inevitable changes that come with growth, though, aren't things we are willing to do. In the spirit of those who have come before us as editors, we are aware of our role as custodians of a journal that has built a solid reputation over so many years, and we strive to uphold and expand that reputation. Respecting the original mission of the journal is a fundamental part of our own mission to remain engaging, relevant, and challenging, as we expand our boundaries to include a diverse range of voices and styles. Recently we published an issue in which prose and visual art originated from contributors across four continents, and the same issue contained poetry ranging from formal to free verse to prose poems, fifty words to ten pages, the absurd to the contemplative. The issue also included references to religious myths, popular children's book characters, 1970s TV icons, and Skee-Lo. We don't wish for the *Southern Review* to look or sound like it did eighty years ago; it shouldn't and it doesn't. The common thread is that it contains exceptional works. We are that somewhat rare place where a poem of any length may be considered for publication and, very consistently, even very long poems will find a home. When, after many years as an assistant editor, Faust began acquiring poetry, she brought to the journal new writers from Poland and Bangladesh, as well as a nineteen-page talk piece by David Antin. Poetry has grown beyond the bounds imagined by the founding editors. As has the prose: alongside its long tradition of literary criticism, the journal's nonfiction has expanded to include essays both modular and memoirist, science writing and sports pieces. Fiction, as well, has expanded its field of possibility.

Even as we celebrate its longevity and high regard, the *Southern Review* is not immune to the global financial difficulties that have affected higher education and state-funded institutions. The year after the United States' entry into World War II, LSU suspended publication of the journal for financial reasons. With the journal closed, Brooks and Warren dispersed to other academic positions, and Albert Erskine, the journal's first business manager, went on to a forty-year editorial career at Random House. The journal would be missed, but its reputation would be solidified for all time, as Katherine Anne Porter wrote in an April 1942 letter to Warren: "Well, it is done, and there is one thing they can't destroy: the record of seven years superb work. That stands. And that is where they fail, always. They can't destroy the record." Brooks remarked, in 1980, that the funding of literary journals is almost "always precarious; and when the university suffers a financial pinch, the university quarterly is usually the first activity to be curtailed. It is deemed a luxury item, a showpiece, a decorative frill."

We are fortunate that administrators agreed to revive the journal in 1965 and that, then and now, they understand that the *Southern Review*, like other leading literary journals, is not a frill: it is a vital forum for a conversation in contemporary literature, and it holds an important role in the university community and in publishing. For those writers who have found homes in academia, journals, many of them university-run, are the places where faculty publish in order to build the resumes that allow them to teach at those very universities. When a journal is lost, so, too, is a place for faculty publications, and this loss jeopardizes a measure that committees have traditionally used in weighing candidates' merits for tenure. For the aspiring story writer, placing stories in journals is often a foundational step in launching the work toward a complete manuscript, an agent, a contract, and ultimately, a published and well-received book. Nevertheless, in recent years, we've seen many journals closed by their home institutions. Editors have been creative in their efforts to find ways to stay afloat and add to the contemporary literary landscape. Along with an eye for talent, a strong sense of grammar, and tact with authors, resiliency is part of an editor's job.

We've made our own necessary changes to adapt to the publishing climate of the twenty-first century, including moving the *Southern Review* from letterpress to digital printing in 2005. This money-saving shift was one kind of loss, in that there is something quite wonderful about the look and feel of letterpress pages. But this very expensive process requires both extra time and money, and the savings from this change allowed the journal to print a full-color cover as well as an insert of contemporary art, to pay authors more, and to spend more time on the editing, rather than printing, stage of production. Like many journals today, we typeset our issues in-house, and then send the final digital file to a printer and distributor.

As the economic crash of 2008 began to take a toll on all units within universities, we also saw our budget tighten significantly. The LSU administration held the journal and its history in high esteem and did not suspend or eliminate publication. Though author payments were reduced and a few marketing mailers and inserts were discontinued, the journal was able to continue producing a quality journal on its regular schedule. A search for synergy among units led the university to urge the *Southern Review* and LSU Press to merge their operations. By joining forces, the two publishing arms of the university pooled their resources and found efficiencies. Further budget cuts did result in a restructuring of the staff, which now consists of a pair of coeditors (who also serve as genre editors) and a graduate assistant. The business manager and designer work for both the journal and the Press, as do the marketing staff and development director. The resident-scholar program was suspended, but we are seeking other funding to reinstate it. There is now one director for both the *Southern Review* and LSU Press, who, among many things, manages the budgets of both units.

With a significantly reduced editorial staff, the workload and responsibilities naturally increased. Brooks explained that he and Warren were given a course release in order to run the journal and that it was too much work. In addition to teaching three courses, they read hundreds of manuscripts and edited the journal. Our positions are now full time and year round, and though we have no formal teaching responsibilities, we do all the work previously done by a larger staff: read all submissions (we have a graduate assistant who helps read prose), acquire artwork, arrange for publication, copyedit and negotiate those changes with writers, determine the layout of each issue, create the digital file for the typesetter/designer, work with marketing and development, write copy and acquire material for the website, attend and participate in conferences and other events. Our submissions last year, even with our now shorter submissions period of three months for prose and five for poetry, topped twenty-three hundred, and we continue to give each manuscript due diligence, which is why our response time is sometimes longer than what we and the writers would like. We aim to write encouraging and helpful notes or letters when we appreciate the work of a writer, especially one we've not yet published but almost did—one of Brooks's and Warren's practices that we like to perpetuate.

Just as it has done for centuries, ever-changing technology has impacted how literature is produced and read, and no matter what one's opinion regarding those effects, some very positive avenues have emerged due to new technology. Corresponding with writers about edits via e-mail, setting an issue in-house, and using digital printing free up time and money for journals and staffs that are already strapped for both. The Community of Literary Magazines and Presses LISTSERV provides a platform where people from all journals may ask questions, seek advice, and hold general discussions about any aspect of producing a journal. It helps editors to know we are not alone in our struggles, to say nothing of the logistical assistance the supportive group offers. We've joined Project MUSE, which bundles journals and distributes them digitally to libraries. This has improved our revenues and increased our subscribers in university libraries around the world.

The *Southern Review* remains a quarterly print journal, which we love and hope never to lose, but there is no denying that if a journal is going to remain a relevant part of the literary landscape, it has to be visible and read in the prevailing technology. While we already have digital subscriptions for institutions, we are working to add digital issues and subscriptions for readers and commercial distributors as an alternative format. To draw potential contributors and subscribers, we have expanded our website and become proactive on Facebook, Twitter, and SoundCloud (where we post our repository of audio clips). Social media and our website have become our primary marketing platforms because they can reach many people cost-effectively as compared to physical mailings of yesteryear. Our website has an audio gallery of writers reading their works, as well as a searchable index of the *Southern Review*'s eighty-year history, and a blog with recent news about our contributors and staff.

Finally, we will point out that, to us, it's interesting that the *Southern Review* has moved offices over the years from one side of LSU's campus to the other, only to find itself housed again across the street from its original location. Likewise, the journal has gone from the original structure of coeditors to a single editor in 2004 and now back to coeditors. What makes a fruitful collaboration? The editors share the work and decision making, but as Brooks pointed out about his relationship with Warren, each one did something maybe the other one didn't do. We have genre specialties, yet we both read everything under serious consideration for publication, and we both copyedit every text that makes it into the pages. While Faust lends her talents to the ordering of each issue (it is still surprising to see back issues in which the poetry was always arranged alphabetically), Nemens specializes in web-based outreach, which is critical to the journal's survival and growth. We both contribute in each of these areas; however, we rely on one another's expertise. It's a true coeditorship.

There is a cycle to things, but there is also change and progression within that cycle. Brooks and Warren were young—twenty-nine and thirty years old—and both Kentucky natives when they began their work at the *Southern Review*. While there have certainly been non-Southern editors since the first series at the *Southern Review*, we now have the unique circumstance of having coeditors—one of whom is a Southerner (the first native-born Louisianan to run the journal) and one who is from the Pacific Northwest—who are both women, with some years between them. One is also a writer and visual artist, the other a single mother and songwriter, and both bring different interests and perspectives to the journal than previous editors did. With these new perspectives, the journal will undoubtedly change and grow. Like our predecessors, we don't care from where a writer hails, we only care how fresh and well-crafted the work is.

We realize that magazines and journals often get tossed into the recycling bin after they are read, because everyone needs to clear a space on the bookshelf or bedside table, but our goal is to continue to make the *Southern Review* not only worth reading but worth rereading and collecting, even if it takes up, as it does in our new offices, the majority of a rather large bookshelf. Brooks stated so well that "authentic literature is impervious to time. That is why we continue to discuss it, and that is the real justification for the ongoing discussion of literature and of literary quarterlies." This observation seems obvious, but in the ongoing struggle to explain the value of editors and to keep literary journals afloat and being read when it seems like we are often having to defend their existence, particularly in print, there's no harm in reminding people. Our roles as editors and literary journals are to help writers craft their best work, promote the work and the writer, and give legitimacy to both by their association with us. Our ultimate goal is that their voices and styles and purposes are exalted and become part of the permanent literary conversation. At the *Southern Review*, we hope that readers and writers still find the work between our covers engaging and challenging enough that the issue holds a space on the shelf, and that when retrieved from that shelf it continues to be worthy of discussion, eighty years later.

WHAT IS THE BUSINESS OF LITERATURE?

Richard Nash

Richard Nash is a strategist and serial entrepreneur in digital media. He led partnerships and content at the culture discovery start-up Small Demons and the story aggregator Byliner. Previously he ran the iconic indie Soft Skull Press. He left in 2009 to found Cursor, now a consulting business for start-ups in publishing, media, and education, and to run Red Lemonade as a pilot for the Cursor project. In 2010, the Utne Reader *named him one of "Fifty Visionaries Changing Your World," and in 2013 the United Kingdom's* Bookseller *magazine picked him as one of the "Five Most Inspiring People in Digital Publishing." His most recent project is Sirens.io, an R&D lab around the future of pretty much everything. "What Is the Business of Literature?" first appeared in the the spring 2013 issue of the* Virginia Quarterly Review.

One of the remarkable deficits in contemporary accounts of both book publishing and Internet business is sociohistorical awareness. That it should be so with the Internet is unsurprising, prone as so many popular tech commentators are to triumphalist or progressive teleologies—one technology replacing another, one company killing another, IBM's dominance unquestioned, then Microsoft unquestionable, followed in turn by AOL, Myspace, Facebook, etc. The implacability of Moore's law is extrapolated from processing power to the social order. Similarly, most current discussions of the book economy rarely reach back earlier than the Golden Era of American publishing in the 1950s, the British one dating back perhaps a little farther, to the 1930s.

While many histories of the book incorporate serious empirical research—Elizabeth Eisenstein's *The Printing Press as an Agent of Change* is an epic example—three have arguably done the best job in applying that rigor to contemporary publishing: J. B. Thompson's *The Merchants of Culture*; Ted Striphas's *The Late Age of Print*, a series of case studies with particular focus on retail; and Laura Miller's *Reluctant Capitalists*, which was almost purely about the retail side. Most other accounts of the contemporary business of literature are autobiographical, hagiographic, or histories of literature, avoiding the business and economics of it all. So why study a business that is sui generis, that isn't even really a business—that, like America, is exceptional?

It is the Exceptionalists, the ones who claim the mantle of defender of the book, who undermine the book by claiming that it is a world unto itself, in need of special protection, that its fragility in the face of the behemoth or barbarian du jour (Amazon, the Internet, comic books, the novel, the printing press, illiteracy, literacy, to name but a handful of purported sources of cultural decline) requires insulation, like the skinny kid kept away from the schoolyard and its bullies. Who are these Exceptionalists? I think we've all read them, so I'll restrict my strawhorses and offer as an example Sven Birkerts, who, in his introduction to the reissue of *The Gutenberg Elegies*, writes that "fiction is under assault by nonfiction"—this despite all the data that demonstrates fiction is disproportionately flourishing in the digital format. More problematic, though, is his characterization of the book as "countertechnology." One may counterpose the book to many things, but technology shouldn't be one of them. The book is not counter-technology, it is technology. It is the apotheosis of technology—just like the wheel or the chair.

Publishing is a word that, like the book, is almost but not quite a proxy for the "business of literature." Current accounts of publishing have the industry about as imperiled as the book, and the presumption is that if we lose publishing, we lose good books. Yet what we have right now is a system that produces great literature in spite of itself. We have come to believe that the taste-making, genius-discerning editorial activity attached to the selection, packaging, printing, and distribution of books to retailers is central to the value of literature. We believe it protects us from the shameful indulgence of too many books by insisting on a rigorous, abstemious diet. Critiques of publishing often focus on its corporate or capitalist nature, arguing that the profit motive retards decisions that would otherwise be based on pure literary merit. But capitalism per se and the market forces that both animate and presuppose it aren't the problem. They are, in fact, what brought literature and the author into being.

The story of the book as technology—the book as revolutionary, disruptive technology—must be told honestly, without triumphalism or defeatism, without hope, without despair, just as Isak Dinesen admonished us to write. A great challenge in producing such an account, however, is the "availability heuristic." This is a model of cognitive psychology first proposed in 1973 by Nobel laureate Daniel Kahneman and his colleague Amos Tversky, which describes how humans make decisions based on information that is relatively easy to recall. The things that we easily recall are things that happen frequently, and so making decisions based on the samples we have at hand would seem to make sense. The sun rises every day; we infer from this that the sun rises every day. A turkey is fed every day; it infers that it will be fed every day—until, suddenly, it isn't. Heuristics are great until they aren't. A person sees several news stories of cats leaping out of tall trees and surviving, so he believes that cats must be robust to long falls. These kinds of news

reports are far more prevalent than ones where a cat falls
to its death, which is the more common event. But since it
is less reported on, it is not readily available to a person for
him to make judgments.

Publishing is tremendously susceptible to the availability heuristic for two significant reasons. First, prior to recent
innovations, manuscripts not published were unavailable
for analysis. So the universe of knowledge we have about
books, literature, and publishing excludes that universe of
books that were never published. It also mostly excludes
those books that were commercial or critical failures. One
doesn't see books that don't sell, not on store bookshelves or
in friends' houses, not on top-ten lists, not on Twitter, not in
the *Times* (London, New York, Irish), and so on.

There are books in the data set now, such as *Leaves of Grass*,
that were self-published, and others, such as *Moby-Dick*, that
were ignored in their time but reappeared through good
luck. The novelist Paula Fox published, vanished, published
again. Her reappearance is a triumph of publishing. But
what about all the unrediscovered Paula Foxes? Or, for that
matter, what about all the books I published at Soft Skull
in the 2000s that had been rejected by ten, twenty, thirty,
sixty publishers? And what about the manuscripts I rejected
at Soft Skull that I would subsequently see published by
prestigious publishers large and small? Is this proof of the
effectiveness of the existing system for the production and
dissemination of literature? It's quite clear that while we do
our best, our output is as much proof of the awfulness of the
system as it is of its strengths. Much like Patty Hearst, we
cannot bear to consider the alternative.

When one speaks of "the system" in relation to the
business of literature, traditionally this has been code for
capitalism. More recent critiques of the system have focused
on the series of mergers that began in the 1960s and begat,

over thirty years, the configuration of publishing that has subsisted for the last twenty years: the Big Six [as of 2013, the Big Five]. Their ownership was initially driven by scale, then by a fad for synergy. (In the end, this was mostly a euphemism for empire building by managers, typically at the expense of shareholders, a phenomenon that has more to do with human nature than capitalism.) Today, only Simon & Schuster remains in a structure (CBS Corporation) conceived of as an entertainment-synergy hybrid. The remaining synergies having been unwound and replaced by a logic of scale, now at a multinational level—German, French, and British-owned, as is frequently and sardonically noted, though it has never been clear why the German, French, or British should be any more contemptuous of literary prerogatives than Americans. In fact, there is little evidence any of these processes has made it any more or less likely for "quality" to be published. What is published is published, and from that pool we choose to celebrate what we celebrate, and we say the system produced these celebrated works because, well, they're available.

. . .

SO WHAT WAS THE BUSINESS of literature, pre-book? There were words, for sure, and there was culture. There were books and there were writers. They were paid, in fact. Very well. But few writers of today would likely forgo the life of the twenty-first-century writer for that of a thirteenth-century writer.

Moreover, the role of the writer before Gutenberg was simply to transcribe. The writer's purpose wasn't to reimagine language—not gainsaying the existence of outliers such as Virgil. Writers were not thought leaders, conjurors of other worlds, conjoiners of emotion and aesthetic. Writers were the machines through which the word of God was reproduced and disseminated. Or, at most, the knowledge that humans had accumulated thus far—the myths, the legends, what is now called "folk wisdom." They captured the store of human knowledge to date. The writer was the printing press. At most, it could be said that the writer was a representative of her generation because, quite literally, the writer faithfully reproduced the stories and beliefs of her time. Such were the trade-offs: a job for life, doing nothing but writing, but you were, in the words of the academics who study this period, a "trained scribal laborer." A calligrapher.

The advent of the book, in the sense of bound typeset pages, was an economic disaster for the writer. It was John Henry *avant la lettre*, the manual laborer supplanted by the machine (albeit without steam for another four hundred years). It was not at all clear at the time that the printing press would transform religion (by eliminating the Church's monopoly on reproducing and interpreting the Bible), art (by allowing innovation in the depiction of three-dimensional objects to spread across the world; in other words, the Renaissance), and science. In this last instance, the printing press essentially made science possible by allowing experiments to be replicated through the introduction of falsification, the ability to prove something wrong. The effects took more than a hundred years to begin playing out (nor have they finished playing out).

If the demand for writers had waned, wouldn't the supply likewise atrophy? One of the ways in which an economic analysis of literature can be useful is to see where it fails to explain behavior. As humans do, when it comes to knowledge, culture, and incipient personal expression, we rose to the occasion. As printing presses flourished, around them clustered scholars, poets, philosophers. The supply of writers in no way withered. The sixteenth-century printers' shops became magnets for people with something to say, as would the eighteenth-century coffeehouses that followed.

A variety of copyright-like regimes sprouted throughout Europe, the first purpose of which was censorship—to thwart the "greate enormities and abuses" of "dyvers contentyous and disorderlye persons professinge the arte or mystere of pryntinge or selling of books," as England's Star Chamber pronounced. The second purpose was to achieve the commercial equivalent of copyright for a cartel of businesses agreeing not to compete with one another, so as to increase their prices when it came to reproducing writing. For much of the seventeenth century, licensed printers earned a return on their investment by mutually agreeing not to pirate one another's books. Then, in 1710, with the Statute of Queen Anne, England's Parliament arrogated unto itself the right to regulate the cartel. Copyright is a legislatively granted, limited right to monopolize the reproduction of a given sequence of words (and later, images and sounds, and nowadays, in some countries, numbers and movements). It was born from corporate self-interest, then was regulated as government sought to balance the prerogatives of both the weak and the powerful in order to maintain social equilibrium. The statute recognized that a balance needed to be struck around the commercial needs of the printer and the needs of society to minimize exploitative monopolies, as did the U.S. Constitution at the end of the eighteenth century. In both instances, the quid pro quo was very clear. The title of the 1710 statute was "An Act for the Encouragement of Learning, by Vesting the Copies of Printed Books in the Authors or Purchasers of such Copies, during the Times therein mentioned" and the copyright provision in the U.S. Constitution makes explicit that it exists "to promote the progress of science and useful arts."

To this day, copyright does not address certain challenges: Is there demand by readers for the writer's unique
arrangements of words? Moreover, the writer may have
a monopoly on the arrangements, but does she have the
means to actually reproduce them? While framed in terms
of the individual creating the words, clearly the purpose
of copyright is suited to the entity that can reproduce the
words, who can make and market a salable thing. What
copyright ensures is that there is a potential return on
investment for the printer or publisher. It provides a guar-
anty to the author not that she will be published, not that
she will make money, only that she can be published, that
there might be publishers who might publish her work.
Indeed, the U.K. law expressly vests the right in either the
author or "purchaser," which refers to the printer; when the
U.S. copyright clause was written in 1787, only the author
was mentioned. Why was it not vested in the author from
the very beginning? Martha Woodmansee, a scholar of literature and law who has written extensively on the invention of authorship, points out that even Alexander Pope,
the first major beneficiary of this new business model and
the first person to earn a living from the sale of books
instead of patronage, continued to see himself as a conduit
rather than a genius. Woodmansee writes:

> In a familiar passage from his "Essay on Criticism"
> (1711), Pope states that the function of the poet is
> "not to invent novelties but to express afresh truths
> hallowed by tradition":

> True wit is nature to advantage dressed;
> What oft' was thought, but ne'er so well expressed;
> Something, whose truth convinced at sight we find,
> That gives us back the image of our mind.

Pope's view of himself was still as a transmitter of culture, not its originator. To originate, we invented genius.

To truly consummate the transformation of writer from scribe to God, and to provide a cultural as well as economic rationale for copyright, we had to invent the Author. Woodmansee offers a comprehensive account of how German Romantic aesthetic theory provided the philosophical underpinnings for authorship; Mark Rose, in his *Authors and Owners: The Invention of Copyright*, does the same for English-language writing and publishing. Rose emphasizes how the construct of authorship was necessary to maintaining copyright—"what finally underwrites the [copyright] system, then, is our conviction about ourselves as individuals." But the reverse is also true—the economic value to be derived from exploiting the copyright monopoly warrants the construction of authorship so as to capture it.

By the early nineteenth century, the two key elements of literature's business model were the business (copyright) and the literature (genius). Innovation continued apace. Advances in printing itself (bigger, faster, more colors), along with allied manufacturing and advances in distribution (faster, higher, further), meant that books were able to penetrate deep into society, woven into the fabric of the everyday. In 1930, in publishers' relentless efforts to find demand for their supply, they retained the ur-genius of public relations, the "father of spin," Edward Bernays. As Ted Striphas describes it in his excellent *The Late Age of Print*, quoting Larry Tye:

> "Where there are bookshelves," [Bernays] reasoned, "there will be books." So he got respected public figures to endorse the importance of books to civilization, and then he persuaded architects, contractors,

and decorators to put up shelves on which to store the precious volumes.

It was a sign, almost one hundred years ago, of the book beginning to achieve what most technology will never accomplish—the ability to disappear. Walk into the reading room of the New York Public Library and what do you see? Laptops. Books, like the tables and chairs, have receded into the backdrop of human life. This has nothing to do with the assertion that the book is countertechnology, but that the book is a technology so pervasive, so frequently iterated and innovated upon, so worn and polished by centuries of human contact, that it reaches the status of Nature.

What is particularly crucial to understand is that books were not dragged kicking and screaming into each new area of capitalism. Books not only are part and parcel of consumer capitalism, they virtually began it. They are part of the fuel that drives it. The growth of the chain model in books offered the twentieth-century public the opportunity to decry the groceryfication of the bookstore, utterly belying the reality, as Striphas outlines in *The Late Age of Print*—by quoting Rachel Bowlby—that the bookstore is in fact the model for the supermarket:

> In the history of shop design, it is bookstores, strangely enough, that were the precursors of supermarkets. They, alone of all types of shop, made use of shelves that were not behind counters, with the goods arranged for casual-browsing, and for what was not yet called self-service. Also, when brand-name goods and their accompanying packages were non-existent or rare in the sale of food, books had covers that were designed at once to protect the contents and to entice the purchaser; they were proprietary products with identifiable authors and new titles.

There are other examples of significant innovation being driven by the publishers—Penguin founder Allen Lane's 1937 paperback vending machine for better commuter distribution being among the most charming—but the point is that books aren't sitting grumpily in economy class on the airplane to the future. They're in the cockpit.

. . .

BY THE TWENTIETH CENTURY, BOOKS, now cheaper and more widely available, had had social and political effects far beyond what the publishing business itself could harness and exploit. Books spread such ideas as the equitable distribution of social, cultural, and economic capital—precisely the resources required to read and write a book. American publishing in the 1950s consisted too often of Ivy League white men publishing one another—Mad Men in tweed. But in the twentieth century, the G.I. Bill, the expansion in education (in general, but college education in particular), the civil rights movement, the decolonization in Africa and Asia, feminism: all were advanced by the power of literature and dramatically increased the number of human beings who had read enough books to (a) want to read more, and (b) be able to imagine writing one themselves.

For the most part, however, the technical and business-model innovations in literature were one-sided, far better at supplying the means to read a book than to write one. The 1970s and 1980s brought supply-chain management. Books flowed from printers to retailers with ever less friction. Wholesalers quickly replenished their inventories of successful books because they could share information with publishers and printers more rapidly and comprehensively; in turn, retailers could rely on publishers and wholesalers to resupply them when the books were "flying off the shelves."

But this also drove hubris. The more seemingly efficient the systems, the more publishers were willing to drive them to achieve greater economies of scale. Yes, inventory management was designed to tell you what you wanted less of and what you needed more of, but mostly it was used for the latter. This was by no means unique to books. The world has also become better at allowing people to buy a desk than to make a desk. In fact, from medieval to modern times, it has become easier to buy food than to make it; to buy clothes than to make them; to obtain legal advice than to know the law; to receive medical care than to actually stitch a wound.

Then things got extreme. The number of titles published had grown significantly since the advent of the printing press, but it was about to get far more dramatic. This dates not to 2007, when Amazon introduces the Kindle, nor to 1993, with the invention of the first popular web browser. If you look to see where the really significant growth in title count begins, you go back to the late 1980s—to July 1985, when a company called Aldus, naming itself after the great Venetian printer Aldus Manutius, releases PageMaker. You put PageMaker on a Mac, put the Mac in a new chain of photocopy shops called Kinkos, and rent them for six bucks an hour, and you've got Publishing 2.0. Exhibit A: Soft Skull Press, a publisher founded in a Kinkos in 1993, and which I ran from 2001 to 2009. Further exhibits: the hundreds of thousands of zines, chapbooks, and books produced since, many of which begat small media businesses, magazines, and book publishers. The number of U.S. titles created by traditional print publishers, whether of the indie variety like Soft Skull or the large corporate publishers, increased from about 80,000 per year in the 1980s to 328,259 in 2010.

Abundance, it turns out, is a much bigger problem to solve than scarcity, or as Clay Shirky frames it: "Abundance breaks more things than scarcity." We learned to handle the first phase of abundance in books: we invented copyright, we built a viable business to manufacture and distribute them, we invented the author, so as to simplify choice. *We don't need to read all words, just the words of these ten important authors.* This was humanity's first stab at artificial scarcity, artful enough that we forgot it was a contrivance. Kurt Vonnegut noticed the contours of this Industrial Revolution phase of the culture business earlier and more cogently than most— and it is its end I am now making an account of. Speaking in *Bluebeard* through the protagonist, painter Rabo Karabekian, he writes:

> I was obviously born to draw better than most people, just as the widow Berman and Paul Slazinger were obviously born to tell stories better than most people can. Other people are obviously born to sing and dance or explain the stars in the sky or do magic tricks or be great leaders or athletes, and so on.
>
> I think that could go back to the time when people had to live in small groups of relatives—maybe fifty or a hundred people at the most. And evolution or God or whatever arranged things genetically, to keep the little families going, to cheer them up, so that they could all have somebody to tell stories around the campfire at night, and somebody else to paint pictures on the walls of the caves, and somebody else who wasn't afraid of anything and so on...[A] scheme like that doesn't make sense anymore, because simply moderate giftedness has been made worthless by the printing press and radio and television and satellites

and all that. A moderately gifted person who would have been a community treasure a thousand years ago has to give up, has to go into some other line of work, since modern communications put him or her into daily competition with nothing but the world's champions.

The entire planet can get along nicely now with maybe a dozen champion performers in each area of human giftedness. A moderately gifted person has to keep his or her gifts all bottled up until, in a manner of speaking, he or she gets drunk at a wedding and tap-dances on the coffee table like Fred Astaire or Ginger Rogers. We have a name for him or her. We call him or her an "exhibitionist."

How do we reward such an exhibitionist? We say to him or her the next morning. "Wow! Were you ever drunk last night!"

The economics of the analog reproduction of culture lead inexorably to the exhibitionist. It is far better, economically, to have the fewest number of authors, the fewest titles. Ideally, there would be one publisher with one title—let's call it the Bible. Regardless of the fact that there would be no competition for reading material, the Bible would be maximally profitable simply because in analog manufacturing, marginal cost always declines (that is, the cost to print each additional book falls). So if the price stays the same, the more you print and sell, the more profitable you are. The most profitable print-publishing business of all would be in a society where everyone reads the same book.

The PostScript output of PageMaker (later to become the more familiar "PDF") undermined the Industrial Revolution model, initiating the digital, post-Industrial phase of abundance, even though, at the time, it appeared to be reinforcing the Industrial model by reforming it. Independent presses could make digital files and send them to offset printers. They still had to deal with the classic economies of scale of analog printing, but they didn't have to deal with the complex, inaccessible, and arcane world of traditional typesetting. The number of publishers began to increase, as did the number of titles, as the creation of a title (by publisher, of course, not by author) became significantly cheaper and began to undo ever so slightly Vonnegut's otherwise accurate analysis of the business of culture. The genius opera singer needed systems to distribute her genius as broadly as possible, and the copyright system combined with analog reproduction made that easy. And it was getting easier for the nonmainstream, too, be that the lover of the avant-garde or the early music or the campy or the local, or the familial (the recording of your grandmother singing opera). The nonmainstream was abetted by the growth of the superstore model of bookstores. The traditional independent bookstore stocked five thousand to ten thousand titles, and so could only handle the new and backlist output of a limited number of publishers. But a Barnes & Noble or Borders superstore could have fifty thousand or sixty thousand or even seventy thousand titles! Indeed, it needed those nonmainstream offerings to fill its shelves. Ironically, while indie, alternative, and literary presses frequently decried the predations of the superstores, the superstores were critical to their existence.

Such is the digital transformation of the business of literature. And it predates the equivalent transformation of the music industry by a good fifteen years. It wasn't until the mid-2000s that one could create a digital master that was as high quality as a record label could—that is, until the music industry had the equivalent of true desktop publishing.

However, the MP3, the means for digital music consumption, significantly predates the Kindle, the first viable mode for digital consumption of long-form text.

Under a digital publishing model, while the costs of creating the text don't vary, the model for reproducing the text for mass consumption is entirely different. The marginal cost is zero: it costs as little to produce the billionth copy as it costs to produce the second copy. As abundant as analog reproduction made books and other cultural artifacts, digital reproduction makes them all the more so—not because it changes the resources required to create, but because it changes what is required to reproduce. Copyright, though nominally instituted to encourage the *creation* of a work, has as its only logical purpose the encouragement of the *reproduction* of the work. What we see again and again in our society is that people do not need to be encouraged to create, only that businesses want methods by which they can minimize the risk of investing in the creation.

Richard Stallman has argued that the central bargain in copyright is that the public gives up a right they couldn't actually use. Until recently, it was more expensive to make a copy of a book than it was to simply buy the book. So when society agreed to grant authors and publishers the monopoly, it was a good bargain. Now that the public can make copies of something, they are giving up a right they could in fact enjoy—or, rather, the public has proceeded to make copies anyway, regardless of the previous bargain, a kind of jury nullification. As with any law that loses the consent of the governed because it no longer reflects the logic of society, the law is not overturned, just ignored. It recedes into the past, like laws forbidding pigs to enter saloons or alcohol to be sold on Sundays or adultery or interracial marriage.

What, therefore, is the business of literature to be if the reading public is willy-nilly making copies of everything?

The primary method of twentieth-century copying—of making, distributing, and allocating *any* given object—is barely a couple hundred years old. There is good reason to believe it may prove to be an anomalous period in human history not just for books and music but for a wide range of human output. Consider 3-D printing, currently at the hobbyist phase of development, much like the computer in the early 1970s. It is a device for printing three-dimensional things, which once meant extruded plastic prototypes of things (toothbrushes, hammers, mechanical parts) but now increasingly means the *actual* thing. In one respect, it's pure science fiction. In another, it's merely a return to pre-Industrial Revolution society, where chairs, horseshoes, and clothes were all made within the village.

In both respects, this phenomenon, a shift from mass (re)production to custom production, has been prefigured by the book, by print-on-demand technology. The first 3-D printer was the laser printer. Again, we see the book not as the antithesis of technology, but as apotheosis—in the avant-garde of how to apply advances in technology to produce new business models. Want another prefiguring from books? Try crowdfunding, its best-known practitioner being the company Kickstarter, which is effectively identical to the eighteenth-century subscription model whereby a book was advertised but only printed once a minimum number of purchasers had paid.

Is there a compelling reason to doubt that once again the book and the business of literature will be at the heart of disruption, as much perpetrator as victim? To be sure, the book won't be the only reproducible cultural artifact, not the only mode for storytelling, just as the chair long ago ceased to be the only device for sitting (the couch, the barstool, the swing, the exercise ball). But can we see how it continues to have cultural salience and how it might point to its own future as well as broader changes in culture and society?

. . .

PREVIOUSLY I SUGGESTED THAT WITH the kinds of friends the book has, it needs no enemies, but of course it does have enemies. It has always had enemies, prior even to its existence in the familiar format of the present.

Several years ago, I met with gaming guru Kevin Slavin, a man who could be assumed to be an enemy, one who might ridicule the stasis of the book. At the end of our coffee, he fell quiet for a second and then said that what books have in common with games is that they reward iteration. The more you play, the more you read, the better you get at it, the more fun you have. The way I have integrated that into my own mode of thinking is: in games you get to wonder what door to walk through; in books you get to wonder what the character was thinking, walking through that door. You get to imagine the color of the door, the material, the kind of doorknob, whether it was warm or cold to the opener's touch.

The lack of video, the lack of audio, the lack of ways to change the forking outcomes of plot (what is rather crudely referred to as "interactivity") is a *feature* of literature, not a bug. And, as it turns out, books are interactive. They're recipes for the imagination. Conversely, video is restrictive—it tells you what things look like, what they sound like.

Books withstood the disruption of new modes of storytelling—the cinema, the TV set. And books have been the disrupter themselves many times, disrupting the Roman Church and upending the French aristocracy, the medieval medical establishment, then the nineteenth-century medical establishment. So the assumption at one extreme end of the Silicon Valley cosmology, that long-form text-only narrative is ripe for disruption (witness Tim O'Reilly's skepticism in his *Charlie Rose* talk, see the continual framing of the book as akin to the horse-drawn carriage, see any number of start-ups offering multimedia platforms designed to replace books), is borderline foolish.

Furthermore, when technologists arrived to embed video in digital text and proclaim the end of print, it was their own rules they were breaking. Any experienced entrepreneur or venture capitalist will warn you not to be a solution in search of a problem. As the Harvard Business School professor Clayton Christensen would ask: What is the job to be done? Many of the companies that entered the publishing industry in recent years, it turned out, were not listening to their own gurus. They were solutions in search of a problem. The book, in Christensen's terminology, was already "good enough." It couldn't tweet, as the *New York Times* best-selling children's book *It's a Book* crowed, and that was fine. The desk I'm sitting at doesn't tweet either. The "job to be done" is to deliver a very large set of words.

However, this is not to say that other jobs to be done won't arise: delivering hundreds of very large sets of words into a single object that permits them to be read, annotated, stored; delivering those sets of words more cheaply, or instantly, as happens with the digital delivery of books. And it furthermore is not to say that the job of making, distributing, and allocating those books need only be performed by an agent-publisher-wholesaler-retailer-supply chain. In this regard, the disruption forecast by technologists is eminently reasonable.

·   ·   ·

WHAT, THEN, IS THE BIGGEST JOB to be done by publishers? There is marketing and discovery, yes, but even though editors are not miracle workers who make their best decisions in a vacuum, the editor is a source of great value in the economics of literature and will therefore remain as valuable, if not more so, than before, even if less privileged. The social thinker Clay Shirky has a rule named after him: "Institutions will try to preserve the problems to which they are a solution." The past five to ten years have witnessed a great degree of anxiety from the editorial class in book, magazine, and newspaper publishing (relatively less so from literary-journal publishing, it should be noted). Some of the anxiety is economic and well-founded: editors have been laid off. Some of it, though, has to do with a perceived loss of relevance, a loss of prestige, and the response has been a series of paeans to the valuable qualities of editorial judgment. Look at all the crap out there, says the editor, you need me to fix it, sort it, curate it.

One value of the editor is clear: making writing better. At its most mechanical and least prestigious, that's the proofreader; at the intermediate phase of prestige, that's the copyeditor, achieving consistency, continuity, grammatical accuracy, ideally dialing into the author's deep style and maximizing it; and there's the acquiring editor, at the highest level of prestige, who may or may not engage in developmental editing, may or may not have junior editors, may or may not be a junior editor herself, who makes product decisions on what to publish, how to optimize it as a product, and in concert with many, many, many others, gestates and births and raises it in the world.

Ironically, the first two categories of activity, while the least prestigious, have a very clear value, and will likely serve as means of employment for decades to come as more social and economic actors (consumer-goods companies, white-collar professionals, advocacy groups, cultural institutions) become de facto publishers, producing ever more sophisticated publications online and offline, designed to deliver their message (buy it, donate to it, believe us, hire me, visit us, vote for me).

Most probably they will seek individuals who can accomplish the first two activities, along with some of the third activity, and they will be called content strategists. This is especially clear in the world of magazines and newspapers. Companies once let magazines and newspapers take care of aggregating the audience they wanted to reach, and paid them to advertise in front of that audience. They now realize it is far more effective to hire the kinds of people who work for those magazines to deliver the message directly.

Editors are also needed to produce books, of course. But beyond their editorial skills, what has kept editors in demand is relationship skills. The skill that is commonly associated with the pinnacle of editorial talent—picking the right book—is, frankly, nonsense. Success, in terms of picking things, is a hybrid of luck with the non-self-evident and money with the self-evident, and even the self-evident often requires luck. This is not to say that people don't work hard on those books that have gotten lucky, but all the retrospective justifications for why, say, *The Da Vinci Code* or the Harry Potter series succeeded are trumped by what really was a matter of luck and network effects. Books, like most entertainment media, live in what Nassim Nicholas Taleb calls Extremistan, a place with vast amounts of commercial failure and spectacularly high and extremely infrequent success. The advent of self-publishing has rendered this ever more visible. The vast majority of the twenty-eight million books currently in print made no money at all, and every few years one author will make more than $200 million: first Dan Brown and J. K. Rowling, now E. L. James. It is remarkable watching people fall over themselves seeking an explanation for their success—there is no explanation, no more than explaining why a particular person won the $550 million Powerball lottery in late November of 2012.

Publishing has no particular ability to discern what is good or not, what is successful or not. This is true not just at the level of predicting commercial success, but also at predicting critical success. I already discussed great writers who almost vanished, books that slipped through the corporate-publisher cracks, and then between the indie cracks. If one could predict a Pulitzer Prize winner, why did Bellevue Literary Press end up with Paul Harding's *Tinkers*, or Soft Skull end up with Lydia Millet's *Love in Infant Monkeys*, which was a finalist that year, too? If great editors could predict National Book Award winners, why did McPherson & Co. publish *Lords of Misrule*, or if editors could predict PEN Award winners, why did Red Lemonade publish Vanessa Veselka's *Zazen*?

This is not a knock on publishing. There's no evidence that stockbrokers can pick good stocks, or touts good horses. In the latter case, that's why any honest financial advisor will tell you to invest in indexed funds, financial instruments that mirror a broad market—no one knows how to beat the market. When you do, it is simply luck, combined with an ability to tell a good ex post facto story about why you were right and the propensity in the human nature to believe in the predictive power of a good story. (Yes, another heuristic.)

And that, as it so happens, points precisely to what publishing can do, to what the business of literature is. It is not about making art; it is about making culture, which is a conversation about what is art, what is true, what is good. What is the business model for the making of culture? What are the implications or the individuals implicated in all that— for the citizens of literature in all their guises, in the writing, in the reading, in the editing, in the teaching, in the hustling, in the gossiping?

The existing product-centric model (as opposed to the culture-centric model) looks like this: imagine *Lorem Ipsum*, a hypothetical book project. It consists solely of placeholder text that a designer uses—the typographic equivalent of Testing, Testing, One, Two, Three. It's text (originally from Virgil), unintelligible, the very definition of gibberish, yet a publisher would be hard-pressed to sell a book of it for much less than ten dollars. Why? A designer needs to lay out the text—which doesn't have to be copyedited, necessarily, but does need to be proofread. *Lorem Ipsum* needs a cover design. It needs jacket copy. It needs to be sent out to other writers for blurbs. It gets a page in the publisher's catalog; the sales reps skim it; the reps waste fifteen seconds with the bookstore buyers enduring their quizzical glances; the reps shrug their shoulders. Advanced reading copies are printed, mailed, passed around by editor, agent, and publicists over lunches. The book is printed, shipped, shelved. It sits for six to eight weeks until our little game is uncovered by the stores, at which point it is recartoned and shipped to a warehouse, then sent to be pulped.

From a publishing standpoint, one can sell *Pride and Prejudice* more cheaply than gibberish because people already know Jane Austen. At minimum, it won't be returned and pulped at the same rate. So why is the margin attributable to the ideas in a book so low, at times in fact negative, whereby the total revenue earned by the book is less than the cost of producing and distributing it? Not because our society doesn't value literature, as so many of us complain, but because it takes so long to discover whether or not you'll actually like the book. Publishers offer the world a massive discount on what should be the true markup on manufacturing and distribution in order to persuade us to try something out, to gamble. To get us to risk wasting our time, they try to minimize the risk that we might be wasting our money. Perversely, publishers are unable to capture the upside. If it turns out we are not wasting our time and do get a wonderful experience, we get it for one to two dollars an hour, an order of magnitude cheaper than film, theater, live music, recorded music, dance, a bar, a restaurant, a museum. We do so because a book is a much more unknown quantity, less susceptible to summary.

How might publishers capture that value? That transformative, transporting, transfixing experience, a value better compared to a trip to another country, to a university seminar, to a lover—yet obtained for the price of a T-shirt? One theory from the creative industries has been to educate the public that content is worth something, and therefore they should pay for it. That notion is everywhere, in trailers before movie screenings and in the pages of magazines, whether they talk about themselves or the book business. As charitable as Americans are, and as willing as Europeans are to subsidize, relying on the notion that one deserves to get paid will fail every time. Imagine that as a dating strategy: I deserve to be desired by you. Apple, Prada, the NFL, the purveyors of widely desired goods and experiences do not "educate" the public that they deserve to be paid. The public simply offers up its money, gratefully. The public will not do so for a basic delivery of a straightforward long-form text experience. If we cannot educate or guilt-trip our way to solvency, then what are we to do?

It has been an irony of recent decades that as capitalist product development shifted to an ever more customized, bespoke mode of production, using more sophisticated manufacturing systems, more flexible supply chains, and more attentive customer-feedback systems, the book supply chain became ever more uniform and bland. As the pressure to have physical books be the primary conduit through which literature reaches its audience begins to fade, the pressure to produce them as cheaply as possible also diminishes. Simultaneously the character of the retailers engaged in the business of retailing literature shifts away from ones where price and breadth of selection are central toward ones that function as a hybrid of culture hub, concierge, and gallery—that is, toward venues optimized to sell higher-end editions. More broadly it means being able to sell at a wide variety of price points: $15 trade paperback, $35 elegant hardcover, $75 slipcase, $250 with the bloody thumbprint of the author on the title page, and so forth. Moreover they are better placed to collaborate with other cultural institutions and lifestyle purveyors, with restaurants, with bars, with museums, with arthouse cinemas, creating thematic connections and cultural nexuses.

We see instances of this throughout the business, and are even starting to see cases where traditional publishing entities are formalizing that process. Several larger U.S. publishers now offer speakers bureau services, which, for poets and for management consultants alike, are far more remunerative than the book. (Even though the book often undergirds the value of the talk, it is not the vehicle through which the actual revenue is conveyed.) O'Reilly, the computer-book publisher, earns more from the conferences it orchestrates than from selling books, although its intellectual reputation and network of connections as a publisher positioned it to create the conferences. The MFA industrial complex is a multibillion-dollar business that typically has been a profit center for universities: the tuition of aspiring poets purchases electron microscopes for physicists. Likewise, Faber in the United Kingdom has been running Faber Academy for five years now, offering creative-writing classes taught by its authors. All universities do is hire publishers' authors to conduct the classes, so why not the publishers themselves? Literary and writers' conferences charge aspiring writers thousands to attend, and in addition to publishers' authors, who else attends as bait for attendees?

Editors. We've seen Penguin deepen their merchandising; if Marc Jacobs can sell books, why can't publishers in turn partner with designers to create shoes inspired by particular characters? Publishers could partner with wine wholesalers to offer wine clubs, with caterers providing literary-themed events, with boutique travel agencies to offer tours.

Selling a book, print or digital, turns out to be far from the only way to generate revenue from all the remarkable cultural activity that goes into the creation and dissemination of literature and ideas. Recall again all the schmoozing, learning, practice, hustling, reading upon reading upon reading that goes into the various editorial components of publishing; the pattern recognition; the storytelling that editors do, that sales reps do, that publicists do, that the bookstore staff does. Recall the average feted poet who makes more money at a weekend visiting-writer gig than her royalties are likely to earn her in an entire year. You begin to realize that the business of literature is the business of making culture, not just the business of manufacturing bound books. This, in turn, means that the increased difficulty of selling bound books in a traditional manner (and the lower price point in selling digital books) is not going to be a significant challenge over the long run, except to free the business of literature from the limitations imposed when one is producing *things* rather than ideas and stories. Book culture is not print fetishism; it is the swirl and gurgle of idea and style in the expression of stories and concepts—the conversation, polemic, narrative force that goes on within and between texts, within and between people as they write, revise, discover, and respond to those texts. That swirl and gurgle does happen to have a home for print fetishism, as it has a home for digital fetishism. This is what literature has always been. Being yoked to the Industrial Revolution's machines for analog reproduction, accompanied by an arbitrary process for selecting what should be reproduced, will prove to be an anomaly in the history of literature, useful as that phase was for the democratization of access to reading. The publisher is an orchestrator in the world of book culture, not a machine for sorting manuscripts and supplying a small number of those manuscripts in improved and bound form to a large number of people via a retailer-based supply chain best suited for the distribution of cornflakes, not ideas.

A business born out of the invention of mechanical reproduction transforms and transcends the very circumstances of its inception, and again has the potential to continue to transform and transcend itself—to disrupt industries like education, to drive the movie industry, to empower the gaming industry. Book culture is in far less peril than many choose to assume, for the notion of an imperiled book culture assumes that book culture is a beast far more refined, rarified, and fragile than it actually is. By defining books as against technology, we deny our true selves, we deny the power of the book. Let's restore to publishing its true reputation—not as a hedge against the future, not as a bulwark against radical change, not as a citadel amidst the barbarians, but rather as the future at hand, as the radical agent of change, as the barbarian. The business of literature is blowing shit up.

Jane Friedman

From 2001 to 2010, Jane Friedman worked at Writer's
Digest, *where she became publisher and editorial director.
Most recently she served as digital editor of the* Virginia
Quarterly Review. *She teaches digital media and pub-
lishing at the University of Virginia and is a columnist for*
Publishers Weekly.

Since the late 1990s, I have been educating writers
about the publishing industry. For the first ten years,
most conversations centered on how to write better,
find an agent, and get a book published (and then another).
The big question on every writer's mind was: Do I have
what it takes? And I would retort with: Do you have grit?
Because dogged persistence was the biggest commonality I
saw among successful writers, at least those who could be
said to make a "living" at it.

By 2008, the weight of the conversation had shifted to
print versus digital challenges. Many of us, both inside and
outside the industry, have become consumed by the question of how long print will last, how much we have to com-
promise our writing and editing time to cultivate an online
presence, and if it's the "most exciting time" to be in publishing or actually the worst.

We've all been in that conversation where we've made a
proclamation about whether we favor print or digital, and
when we favor it, and why we favor it. We muse on the difference in hand feel, smell, navigational memory, marginalia,
and attention. And all of these things are intertwined with

childhood associations, emotional milestones, and matters of personal identity.

But this talk is ultimately a distraction from the real challenges faced both by writers and publications—and especially by literary publishing. The problem is not whether print will survive, but how literary publishing adapts to a world where to publish something has lost value. As Clay Shirky writes, in *Here Comes Everybody*:

> In a world where publishing is effortless, the decision to publish something isn't terribly momentous. Just as movable type raised the value of being able to read and write even as it destroyed the scribal tradition, globally free publishing is making public speech and action more valuable, even as its absolute abundance diminishes the specialness of professional publishing. For a generation that is growing up without the scarcity that made publishing such a serious-minded pursuit, the written word has no special value in and of itself. . . . If everyone can do something, it is no longer rare enough to pay for, even if it is vital.

At a 2014 AWP panel, Morgan Entrekin, president and publisher of Grove/Atlantic, identified two primary challenges facing literary publishing going forward: distribution and discoverability. But these challenges are not unique to literary publishing—they affect every single producer of media, large and small, and they've been long-term, persistent challenges. Furthermore, distribution is only a future challenge insofar as literary publishing is focused on print retail and bricks-and-mortar bookstores. Access to online distribution is now available to every author, business, and publishing company. *This* is what increases discoverability complications. The self-service, plug-and-play tools to publish *and* distribute have created not just a crowded marketplace, but a decreased value on the function and process of publishing. This has become a dilemma for commercial publishers in particular, who face increased competition from self-publishing authors, digital presses, and Amazon's own publishing program. Hachette, one of the Big Five, was even compelled to leak a document in 2011 explaining why publishers are relevant. Could such a thing even have been fathomable twenty years ago?

To be fair, Entrekin's comments focused on how publishing needs *diversity* in distribution channels. Opportunities for books to get discovered by readers are disappearing and becoming limited to a few big companies, such as Amazon, Apple, and Google. It's largely Silicon Valley companies and the tech industry that drive what the future of book distribution and discoverability look like. A 2012 Bowker report revealed that where readers purchase books has dramatically shifted. In 2010, about 25 percent of books, whether print or digital, were purchased through online channels (that means Amazon, mostly). By the end of 2012, that percentage was closer to 44 percent. Most industry experts estimate we're now at 50 percent.

One of a publisher's primary strengths has been getting an author's books distributed to every bookstore or appropriate retail channel. As bookstores and physical retail become less and less important to book sales—and to an author's discoverability—what purpose does a publisher serve?

For literary publishing in particular, the imprimatur of a house remains important. It's not enough simply to publish; literary authors must be published by a certain *someone* to achieve the "right" types of reviews, coverage, awards, and attention. Literary authors are also concerned with quality editorial relationships that can nurture and support their careers for the long term, which presumably a literary publisher cares about too, and is more able to offer, as opposed to a commercial house, which is less likely to be patient in the pursuit of profits.

In this way, an independent, literary press is often in a better position than conglomerate-driven publishing. They can more readily play the long game, be happier with small or "quiet" books, and focus on cultivating what I'll argue is imperative in the Internet era: community. But doing that effectively means that editors and authors have to give up some long-held beliefs and myths about online marketing and what it means to develop . . . dare I say the dirty word? . . . a *brand*.

.   .   .

In 2011, the editors of *Triple Canopy* wrote a long essay on publishing in the digital age, "The Binder and the Server." In it, they spend a great deal of time explaining their efforts to design their online publication in such a way as to "slow down the Internet" and allow readers to focus. This will become important later on; for now, I want to bring forward a facet of their discussion, where they explain why their publication doesn't allow comments:

> Even after our redesign, which further facilitated our connectivity to social-networking sites, there is no way to "talk back." Everything published is carefully edited, often elaborately produced, and properly attributed. As far as the website is concerned, *Triple Canopy* has only authors, no friends. . . . If online publishing is to distinguish itself from the rest of the Internet's information stream, it mustn't settle for

the easy terms of online friendship. It needs to maintain a degree of idiosyncrasy and difficulty.

Plainly illustrated, there you have the biggest threat to literary authors, editors, publishers, and supporters: outright
hostility toward readers and discouragement of community.
This position is *not* unique to *Triple Canopy*; it is commonplace
in literary publishing. Regardless of what philosophical line
of reasoning might justify it, the result remains the same:
standoffishness and the overriding attitude that engagement or interaction is a suspicious activity. The primary
focus should be on the art; the rest is base. It is distraction.

Yet, by the end of their essay, *Triple Canopy* discusses their
additional focus on readers:

> . . . we have begun to address a third constituency,
> our readers, in a manner that we hope changes how
> they conceive of their relationship to *Triple Canopy*.
> Our readers have provided much in the way of moral
> support, but little of the material variety; for the sake
> of *Triple Canopy*'s long-term sustainability, we believe
> some percentage of our public need to think of them-
> selves as subscribers. . . . We're hopeful for the sub-
> scription model, if not necessarily optimistic. As a
> first attempt at attracting broad support, we recently
> organized a Kickstarter campaign. . . . We were heart-
> ened that 338 individuals pitched in, and grateful for
> the thirty-five thousand dollars raised.

Triple Canopy could rightly point out that not settling for the
easy terms of online friendship has not apparently hurt their
cause, though I have to wonder how much more support
they would have garnered if they didn't seek to build difficulty into the experience of their publication. Regardless—

and maybe surprising themselves at what they've built—
Triple Canopy succeeded in building a community that has
translated into sustainability for their publication. My
theory is that they offer something essential that everyone
seeks, online or off: *meaning*. It's not so important what *Triple
Canopy* offers, but *why* they offer it. Whether I agree with
their philosophy or attitude or not, they've attracted a following—online friends!—who believe in their mission and
why they do what they do. Further, the people they attract
have something in common with each other, which is the
start of a community. *Triple Canopy* could take that same mission and produce a Tumblr, a newsletter, an annual event, an
intellectuals-only café in Brooklyn, a line of clever stuffed
animals, and serve that community through a variety of
mediums and channels. People don't care as much about the
what as the *why*, and this is the hope and strength of literary
publishing. (Notice this has nothing to do with print versus
digital; each is simply a substrate through which to serve a
readership.)

This is where conversations about brand have to start,
and why brand doesn't have to be a dirty word. Brand should
evoke an immediate and clear response that's not about
sales, marketing, or promotion. The brand should evoke
and emphasize the *why*—what the publication or publisher
stands for. This takes time and is not an overnight process,
and it's partly built on what *other* people say about you or
what they value you for.

Perhaps the most important reason why this has become
so critical—putting aside the fact we now live in a time
where no one need struggle to find something quality to
read, *even if we limited ourselves to reading only that which is free*—is
disaggregation.

Being able to cherry-pick an essay from *ABC Review*, a
poem from *DEF Review*, then a short story from *GHI Review*,

and consume them seamlessly and distraction-free in a long-form-reading environment such as Pocket, leads to three industry-changing behaviors: (1) readers have less reason to consume a publication in its entirety if they're not 100 percent committed to its reason for being (the *why*), (2) readers are less committed to any single publication if it doesn't interest them from cover to cover, and (3) a publication's design and reading environment, or an issue's larger context, become meaningless. This brings us back to *Triple Canopy*'s essay that focused on its extensive efforts to "slow down" the Internet reading experience. Today, it is largely irrelevant how a site presents content, because avid readers will increasingly import content into their preferred reading environment, usually when they are prepared to "lean back" into reading, a phrase coined by the *Economist* to signify that moment when we focus attention on reading (as opposed to "leaning forward" as part of a multitasking work environment).

While disaggregation has a more powerful and immediate effect on literary journals, magazines, and online publications, book publishers face the challenge, too; the proliferation of endless (and quality) digital content that we can save and read for later can take us away from the to-be-read pile on the nightstand or what's hidden behind our reading-app icon. One can easily fill all available reading time by simply keeping up with a self-curated list of articles saved to Pocket, scrolling through friends' links from Facebook or Twitter, or opening up Candy Crush. The less visible and immediate physical books are in our lives (because bookstores disappear, because books become digital, because of the competition from other media), the more important it becomes for every publisher to think beyond the next book on the release schedule, and consider how to engage their community in a variety of media and channels. The words on a screen or a page may remain central, but they become one expression of the brand, not the *only* expression.

In an essay that remains as relevant (and unheeded) as it was the day it was published, "Context, Not Container" by Brian O'Leary offers one of the secrets to any type of successful publishing of the future: we have to stop being so attached to our containers, and think more about how we're relevant to our reading community, who now turn first to digital tools for discovery, information, and entertainment.

. . .

IN CLAY CHRISTENSEN'S NOW-CLASSIC business text, *The Innovator's Dilemma*, he describes how low-quality upstarts in any industry are, at various stages, ignored, ridiculed, feared, and eventually (when it's too late) imitated. The legacy players within an industry are rarely able to innovate in the same manner as a new entrant, and the new entrants ultimately disrupt the traditional business and enter the high-quality range of the market. In print journalism, we've already seen this disruption at work with the rise of news sites like the *Huffington Post* and the decline of newspapers and periodicals such as *Newsweek* and *Time*.

We can either ignore or ridicule Buzzfeed, Upworthy, and similar sites for their low quality, or for headlines such as "It's Often a Controversial Issue, but One Stunningly Illustrated Picture Book Handles It With Grace." Or we can take a page from their book, because they've got at least one thing right: most of us want to read, watch, or feel something that has meaning and potential to provoke a life change, or help us see the world anew. If faced with a choice between reading "A Mind-Blowing Short Story That Changes How You View Love" and the spring 2014 issue of *ABC University Literary Journal,* which would you choose? Chances are you're

going with the experience that has offered you some context, unless you're already a devoted community member of
ABC *University Literary Journal*. And therein lies my point.
Without a framework and context for what is published,
literary publications can feel virtually indistinguishable
from one another. Journals especially are guilty of making
work available but not known. One might say there's a good
excuse for the failing: literary publishing's mission or calling
usually relates to producing art, not marketable commodi-
ties. But then this mission or calling needs to be defined and
marketed to a target reader community that is engaged and
committed to the survival of that mission.

The good news is that the digital era has dramatically
fragmented the audience for media: we don't have to consume
only what is best marketed and advertised. We each have
more tools than ever to find exactly the right book, magazine,
or experience that fits our mood, interest, or aspirations. The
algorithm, silently at work behind millions of online transactions, is getting more and more powerful at identifying what
each of wants to see next, and this is an opportunity for every
publisher. You can identify and directly reach your potential audience, without needing special distribution, without needing a large advertising budget, and without having
a print book. But doing this requires what is often missing
from the equation: the brand that knows what it's about and
can convey that to an intended market. It takes time to build
a brand and audience, and develop a real, valuable connection with readers, and it's a very different game than the one
that is (and will be) played by the Big Five in New York. As
Richard Nash once theorized at his own website:

> Basically, the best-selling five hundred books each
> year will likely be published like Little, Brown pub-
> lishes James Patterson, on a TV production model; or

like Scholastic did Harry Potter and Doubleday Dan Brown, on a big Hollywood blockbuster model.

The rest will be published by niche social publishing communities.

Literary publishers produce niche work, and are poised to become leaders of the community of readers *and writers* who have matching missions and belief systems. Literary publishers can add value and credibility to niche communities, through the act of publishing of course, but also through other forms of leadership and support that go beyond print and extend into events, services, grants, fellowships, reading groups, etc. Building community is primarily about intimate knowledge of and respect for a community, combined with creativity and imagination in serving it. Publishers that survive, whether they focus on traditional publications or digital media, must become indispensable to the communities they serve. While at one time a publisher might have been indispensable by communicating quality ideas and stories by remarkable authors, a publisher who does that today—and nothing more—can be seen as merely adding to the burden we all now face. There are too many wonderful things to read, and too few signposts as to what's worth our time. Thus, the literary publisher needs to be a beacon, to offer a strong signal amidst all the noise, and organize ideas, content, and stories within an identifiable and useful context. Otherwise, many of us will turn away because we simply can't find the time to understand or discover the meaning or the quality of what's presented to us.

NOTES

INTRODUCTION

VIII   *According to a 2000 article*   MH Munroe, "Which Way Is Up? The Publishing Industry Merges Its Way into the Twenty-First Century," *Library Administration & Management* 14, no. 2 (Spring 2000).

VIII   *the Council of Literary Magazines and Presses*   Now called the Community of Literary Magazines and Presses.

IX   *Between 2000 and 2007*   Yvonne Zipp, "The Novel Resurgence of Independent Bookstores," *Christian Science Monitor*, March 17, 2013, http://www.csmonitor.com/USA/Society/2013/0317/The-novel-resurgence-of-independent-bookstores.

IX   *In 2014, Kirshbaum departed*   See George Packer's detailed article "Cheap Words" in the *New Yorker*, February 17, 2014.

IX   *According to a September 2014 article*   Zachary Karabell, "Why Indie Bookstores Are on the Rise Again," *Slate*, September 9, 2014, http://www.slate.com/articles/business/the_edgy_optimist/2014/09/independent_bookstores_rising_they_can_t_compete_with_amazon_and_don_t_have.html.

IX   *a paradoxical place*   Jordan Weissmann, "The Decline of the American Book Lover," *Atlantic*, January 21, 2014, http://www.theatlantic.com/business/archive/2014/01/the-decline-of-the-american-book-lover/283222/.

Reading the Tea Leaves: Notations on the Changing Look of the Literary

8   *Writer Nicholas Carr* Nicholas Carr, "Is Google Making Us Stupid?," *Atlantic*, July/August 2008, http://www.theatlantic.com/magazine/archive/2008/07/is-google-making-us-stupid/306868/.

9   *In a 2014 article* Matt McFarland, "Books Are Losing the War for Our Attention," *Washington Post*, March 19, 2014, https://www.washingtonpost.com/news/innovations/wp/2014/03/19/books-are-losing-the-war-for-our-attention-heres-how-they-could-fight-back/.

10   *David Streitfeld published an article* David Streitfeld, "Web Fiction, Serialized and Local," *New York Times*, March 24, 2014, http://www.nytimes.com/2014/03/24/technology/web-fiction-serialized-and-social.html?_r=0.

The Amazon Effect

40   *One thing, however, is certain* As of this book's publication—four years after the essay was written—e-book sales appear to have plateaued.—Eds.

The View from a University Press

67   *Sales have not increased* American Association of University Presses Financial Statistics, 2013.

69 *"The most important evidence . . . "* University of Oregon Program in Creative Writing, Promotion and Tenure Guidelines, revised and approved November 2005.

POETRY IN TRANSLATION: HEMISPHERIC PERSPECTIVES

83 *the public dialogue* Latino Cultural Center, Dallas, Texas, April 11, 2013.

87 *Beginning with issue 6* Guest edited by Esther Allen.

87 *journals like* El Corno emplumado Edited from 1962 to 1969 by Margaret Randall and Sergio Mondragón.

HOLD THE DAMN DOOR OPEN: IDEALISM IS NO CURRENCY

133 *On the Best American Poetry blog* In an April 16, 2015, comment reply on his April 15 post, "Clowns Against Submission Fees," at the Best American Poetry blog, Timothy Green wrote:

And when you pay just to submit, there's no way to even know that your poems were READ at all. Literary magazines are different from other publications, because it's a highly interactive niche art—almost all readers are writers; it will never be self-sustaining unless we find an audience outside of poets, but that's hard, because reading poetry makes you want to write it. If it were a regular business, it just wouldn't exist, couldn't exist. That's why these are social benefit

organizations, and as such, we have to hold to a higher
ethical standard, I think.

139   *Richard Nash alludes to this*   Richard Nash, "What Is
the Business of Literature?," *Virginia Quarterly Review*
89, no. 2 (spring 2013), http://www.vqronline.org/
articles/what-business-literature. The article is also
included in this collection, beginning on page 252.

140   *A 2014* Ploughshares *blog post*   Peter Kispert, "Round-
Down: A Look at the Crowded Literary Journal
Landscape," *Ploughshares* (blog), December 23, 2014,
http://blog.pshares.org/index.php/round-down-more-
literary-journals-more-possibility-2.

151   *Dan Brady of* Barrelhouse *writes*   Dan Brady, "How
and Why *Barrelhouse* Pays Poets," *Poetry Has
Value* (blog), February 11, 2015, http://poetryh-
asvalue.com/post/110737396691/how-and-why-
barrelhouse-pays-poets-by-dan-brady.

DIVERSITY IS NOT ENOUGH: RACE, POWER, PUBLISHING

156   *Christopher Myers wrote*   Christopher Myers, "The
Apartheid of Children's Literature," *New York Times*,
March 15, 2014, http://www.nytimes.com/2014/03/16/
opinion/sunday/the-apartheid-of-childrens-litera-
ture.html.

157   *author Walter Dean Myers, wrote*   Walter Dean Myers,
"Where Are the People of Color in Children's Books?,"

New York Times, March 15, 2014, http://www.nytimes.
com/2014/03/16/opinion/sunday/where-are-the-
people-of-color-in-childrens-books.html.

161   *CNN recently published an article*   Ashley Strickland,
      "Where's the African-American Harry Potter
      or the Mexican Katniss?," CNN, July 2, 2014,
      http://www.cnn.com/2014/04/09/living/young-
      adult-books-diversity-identity/.

161   *Nancy Larrick begins her essay* Nancy Larrick, "The All-
      White World of Children's Books," *Saturday Review,*
      September 11, 1965.

THE OPEN REFRIGERATOR

198   *"MFA vs. NYC"* "MFA vs. NYC," *n+1* 10 (Fall 2010): 1-12,
      https://nplusonemag.com/issue-10/the-intellectual-
      situation/mfa-vs-nyc/.

201   *In his generous review* Alfred A. Knopf, "The Man Who
      Made Great Novels Greater," *New York Times Book
      Review,* March 26, 1950.

THE *SOUTHERN REVIEW* AT EIGHTY

240   *"some kind of personality and character"*   Cleanth Brooks,
      Beyond Words: The Story of the Southern Review, directed
      by Peggy Scott Laborde (WLAE-TV, 1986), VHS.

240   *As second series* Ibid.

240 *"Why, it just gave me . . ."*   "The Interior World: An Interview with Eudora Welty," by Charles T. Bunting, *Southern Review* 8, no. 4 (Autumn 1972): 711-35.

241 *"very little, little magazine"*   Cleanth Brooks, "The Life and Death of an Academic Journal," *The Art of Literary Publishing*, ed. Bill Henderson (Yonkers: Pushcart Press, 1980).

242 *"does not have to be attached . . ."*   Ibid.

243 *"I have no regrets . . . "*   Ibid.

244 *"Well, it is done . . . "*   Porter to Robert Warren, April 19, 1942, in *Letters of Katherine Ann Porter*, ed. Isabel Bayley (New York: Atlantic Monthly Press, 1990).

244 *"always precarious . . ."*   Brooks, "The Life and Death of an Academic Journal."

246 *Brooks explained that*   *Beyond Words: The Story of the Southern Review*, VHS.

What Is the Business of Literature?

257 *Woodmansee writes*   Martha Woodmansee, *The Author, Art, and the Market: Rereading the History of Aesthetics* (New York: Columbia University Press, 1993).

258 *Rose emphasizes*   Mark Rose, *Authors and Owners: The Invention of Copyright* (Cambridge, Massachusetts: Harvard University Press, 1993).

258 *Ted Striphas describes*   Ted Striphas, *The Late Age of Print: Everyday Book Culture from Consumerism to Control* (New York: Columbia University Press, 2009).

259 *As Striphas outlines*   Ibid.

THE FUTURE VALUE OF A LITERARY PUBLISHER

278 *As Clay Shirky writes*   Clay Shirky, *Here Comes Everybody* (New York: Penguin Press, 2008).

278 *At a 2014 AWP panel*   2014 Association of Writers & Writing Programs Conference, "The Business of Literary Publishing in the Twenty-First Century."

279 *This has become a dilemma*   For five years straight, Harlequin has reported declining revenues despite being one of the strongest commercial publishing brands in North America. Reasons for the decline include increased competition from independent authors, extremely competitive pricing, and decreased physical bookshelf space, among other factors.

280 *In 2011, the editors of* Triple Canopy   *Art Journal* 70, no. 4 (Winter 2011): 40-57, http://artjournal.collegeart.org/?p=2644.

282 *People don't care as much*   Here I must credit the ideas and talks of Simon Sinek, author of *Start With Why: How Great Leaders Inspire Everyone to Take Action* (New York: Portfolio, 2011).

284   *In an essay that remains*   Brian O'Leary, "Context, Not Container," in *Book: A Futurist's Manifesto*, ed. Hugh McGuire and Brian O'Leary (Sebastopol, California: O'Reilly Media, 2011), http://book.pressbooks.com/ chapter/context-not-container-brian-oleary.

ACKNOWLEDGMENTS

Unless otherwise noted below, all essays in this book appear with the permission of their authors.

"The Amazon Effect," by Steve Wasserman, previously appeared in the *Nation* on May 29, 2012, and is printed with the permission of Steve Wasserman.

"Diversity Is Not Enough: Race, Power, Publishing," by Daniel José Older, previously appeared on Buzzfeed Books on April 18, 2014, and is printed with the permission of Daniel José Older.

"The Art of Agenting: An Interview with Chris Parris-Lamb," by Jonathan Lee, previously appeared on *Guernica* in spring 2015 and is printed with the permission of Jonathan Lee.

"What Is the Business of Literature?" by Richard Nash, previously appeared in the *Virginia Quarterly Review* in spring 2013 and is printed with the permission of Richard Nash.

Interior design & typesetting by Mary Austin Speaker

Typeset in Requiem

Requiem was designed in 1992 by Jonathan Hoefler, who used
as his inspiration an Italian writing manual from 1523, *Il Modo
de Temperare le Penne*, which depicts the *cancelleresca corsiva*
handwriting style used by Vatican scribes.